Benedict Rogers is a writer and advocate working for the international human rights organisation CSW. Specialising in Asia, he is a regular contributor to international media including the *Wall Street Journal*, *International Herald Tribune*, *New York Times*, *Australian*, *Asahi Shimbun*, *Huffington Post*, *Guardian* and *Daily Telegraph*, as well as the BBC, CNN, al-Jazeera and Sky. Invited to give briefings and speeches round the world, he has addressed audiences at venues such as the White House, European Parliament, House of Commons, Japanese Parliament and Oxford University. Currently living in London, his focus has been on Burma for many years, travelling some forty times to the country and its borders.

By the same author:

Than Shwe: unmasking Burma's tyrant

*A Land without Evil: stopping the genocide of
Burma's Karen people*

Burma

A Nation at the Crossroads

Benedict Rogers

LONDON • SYDNEY • AUCKLAND • JOHANNESBURG

1 3 5 7 9 10 8 6 4 2

Rider, an imprint of Ebury Publishing,
20 Vauxhall Bridge Road,
London SW1V 2SA

Rider is part of the Penguin Random House group of companies
whose addresses can be found at global.penguinrandomhouse.com

Copyright © Benedict Rogers 2012, 2015

Benedict Rogers has asserted his right to be identified as the author of this Work in
accordance with the Copyright, Designs and Patents Act 1988

First published by Rider in 2012. This revised edition first published in 2015.

www.eburypublishing.co.uk

A CIP catalogue record for this book is available from the British Library

ISBN 9781846044465

Printed and bound by CPI Group (UK) Ltd, Croydon CR0 4YY

Penguin Random House is committed to a sustainable future
for our business, our readers and our planet. This book is made from
Forest Stewardship Council® certified paper.

For the people of Burma, that they may know true freedom, real peace and genuine democracy, and that they may celebrate the beauty of unity in diversity.

Contents

Acknowledgements

M ANY BURMESE OF different ethnicities have helped me considerably in the course of my work for Burma, and for the research involved in writing this book. Some cannot be named, for their own security, but they know who they are and to them I express my deep respect, admiration and gratitude.

Those who can be named and who have helped me specifically with this book, either by providing information or sharing their own personal experiences with me, include former political prisoners Khun Saing, Su Mon Aye, Yee Yee Htun, Moe Aye, Tin Aye, Htein Lin and Nyi Nyi Aung; the daughter of a former political prisoner, Waihnin Pwint Thon; Aung San Suu Kyi's former 'Tri-color' security guards, Phone Myint Tun and Moe Myat Thu; elected Members of Parliament U Bo Hla Tint and Lian Uk; Dr Thaung Htun, UN representative of the exiled government, the National Coalition Government of the Union of Burma (NCGUB); the former General Secretary of the Ethnic Nationalities Council (ENC) and Chin activist, Lian Sakhong; the former General Secretary of the ENC and Kachin activist, U Hkun Sa; former '88 Generation activist Khin Ohmar; the former General Secretary of the Karenni National Progressive Party (KNPP), Rimond Htoo; the Joint Secretary-1 of the KNPP, Khu Oo Reh; the former Vice-President of the Karen National Union (KNU), David Thackerbaw; the Vice-President of the KNU, Naw Zipporah Sein; Zoya Phan, Campaigns Manager at Burma Campaign UK and daughter of former KNU General Secretary, Padoh Mahn Sha Lah Phan; Charm Tong, of the Shan Women's Action Network (SWAN); Victor Biak Lian,

Bawi Lian Mang and Za Uk Ling of the Chin Human Rights Organisation (CHRO); Hkanhpa Sadan, Kachin National Organisation (KNO); Nurul Islam, President of the Arakan Rohingya National Organisation (ARNO); U Aung Htoo, General Secretary of the Burma Lawyers Council; Harn Yawnghwe, Director of the Euro-Burma Office; Nancy Shwe, Director of Radio Free Asia Burmese Service; Thant Lwin Htut, Director of Voice of America Burmese Service; Nita May, BBC Burmese Service; Soe Myint, Editor of *Mizzima News*; Thin Thin Aung of the Women's League of Burma; Zaw Min of the Democratic Party for a New Society (DPNS); Ka Hsaw Wa, founder of EarthRights International; Aung Saw Oo; Inge Sargent; and Louisa Benson Craig, who sadly died in 2010.

I am also indebted to friends outside Burma who work tirelessly for Burma's freedom and have provided invaluable insights and information. They include Mark Farmaner, Director of Burma Campaign UK; John Jackson, co-founder of Burma Campaign UK; Yvette Mahon, former Director of Burma Campaign UK; Debbie Stothard of ALTSEAN-Burma; Jared Genser of Freedom Now; Dr Chris Beyrer of Johns Hopkins Bloomberg School of Public Health; David Eubank of the Free Burma Rangers; John Bercow MP; Andrew Mitchell MP; Baroness Cox; Lord Alton; Dr Martin Panter; and James Mackay. Past British, American, Australian, Thai and Japanese diplomats have been generous in sharing their recollections and analysis, not least former British Ambassadors Sir Nicholas Fenn, Martin Morland, Robert Gordon and Mark Canning, and former British Council Director Tom White. Journalist Dominic Faulder, previously of *Asiaweek*, has been exceptionally helpful in providing news articles and information regarding the period from 1988–1996. I am also grateful to the staff of St Hugh's College, Oxford University, for opening up their archive of press cuttings and other information about Aung San Suu Kyi and Burma.

I owe a special debt of gratitude to several volunteers who devoted many hours to painstakingly transcribing interviews for me: Kirk Acevado, Liam Allmark, Sarah Armitage, Chris Beanland, Myra Dahgaypaw, Pippa DeWitt, Claire DeWitt, Kate Gwynn, Rita Lobo, Daniella Lock, James Mackay, Sally Pearson, Jacqueline San, Gabi Sibley, Chloe Simons and May Pearl Tun. I am also grateful to friends who read the draft manuscript and suggested improvements, including Mark Farmaner, Debbie Stothard,

James Mackay, Chris Lewa, Martin Morland, Juliet Rogers and Julia Evans.

My own employers, Christian Solidarity Worldwide (CSW), have been exceptionally generous in providing time, space and resources to conduct the research and to write this book, and without their support it would not have been possible. All of the travel involved in researching this book has been made possible by CSW.

I am grateful to my publishers, Random House, and particularly Judith Kendra and all her colleagues, for recognising the value and significance of this book, taking it on so enthusiastically, and providing guidance, wise counsel, editorial expertise and warm encouragement throughout the process.

I am also grateful to the Göttweig Abbey, a Benedictine monastery near Krems, Austria founded in 1083, and to my parents in the rolling English countryside in Dorset, for providing beautiful places of peace and tranquillity in which to read, research and write.

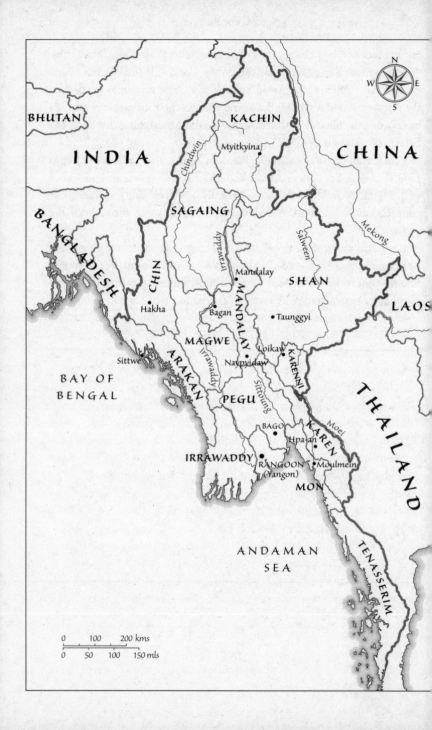

Author's Note

O N 26 MAY 1989 the military regime in Burma changed the name of the country to 'Myanmar'.[1] The democracy movement and the leaders of the ethnic resistance organisations, however, continue to use 'Burma', and have urged the international community to do the same. They argue that the regime had no mandate to change the name of the country. In this book, therefore, I use 'Burma' and not 'Myanmar', except in direct quotations from other sources.

The regime also changed the names of various cities and divisions. Rangoon became 'Yangon', the Irrawaddy Division became 'Ayeyarwady' and Maymyo became 'Pyin Oo Lwin'. Karen State is called 'Kayin', while Karenni is 'Kayah'. I have generally used the older names – Rangoon instead of Yangon, Irrawaddy instead of Ayeyarwady and Karen rather than Kayin, because they are more easily recognisable for international readers.

The Burma Army is commonly known as the Tatmadaw, and so I use the terms 'Burma Army' and 'Tatmadaw' interchangeably. The regime was officially called the State Law and Order Restoration Council (SLORC) from 1988–1997, and then the State Peace and Development Council (SPDC) until 2010, and so in some parts of the book I use these terms.

All references from other works are sourced in the endnotes. Any unsourced material should usually be understood to have come from direct interviews conducted by the author with sources, whether named or unnamed.

Glossary

AAPP	Assistance Association for Political Prisoners
ABMA	All Burma Monks' Alliance
ABMRC	All Burma Monks' Representative Committee
ABSDF	All Burma Students' Democratic Front
ABSDMO	All Burma Students' Democratic Movement Organisation
AFPFL	Anti-Fascist People's Freedom League
ARNO	Arakan Rohingya National Organisation
ASEAN	Association of Southeast Asian Nations
BSPP	Burma Socialist Programme Party
CHRO	Chin Human Rights Organisation
CNF	Chin National Front
CNLD	Chin National League for Democracy
CPB	Communist Party of Burma
CPCS	Centre for Peace and Conflict Studies
CSW	Christian Solidarity Worldwide
DAB	Democratic Alliance of Burma
DDSI	Directorate of Defense Services Intelligence
DFID	Department for International Development
DKBA	Democratic Karen Buddhist Army
DKBO	Democratic Karen Buddhist Organisation
DPNS	Democratic Party for a New Society
DSA	Defense Services Academy
DVB	Democratic Voice of Burma
EAT	Emergency Assistance Team
ENC	Ethnic Nationalities Council
ICRC	International Committee of the Red Cross
IPAD	Institute for Political Analysis and Documentation

IRC	International Rescue Committee
KDNG	Kachin Development Networking Group
KIA	Kachin Independence Army
KIO	Kachin Independence Organisation
KNO	Kachin National Organisation
KNDO	Karen National Defence Organisation
KNO	Karenni National Organisation
KNU	Karen National Union
KNLA	Karen National Liberation Army
KNPP	Karenni National Progressive Party
MNDAA	Myanmar National Democracy Alliance Army
MPF	Mon People's Front
NCGUB	National Coalition Government of the Union of Burma
NCUB	National Council of the Union of Burma
NDF	National Democratic Front
NLD	National League for Democracy
NMSP	New Mon State Party
NUP	National Unity Party
NUPA	National United Party of Arakan
RANIR	Relief Action Network for IDP and Refugee
RPF	Rohingya Patriotic Front
RSO	Rohingya Solidarity Organisation
SHRF	Shan Human Rights Foundation
SHAN	Shan Herald Agency for News
SLORC	State Law and Order Restoration Council
SNLD	Shan Nationalities League for Democracy
SPDC	State Peace and Development Council
SSA	Shan State Army
SWAN	Shan Women's Action Network
UNDP	United Nations Development Programme
UNHCR	United Nations High Commissioner for Refugees
USDA	Union Solidarity Development Association
USDP	Union Solidarity and Development Party
UWSA	United Wa State Army
WFP	World Food Programme
WPN	Wanpawng Ninghtoi

Foreword by
The Most Reverend Desmond M. Tutu

THE PEOPLE OF BURMA have been struggling for almost fifty years against two twin challenges: a brutal military dictatorship among the very worst in the world, and the apathy and inaction of too many people in the rest of the world.

Drawing on his own many travels to Burma, Benedict Rogers has provided a comprehensive, vivid and powerful account of the suffering of its people, weaving together the story of the democracy movement and the plight of the ethnic nationalities along all Burma's borders. An important introduction to Burma and a vital call to action.

Introduction

ON 11 FEBRUARY 2008 I spent half a day with Padoh Mahn Sha Lah Phan, then the General Secretary of the Karen National Union (KNU), the major resistance organisation struggling on behalf of Burma's Karen people, one of the largest of the country's ethnic groups. I knew him well, and always visited him whenever I was in Mae Sot, a town on the Thailand–Burma border where many exiled Burmese democracy groups are based. His daughters are friends of mine.

That particular day, Padoh Mahn Sha had arranged for me to meet some former child soldiers from the Burma Army who had escaped and sought refuge among the Karen. He was giving them shelter. From 8 a.m. until 1 p.m., I was in his home. After interviewing the former child soldiers, I had a meeting with Padoh Mahn Sha and other senior KNU leaders. Then he invited me to stay for lunch. He was at his best – relaxed, speaking softly but firmly about the political and humanitarian situation for his people, joking about the improvement in his English language ability, and reflecting with pride on how his children living abroad have become involved in the struggle.

Three days later on Valentine's Day, gunmen came to his home and shot Padoh Mahn Sha dead. They entered the gates and walked up to the veranda where he was sitting – the veranda where I had sat with him three days previously. They greeted him in Karen, and offered him fruit. And then they shot him.

Although Burma may now be beginning to change, for over half a century its people have lived as captives in their own nation, and even when they fled to the borders with neighbouring countries, they were not safe. In spite of recent reforms, fear and suspicion prevail, particularly among the ethnic nationalities. Padoh Mahn Sha was assassinated by Burma's military regime, in broad daylight, across the border in Thailand. The gunmen were believed to be Karen, and he may even have known them personally, but there is little doubt that they were acting as proxies for the junta. Padoh Mahn Sha was killed because he was one of the strongest opponents of the regime which has terrorised its people for almost half a century. He was one of the few ethnic leaders who bridged the divides of ethnicity, religion and politics, and was able to unite people in pursuit of a common cause: federal democracy and equal rights for all Burma's people.

In contrast to some other Karen leaders, who sometimes focus narrowly on their own specific Karen struggle, Padoh Mahn Sha saw the bigger picture for Burma, and worked closely with the broader Burman-dominated democracy movement and with the other ethnic nationalities, without ever compromising on his devotion to his Karen people. He skilfully mediated between different factions within the KNU and the wider democracy movement, trying to achieve agreement between the so-called 'hardliners' wedded to armed struggle, international sanctions and no compromise, and the 'engagement' faction which believed that the struggle could never be won militarily and that a negotiated, political settlement with the regime should be sought. He was an Animist, among a predominantly Christian leadership and a primarily Buddhist people, and was able to bridge the religious divides. He had good access to international media, politicians and human rights non-governmental organisations (NGOs), and was a prominent and articulate voice for his people. In the run-up to the regime's planned referendum on a new constitution, Padoh Mahn Sha was seen as a threat to the junta. His assassination is an example of the lengths to which Burma's military regime would go to silence its critics.

For more than fifty years, Burma has been ruled by a succession of brutal military regimes that rank among the worst dictatorships in the world. Accused of crimes against humanity, successive regimes have used torture, rape as a weapon of war, forced labour, people as minesweepers and have forcibly conscripted child soldiers on a widespread and systematic basis. The nominally civilian government which has ruled since 2010 is led by former generals, who took off their uniforms in 2010 and held elections for the first time in two decades. The 2010 elections were a blatant sham; five years later the approach has been more sophisticated, with some semblance of the instruments of democracy beginning to emerge. Yet behind the scenes, the military is still in power.

After a decade of democracy following independence in 1948, the civilian government was replaced by military rule led by General Ne Win in 1958, with the purpose of restoring order to a nation torn apart by armed uprisings by the communists and several ethnic groups. In 1960, fresh elections were held and the previous government led by Prime Minister U Nu was returned to power. Two years later, however, Ne Win launched a coup d'état and the military have ruled the country ever since, making it the world's longest-ruling military regime. Yet with the demise of other military dictatorships, notably the regimes across the Arab world, Burma's junta appears at last to be embarking on a new path. In 2009, Bertil Lintner noted that of the military regimes which had taken power around the world since 1962, only two remained in existence: Burma and Libya.[1] Two years later, Libya's regime fell, and Burma's regime appeared to be changing. The reforms, however, are largely atmospheric rather than substantial. Without institutional, legislative and constitutional reform Burma will not be truly free and, crucially, without a political process that results in a political settlement for the country's ethnic groups, Burma will never be at peace. The emergence of a powerful movement of Buddhist nationalism, resulting in a campaign of hate speech, discriminatory legislation and anti-Muslim violence, threatens the nascent, fragile freedoms that have begun to emerge.

A nation of approximately 51 million people – according to a controversial census in 2014 – Burma is one of the most ethnically and religiously diverse in South East Asia. Besides the Burman, Burmese-speaking majority, there are seven major ethnic groups. These are the Karen, Karenni, Shan and Mon, who inhabit eastern and southern Burma along the border with Thailand (although the majority of Karens are in the Irrawaddy Delta, Tenasserim Division and Rangoon); the Kachin in northern Burma along the border with China; the Chin, in western Burma straddling the Indian and Bangladesh borders; and the Arakan or Rakhine, along the border with Bangladesh. There are numerous other sub-groups, such as the Pa-O, Lahu, Lisu, Naga, as well as smaller groups such as the Wa, the Chinese-speaking Kokang, and the Muslim Rohingyas, who are among the most persecuted people in the country. For much of the time since Burma's independence from British colonial rule in 1948, many of these ethnic groups have fought an armed struggle against the Burman-dominated central government – fighting in some cases initially for secession and independence, but in almost all cases today for autonomy, equal rights and federal democracy within the Union of Burma. Many signed ceasefires with the regime in the 1990s, but some, such as the Karen, Karenni, Shan and Chin continued, to varying degrees, to fight until preliminary ceasefire agreements were reached towards the end of 2011 and the beginning of 2012. In contrast, the Kachin had seventeen years of ceasefire from 1994 until the regime launched a fresh and brutal offensive against them in 2011. Efforts to secure a nationwide ceasefire have progressed painfully slowly.

The Burman majority population has also been engaged in a struggle for democracy, manifested in protests in 1962, 1967, 1970, 1974, 1988, 1996 and 2007. The movement in 1988 sparked the most organised opposition to the regime, led by Aung San Suu Kyi, daughter of the leader of Burma's independence movement, Aung San. In 1990, the regime held elections, which were overwhelmingly won by Aung San Suu Kyi's party, the National League for Democracy (NLD) – but instead of transferring power to the legitimate representatives of the people, the junta reneged on its promise to respect the results, imprisoned the victors and intensified its grip on power. Aung San Suu Kyi, recipient of the Nobel Peace Prize in 1991, was put under house arrest in 1989, prior to the elections, and was held in detention for almost fifteen of the following twenty-one years. Her most recent period of detention was from 2003 until 2010, when she was released immediately after the country's first elections in twenty years. An estimated 2,000 political prisoners were jailed for much of the past two decades as well, but towards the end of 2011, and in early 2012, hundreds were released, as the regime tried to convince the world it was changing. The releases, however, were not unconditional; many were freed on parole rather than under an amnesty, and many have been left with unjust criminal records, unable to find work and with no rehabilitation offered. Furthermore, at the time of writing, hundreds of new political prisoners remain in jail.

For years, Burma's plight was one of the most under-reported tragedies of the second half of the twentieth century. Aung San Suu Kyi helped to change that a little, and since 1990 she has become the face of Burma's democracy movement. Yet even her face and name, adorning T-shirts and posters and championed by world figures such as Archbishop Desmond Tutu and former Czech President Václav Havel, celebrities such as Bono and his band U2, the former US First Lady Laura Bush and Indian economist Amartya Sen, and politicians such as former British Prime Minister Gordon Brown, former Norwegian Prime Minister Kjell Magne Bondevik and former US Secretary of State Hillary Clinton, still go unrecognised by many. A movie, *The Lady*, in which Michelle Yeoh plays Aung San Suu Kyi, a play, *The Lady of Burma*, a piece of music called *Letters from Burma*, and several biographies have all been produced, but still many people are unfamiliar with her story.

Even more unknown, or at least ignored, are the ethnic peoples, suffering from crimes against humanity and, in some areas, war crimes and perhaps a form of attempted genocide. From 1996 to 2011, over 3,700 villages in eastern Burma were destroyed by the military, and more than a million people internally displaced, yet only those who had an interest in such issues were aware. And in terms of achieving levels of global awareness, the Karen are better off than the other ethnic groups. Of all the borders, Thailand's is the most accessible, and over the years more and more journalists, activists, politicians, celebrities and NGOs have visited the Karen refugees and drawn much-needed attention to their plight. The Karen continue to need more attention, but the Karenni, Shan and Mon along the same border have received far less, and those on other borders are even more neglected. Few have travelled to the ethnic peoples living along Burma's borders with China, India and Bangladesh – and these people continue to suffer almost in silence, virtually unheard, unknown and un-helped.

Between 2007 and 2010, the people of Burma experienced some of the worst years of political turmoil and humanitarian crisis. Burma's absence from the international headlines changed dramatically in September 2007, when thousands of Buddhist monks took to the streets in what became known as the 'Saffron Revolution'. In the largest demonstrations since 1988, monks and Burmese civilians marched in protest at fuel price rises –

and called for dialogue with the regime and a transition to democracy. The regime, then known as the State Peace and Development Council (SPDC), responded true to character, as it has always done. Monks and civilians were arrested, severely beaten, jailed, tortured and in some cases shot in the streets. The difference between 2007 and 1988 was that in 2007, the events were captured on video and in photographs, and released to the world's media within minutes, by email and mobile phone. In 1988, the international community was not aware of the severity of the crackdown until after the events; in 2007, the world could see what was happening, in real time.

Eight months later, Burma again dominated the news, when Cyclone Nargis struck the country, causing death and devastation. Astonishingly, the regime initially failed to respond to the humanitarian disaster that had hit its shores, and refused international aid, compounding the suffering. Only after intense international pressure, largely led behind the scenes by the United Kingdom, the United States and France, and fronted by UN Secretary General Ban Ki-moon and Burma's neighbours in the Association of South East Asian Nations (ASEAN), did the regime relent and permit aid and relief workers. It took coordinated diplomatic and political pressure, supported by threats to invoke the UN's 'Responsibility to Protect' (R2P) mechanism and the presence of French, British and American naval ships off Burma's coast, to achieve this. Even then, access to the affected areas remained restricted, and there were widespread reports of relief supplies being stolen or diverted.

In the immediate aftermath of the cyclone, the regime held a referendum on a new constitution – one which simply enshrined military rule and denied Aung San Suu Kyi any role in government. The referendum was recognised by almost all observers as a complete sham, with numerous widespread reports of ballot rigging. The basis upon which the 2008 referendum was carried out offered no hope for Burma's future democratic prospects.

As these events brought Burma to the world's attention, humanitarian crises were developing in other parts of the country. The regime intensified its offensive against civilians in Karen State, shooting women and children on sight and displacing thousands. In western Burma, the flowering of bamboo attracted a plague of rats, which wrought death and destruction on the Chin people by destroying all their crops. At least 100,000 Chin

people in more than 200 villages faced a chronic food shortage as a result.[2]
And then, in 2009, Aung San Suu Kyi was put on trial just as her period of
house arrest was due to expire. The scenario was ludicrous – an American
Mormon and Vietnam veteran, John Yettaw, swam across Inya Lake to
Aung San Suu Kyi's home. Despite pleading with him to leave, Aung San
Suu Kyi was charged with breaking the terms of her house arrest, put on
trial and given three years in prison with hard labour, reduced to eighteen
months under house arrest. Yettaw was also given a jail sentence, but was
deported a few days later after a visit to Burma by US Senator Jim Webb.
On 7 November 2010 this litany of horrors came to a crashing crescendo
with a sham charade of an election. In the months preceding the poll,
designed to perpetuate the military's rule, election laws were published
which excluded Aung San Suu Kyi and made it impossible for the NLD to
participate. As a result the NLD was deregistered as a political party and
deemed illegal.

It therefore caught almost everyone by surprise when in August 2011
Burma's new President, Thein Sein, met with Aung San Suu Kyi, and
she emerged to say that he was a man of integrity whom she could trust,
although this was an opinion she subsequently revised. Thein Sein began to
unveil a reform process that has resulted in some relaxation of restrictions
on media and political activity, the release of political prisoners, the
beginning of ceasefire talks with the ethnic groups, and the re-registration
of the NLD. Within the course of a year, Aung San Suu Kyi and her party
went from being illegal and completely outside the established system, to
contesting parliamentary by-elections and winning seats in Parliament.
In 2012 she travelled to Thailand, Britain, Norway, Ireland and Geneva,
and has subsequently visited the United States, Australia, India, Japan and
Korea – and yet her perceived reluctance to speak up on some of Burma's
key challenges has tarnished her image internationally and lost her trust
among some in Burma. For that reason alone, it is fair to say that Burma is
a nation at the crossroads.

Since 2000, I have travelled many times to Burma and its borderlands
– at the time of writing, I have made over forty fact-finding visits. I
have been to almost all of Burma's borders, spent time with internally
displaced peoples (IDPs) in the jungles of eastern Burma, met former
political prisoners, defectors from the Burma Army, Buddhist monks who

participated in the Saffron Revolution and ethnic resistance leaders. I have looked into the eyes of desperate Rohingya refugees in Bangladesh, who have been denied citizenship in Burma despite living there for generations. I have experienced the tensions which the ethnic ceasefire groups have to face, living with a degree of peace but no real freedom. I have also travelled many times inside the country, to Rangoon, Mandalay, Maymyo, Bagan (formerly Pagan), Inle Lake, Bago, Kyaiktiyo (the 'Golden Rock'), Myitkyina, Lashio, Hsipaw, Hakha, and the new capital of Naypyidaw, and talked discreetly with brave dissidents. I have sat with the 'Moustache Brothers', courageously outspoken comedians in Mandalay, and watched a video of Aung San Suu Kyi enjoying one of their shows, enjoyed many conversations with Zarganar, Burma's best-known political comedian, and I have met some of Aung San Suu Kyi's closest associates, including her lawyer, U Nyan Win, and the prominent journalist and dissident U Ludu Sein Win. I have enjoyed many discussions with Burma's first-ever cardinal, the outspoken Archbishop Charles Maung Bo. And I have been inspired by the courage and commitment of many activists from Burma, along its borders and outside. They include those who continue to defy the regime, express dissent in various creative ways, document human rights violations at grave risk to their own lives, provide humanitarian support to their own people unreached by the major aid agencies, and provide a voice for their people in the wider international community. They are the heroes of Burma's struggle, and it is their stories that inspire my work and provide the heart of this book.

In March 2011, I spent a week in Rangoon. I had arranged an appointment to meet Daw Aung San Suu Kyi on my final day. At about 10.45 p.m. the previous night, having completed all my activities that day, I went into the hotel bar to listen to some live jazz. I thought I would relax for a few minutes. I had almost made it, and just had one more day, and the most important meeting, left. No more than five minutes after I sat down in the bar, I heard the words every activist in Burma fears: 'Mr Rogers, the authorities want to speak to you.' Outside my room, six plain-clothes military intelligence agents were waiting for me. Calmly, I finished my beer and went upstairs. Inside, I was apprehensive, but I tried not to show it.

I greeted the six men and invited them into my room. 'I understand you would like to speak to me,' I said. I invited them to sit down. 'How can I help?' Immediately, one man informed me that they had instructions from the capital, Naypyidaw, to deport me from the country the following morning. Initially, they claimed they did not know the reason, although as they searched my hotel room and luggage, I saw one of them flicking through his file which contained a photocopy of the front cover of my previous book, *Than Shwe: Unmasking Burma's Tyrant*, a biography of the previous dictator. They checked my camera. 'These are just tourist pictures,' one exclaimed. 'Yes I told you I am just a tourist,' I said. They asked to copy them, and I asked why. 'We have to show our superiors something.' They searched my luggage, but found nothing. They examined a large pile of books, including Barbara Demick's *Nothing to Envy: Real Lives in North Korea*, which I had brought as gifts. 'Nothing to Envy,' one man read out slowly. Then he put it aside. The pile also contained a book and a film about the life of Dietrich Bonhoeffer, the German pastor who stood up against Hitler and was executed. There was also a DVD called *Nine Days that Changed the World*, about Pope John Paul II's visit to Poland which sparked the Solidarity movement and ultimately led to the collapse of communism. They appeared not to know the significance of these. They took several photos. I reminded them that I had committed no crime. 'Of course,' said one with an insincere smile. 'If you had committed a crime you would be in prison.' Looking at my Bible, in a cover made by Karen ethnic people, they asked: 'Is it an iPad?' They examined my Kindle with interest and asked me to show them how it works. 'Ebook?' they exclaimed. Yes, ebook.

At midnight they finished, and told me to be ready at 7 a.m. They left, but five minutes later one man returned. 'I left my notebook,' he said. It felt like a French farce or a scene from Monty Python. After anxiously searching for a while he found it in my suitcase. He must have put it in there accidentally while replacing my belongings.

The following morning, I was escorted to the airport by two men, in a taxi. I asked again what the reason for my deportation was. 'We'll tell you at the airport.' One man offered me a cigarette, which I declined. They paid for the taxi.

I was met by a large group at the airport – plain-clothes military intelligence, uniformed immigration officers, a few police. Every step I made I was surrounded by three or four men with cameras, and they took dozens of pictures. One unpleasant little man was a bit officious, barking orders at me and others, but most of the people were civil, and one or two were quite cheery. I said I wanted a cup of coffee, and one of them fetched one for me.

When the procedure was complete, two men sat down with me. 'I can now inform you the reasons for your deportation. We know you have written several books about Myanmar, including *Than Shwe: Unmasking Burma's Tyrant.*' With no sense of irony, he quoted the title in full.

I decided to ask them a few questions. Paul McCartney's song 'Freedom' was echoing in my head. I remained polite, but my conscience would not allow me to go silently. I wanted them to know what I thought, but also that I didn't blame them personally, I blamed the system. 'Is it a crime to write a book?' I asked. He looked surprised, and confused. Then, feigning ignorance and naivety, I continued. 'In November, Myanmar held elections. So I thought Myanmar was becoming a democracy. In a democracy, it is very normal to write books freely, and very common to write books about leaders. Some books are positive, others are critical. But the fact that you are deporting me for writing a book suggests that Myanmar is not a democracy. So, I am confused. Can you tell me, is Myanmar becoming a democracy or not?' He hesitated. 'Myanmar will be a democracy one day, but slowly, slowly. We are in transition period.' OK, I said, but transition implies change. 'I thought Myanmar was changing. But deporting a foreigner for writing a book suggests no change. So is that correct – no change?' He nodded enthusiastically. 'Yes yes, no change, no change.'

I asked if he deports many foreigners. He smiled. 'Yes, many.' I asked if he thought my deportation was fair. He said he had not read my book, so he could not comment. 'Do you have a copy of your book with you? I would be interested to read it.' I laughed, and said I did not, but I offered to send it to him if he gave me his address. He didn't take me up on the offer. He asked whether I had any plans to write more books about Burma, and I told him I had just completed another, which had not yet been published. With his pen and notebook at hand, he said: 'Ah. What is the title?' I wasn't going to help him that much, so I told him he could wait until it was published. This is the finished product.

I told him it was a shame they were deporting me, because if they had allowed me to stay just one more day, I may have gone away with a more positive impression. Now, I would have no choice but to tell my friends that the regime in Burma was not changing at all. He looked at me impassively. I asked if he enjoyed working for a government that treats its people so badly, and if he knew that the ethnic nationalities in Burma were particularly suffering under this regime. This drew no response.

I asked what he thought about the events in Egypt, Tunisia and Libya. 'I don't like this kind of change. I think it was created by al-Qaeda. Do you think it was created by al-Qaeda?' No, I said, I did not. I acknowledged the risk of extremists taking advantage, but I said the movements in these countries were led by ordinary people who don't like dictatorship. 'But democracy gives al-Qaeda opportunities.' No, I disagree. 'Democratic, open societies are a better way to challenge extremism and terrorism than dictatorship.'

Then they told me I could go through to the gate for boarding. But they still had my passport, which they had taken, along with my air tickets, the night before. I reminded them that they had my passport, and they had a few minutes of confusion over what to do. I said with a smile: 'No passport, I stay in Myanmar, OK?' and we all burst out laughing.

They shook my hand and said goodbye. Looking them straight in the eye, I uttered my last words before leaving Burma: 'Thank you for treating me well. I know that your government does not treat your own people well at all, but I am grateful that at least you treated me well.' I know that if I had been Burmese, I would have been treated far worse. I might not even have survived.

Within hours of my deportation, the news had reached the exiled Burmese media. I did not seek publicity, but I started to receive calls from Radio Free Asia, Democratic Voice of Burma, *Mizzima* and other exiled media. Only once the media were running the story anyway did I decide I should speak about it, in order to ensure that the story did not descend into wild rumours which could make things worse. People inside Burma also asked me to speak out, to let the world know that nothing very much had changed.

Four days later, I sat in a refugee camp on the Thailand–Burma border and watched Karen students graduate from a Bible school. They sang the 'Hallelujah' chorus from Handel's *Messiah*, in a bamboo church at the foot of a mountain. The contrast between such physical and spiritual beauty, the suffering that these people had endured, and the secret police

I met just a few days before was hard to absorb. One young Karen gave a graduation speech titled 'Rebuilding Our Land'. He said: 'The dictators want to make our people disappear from this world.' The principal, Pastor Simon, uttered the cry of people across Burma: 'We want peace, justice and freedom for all the people of Burma. We want the regime to respect and treat us as brothers and sisters, not as enemies or slaves. We want the whole world to help. We want to go home – please help us.'

In contrast, I hadn't wanted to go home – I wanted to stay just one more day. But the fact that I was forced to leave has given me a deeper empathy with the people of Burma, and reinforced my commitment to support their struggle for freedom. One man I met told me I was 'very dangerous'. But, he added, 'I like what you do. Keep doing it. This regime is like a psychiatric patient, who needs electric shock treatment. You give them electric shocks.'

It was surprising that I had been able to obtain a visa – and when I asked the military intelligence agent why I had been given a visa, if my book was a problem, he replied solemnly: 'We are also asking that question.' He asked whether this was my first visit, and appeared rather shocked when I told him I had been several times before. Indeed, on my previous visit I had an unnerving encounter at Bangkok airport where I bumped into a Chin friend on my way to Rangoon. He did not know that I was travelling into Burma, and so merrily produced from his bag a copy of the print-version of *Mizzima News*. To my horror, on the front page was an article about my forthcoming biography of Burma's dictator, and a photograph of me. I told my friend that where I was travelling it would not be wise for me to carry that, and he nodded knowingly. Despite that, I encountered no personal difficulties inside the country, until 2011.

Less than ten months after my deportation, I decided to apply for another visa, not expecting to be granted one but believing that I had nothing to lose by trying. To my astonishment, not only did I receive a visa, but I encountered no difficulty upon arrival in Rangoon or for the eight days I spent there. I had expected the immigration officials to have a record of my deportation and at least to question me, but my passport was stamped in the normal way, with not even an eyebrow raised. For the following eight days I met some of the most high-profile and sensitive people in Burma, including Aung San Suu Kyi, her colleagues U Tin Oo and U Win Tin, and leaders of the '88 Generation Student Movement, including Min Ko Naing, Ko Ko Gyi, Ko Jimmy, Ko Mya Aye and Ko Htay Kywe, who had been released from prison just a fortnight before. The fact that I could return to the country less than a year after being expelled is just one sign of the change taking place.

However, the previous week I visited Kachin State on the China–Burma border, where I heard some of the worst stories of human rights violations I have ever heard, in fifteen years of working on Burma. Juxtaposing the mood of optimism in Rangoon with the situation in Kachin State, the opening line of Charles Dickens's *A Tale of Two Cities* comes to mind: 'It was the best of times, it was the worst of times.' While it would be an exaggeration to describe the situation in Rangoon as 'the best of times', as there is still a long way to go, it was markedly more open and hopeful than at any time in the previous twenty years. Yet in Kachin State, a brutal war is being waged against ethnic civilians.

As I have travelled around Burma, I have become increasingly convinced of the need to see Burma as a whole. There is certainly a place for specialisation, for those who choose to devote their energy and resources to one particular ethnic group or theme. However, there is also a need to put all the pieces of the patchwork quilt into place and see not just one or two parts, but the entire picture, or as much of it as possible. For all the peoples of Burma have been oppressed by the same regime and all are fighting for the same principles of freedom, democracy, justice, peace and basic human rights. The tactics of the regime towards each group may vary, the experiences and opinions of each individual group may not be completely identical, but ultimately all have a common enemy: a brutal military regime that has sought to maintain power and deny them freedom at all costs. Furthermore, that regime's most favoured tactic is divide and rule. It loves to sow division within ethnic and political groups, to divide and subdivide its opponents. The more the people of Burma can unite, and outside observers can see and understand Burma holistically, the better equipped they will be to secure freedom for Burma.

This is the main reason for writing this book. Much of the available literature tends to be one-dimensional. Books often concentrate either on various aspects of the regime, Aung San Suu Kyi, the democracy movement and life within urban Burma, or the ethnic nationalities. Many of these books provide a valuable contribution to the study of Burma, but few approach Burma holistically.

I have therefore sought, within the constraints of time and resources, to weave together as comprehensive, holistic and accessible a picture as possible, to tell the story of the peoples of Burma, both Burman and non-Burman, their struggle for democracy and human rights, and the contribution of others in the international community to that struggle. The book is about them, but it is to a large extent informed by my own experiences and by the people I have had the privilege of meeting. Naturally, as an activist, my allegiance is clear and I am not a neutral observer. But as I have already declared in my previous books, I am not biased in favour of one or other ethnic, religious or political group, but rather in favour of the basic values of freedom and human rights. I have a moral framework, informed by my own personal faith and humanity, which tells me that rape, torture, forced labour, the conscription of child soldiers and the use of human minesweepers are wrong, and that we are all entitled to express our political or religious beliefs freely, without hindrance, and without fear of discrimination, detention or death. It is those values which inform this book.

In following Burma, there are two key dangers, both of which I have sought to avoid. On the one hand, there is the risk of over-simplification. It is very easy to paint the regime as the bad guys, and Aung San Suu Kyi, the democracy movement and the ethnic resistance groups as the good guys. It is my profound belief that the balance of evil does indeed weigh heavily on the regime's side of the equation. Their record of brutality, corruption and inhumanity far outstrips that of anyone else in Burma. Whereas the people struggling for democracy and human rights, from all ethnicities, have in my experience shown truly extraordinary courage, dignity, sacrifice and goodness. The values for which they struggle are good, and in that sense it is indeed a struggle between right and wrong. Yet they are all human beings, and as Aleksandr Solzhenitsyn said, the line between good and evil passes through every human heart. The democracy and ethnic movements have made mistakes. Sometimes they have treated some of their own people badly, and allowed unnecessary divisions to grow, giving the regime opportunity to widen the divide. More recently, they have been accused of staying silent in the face of extremist religious nationalism and other serious human rights violations. And there are indeed tensions between the Burmans and the non-Burmans which go beyond the regime. As Christina Fink has observed, 'Some ethnic nationalist leaders worry that a democratic government would not safeguard minority rights. At the same time, some Burman pro-democracy activists are uncomfortable with the ethnic nationalists' demands for autonomy, which they perceive as potentially leading to the break-up of the country. In recent years, many of the opposition groups have come to see the creation of a federal, democratic union as the best solution for all, but the regime's divide-and-rule tactics have made it difficult for them to work together.'[3] Burma is complex, not least in the multiplicity of ethnic groups, political groups and rivalries. The democracy movement, moreover, has formed an alphabet soup of coalitions and umbrella groups, which will become apparent throughout this book. Simply learning the various abbreviations and acronyms illustrates the fact that Burma is not simple.

On the other hand, there are some within the worlds of academia and diplomacy who appear to make a virtue out of over-complicating the situation. They get lost in a fog of Burma's complexity, and lose sight of the truth. Complexity is no excuse for inaction against the regime's crimes. As I have argued above, there are such concepts as right and wrong, and we should not forget them.

In this book, therefore, I hope to offer an up-to-date, comprehensive, holistic account of Burma's struggle for freedom. It is intended to be a resource both for the beginner, as an introduction to Burma, and for those who are already well acquainted with these issues, as a contribution to furthering the debate about the future of the country. It will provide some brief, basic historical background, in order to put the current situation in context, but will focus primarily on the current situation, and draw largely on the human stories of suffering and courage that are the reality of Burma today. Like my previous work, it is more an activist's text than an anthropologist's study, but I have sought to make it academically and intellectually credible. It is supported primarily by first-hand evidence, or by information provided by reliable sources. It is my hope that it will not be an abstract piece of literature that only provokes interest and discussion, but also a book that will motivate action, whether in support or aid. While writing it, the words of a young Shan boy I met in 2002 continue to ring in my ears. He described to me how he had seen his father shot dead in front of him as he worked in his paddy field. The boy waited until the soldiers had left, and then took his father's body back for burial. Just two weeks later, the Tatmadaw struck again, this time killing most villagers including his mother, and burning down the entire village. He was taken as a porter and ordered to carry heavy loads of supplies and ammunition for three days, walking long distances and denied food and water. At the end of three days he collapsed with exhaustion, and the soldiers beat him for half an hour, until he fell unconscious. When he regained consciousness, he found the troops had moved on and he was able to make his escape. For two weeks he walked through the jungle, surviving on tree bark and banana pulp, before reaching a camp for internally displaced people near the Thai border. As he told his story, he looked into my eyes and said words that are ingrained in my mind: 'Please tell the world to put pressure on the military regime to stop killing its people. Tell the world not to forget us.' In writing this book, I hope I have at least partially responded to his request.

When I met Aung San Suu Kyi in January 2012, I told her about this book. I also told her that I had changed the title. Originally, the book was to be called *Burma: A Captive Nation*. She responded by commending the new title, saying that Burma truly is at a crossroads and people must shed their status as captives. She went on to say that in her view, in the debate over Burma's future, there are three types of people: those who are unquestioningly euphoric and enthusiastic about the process of change; those who are supportive of her decision to engage with the regime and in the political process, but are cautious, sceptical and weighing the evidence; and those who, for whatever agenda of their own, simply do not even want the process to be tried. It is the second category that she values, and she made it clear that she does not understand and has no time for the first or the third.

I returned from Rangoon in 2012 with a sense of cautious optimism, with equal emphasis on both words. This could be a moment of breakthrough for Burma, the first opportunity in decades for genuine change to develop, but we must test the evidence and ensure that the atmospheric changes occurring at the moment lead to a process that is more substantial, rooted in the institutional, legislative and constitutional reforms needed to make change truly irreversible. The process is fragile, much is riding on the shoulders of two individuals, President Thein Sein and Aung San Suu Kyi, and it is not certain that Thein Sein is strong enough – or sincere enough – to neutralise the hardliners within the regime and secure wider support within the military for his reforms. Genuine peace and true political reform have yet to come, and there is a long way to go. Nevertheless, the change in atmosphere is an important first step, and as Chinese philosopher Lao-tzu said, a journey of a thousand miles must begin with a single step. For perhaps the first time in decades, the question is not whether Burma is changing, but how deep, how substantial and how long-lasting the changes are. Burma is at a crossroads, and the world is watching to see in which direction it will go and how far down the road to change the Generals are willing to travel.

In this new edition, with a new epilogue, I try to look at some of the challenges that have emerged since the publication of the first edition in 2012 and, as Burma goes to the polls for only the third time in twenty-five years, to continue to ask the question: where does it go from here?

1

From Rice Bowl to Basket Case

'This is Burma and it will be quite unlike any land you know.'

Rudyard Kipling, 'Letters from the East' (1898)

A T 4.20 A.M. on 4 January 1948 Burma regained its independence. Following just over a century of British colonial rule, and several years of Japanese occupation, the country had finally shed its shackles and won its freedom. 'This early hour was selected by Burmese astrologers as the most propitious for the country's new beginning,' writes Christina Fink.[1]

Only a few days prior to this event, when people should have been celebrating their impending liberty, a well-educated, middle-class Burmese family near Mandalay gathered outside for drinks. A guest, who was also educated, was agitated. 'He was adamant that the wrong date had been chosen for independence,' recalls one of those present. 'He predicted that because of this date and time, there would be nothing but bloodshed and fighting among ourselves, and that we would not be able to do anything to change this. He had done all the astrological calculations.'

Astrology is taken extremely seriously among many Burmese people, as are other forms of spirituality and superstition, including numerology, and a belief in *nats* or spirits. Yet whether or not the astrological dangers of the date chosen for Burma's independence mean anything, other factors contributed to a fragile birth. Just six months prior to independence, on 19 July 1947, the man who had led Burma's struggle against colonial rule, General Aung San, was assassinated, along with half his cabinet. 'Burma's most competent leaders, who had been preparing to take over from the British, were dead before the country had even become independent,' writes Kin Oung in his book *Who Killed Aung San?*[2] Sir Nicholas Fenn, who served in Rangoon in the early 1960s and again as Ambassador twenty years later, says that the assassination of Aung San and half his cabinet meant that Burma came into being as an independent nation 'with a second-eleven cabinet'.

Interestingly, Aung San predicted his own death when he met the British Governor Sir Reginald Dorman-Smith in 1946. 'How long do national heroes last?' Aung San reportedly asked. He then answered his own question, saying: 'Not long in this country; they have too many enemies. Three years is the most they can hope to survive. I do not give myself more than another eighteen months of life.'[3] Aung San is respected to this day in Burma as the father of the nation and the founder of Burma's army; he was also the father of Burma's current democracy leader, Nobel Peace Prize-winner Aung San Suu Kyi. In 1998, she wrote an article about him for *Asiaweek*, describing her father's greatest strengths as 'the largeness of his spirit and an immense capacity to learn from his experiences. He recognized his faults and worked hard to remedy them.' His vision for the army he founded, she concludes, was very different from the one today's Burma Army pursues. 'My father made it abundantly clear that the army was meant to serve the people, that it should abide by principles of justice and honour, and that unless it could win and keep the trust and respect of the people, its purpose would be vitiated,' she wrote. 'He never intended the army to meddle in government. A liberal and a democrat, he saw from the fascist Japanese army the dangers of military absolutism.'[4]

Aung San was perhaps the one Burman capable of uniting the country's different ethnic peoples, despite having fought against them during the Second World War when he sided with the Japanese. In February 1947, Aung San attended a conference at Panglong, Shan State, to seek a constitutional way forward that would be based on equal rights for all the ethnic nationalities of Burma. In a speech in Jubilee Hall in Rangoon a few months later, Aung San explained the vision of Panglong: 'When we build our new Burma, shall we build it as a Union or as a Unitary State? In my opinion it will not be feasible to set up a Unitary State. We must set up a

Union with properly regulated provisions to safeguard the rights of the national minorities.'[5]

Although the Karen people boycotted the process, the Arakanese and Mon were not invited, and the Nagas, Was and other ethnic groups were excluded, the Panglong Agreement was signed on 12 February 1947 by the Shan, Kachin, Chin and Karenni, with the promise that 'full autonomy in internal administration for the Frontier Areas is accepted in principle'.[6] In addition, the Shan and Karenni, who had been largely independent during the pre-colonial and colonial periods, secured the right of secession after ten years. The status of the Karen was left to be resolved after independence.

The Panglong Agreement was part of a rapid process towards independence, from the defeat of the Japanese and Britain's restoration of colonial rule in Burma in 1945 to British Prime Minister Clement Attlee's agreement with Aung San on 27 January 1947 to grant Burma independence 'as soon as possible'.[7] Burma had been gradually occupied by the British in the nineteenth century through three Anglo-Burmese wars – 1824–1826, 1852 and 1885 – ultimately leading to the overthrow of the Burmese King Thibaw. During the early twentieth century, an active Burman nationalist movement developed in protest at the colonial occupation, beginning with the formation of the Young Men's Buddhist Association (YMBA) by students in 1906. The YMBA is regarded as Burma's first modern political organisation. An armed rebellion against the British led by a traditional medicine man known as Saya San began in 1930, and lasted two years. Saya San, who had been commissioned by the YMBA's successor organisation, the General Council of Burmese Associations (GCBA), to carry out an investigation into the conditions of farmers in rural Burma, declared himself King and urged people to refuse to pay tax to the British. His army, which numbered 3,000 by the time it was crushed two years later, led what Thant Myint-U describes as 'a passionate, desperate revolt'.[8] It took the British seven battalions and more than 8,000 soldiers to defeat Saya San, who was then hanged for treason.[9] His defeat, however, did not diminish the determination of Burman nationalists, who found fresh impetus in the movement established by Aung San in 1938, known as the *Dohbama Asiayone* or 'We Burmese Association'.[10]

Aung San and his fellow student leaders each adopted the title of *thakin* or 'master', and continued to agitate for change. In 1941, as a Japanese invasion of Burma appeared likely, he joined twenty-nine other nationalist activists on a journey to China, to receive military training from the Japanese. Known as the 'Thirty Comrades', they formed the Burma Independence Army (BIA) and paved the way for the Japanese invasion of Burma. On 8 December 1941 Japan declared war on Britain, and with BIA forces providing vital military and intelligence support, overran Burma during the following three years.

Some of the seeds of today's tensions between the Burman and non-Burman ethnic groups were sown during this period. The non-Burman ethnic nationalities, particularly the Karen, Karenni, Chin and Kachin, and the Rohingyas, not only sided with the British and American allies against the Japanese, but actively fought alongside them. Even prior to the Second World War, some of these ethnic groups had been favoured by the British over the Burman majority, and were perceived to be stooges of the colonialists. The BIA showed little restraint in attacking them, committing many atrocities and several massacres of the Karen. The fact that many of these ethnic groups were not Buddhists added to the Burman feeling that they were traitors. Many Karen Christian congregations were particularly targeted.

Japan granted Burma, under Aung San's BIA, independence, but that soon proved no more than nominal. By 1944, frustrated that their expectations of liberation under the Japanese had not borne fruit, and recognising that the tide had turned and the Allies were advancing, Aung San decided to switch sides. Taking his soldiers from their base at Pyinmana, the site of the SPDC's new capital sixty years later, Aung San established the Anti-Fascist People's Freedom League (AFPFL), and ensured that word reached the Allied commanders Generals William Slim and 'Vinegar' Joe Stilwell that he wanted to help eject the Japanese from Burma. Slim then met Aung San, and accused him of only turning to the British because they were winning. He was amused when Aung San swiftly retorted that it would not be much good to come to him if they were losing. 'I was impressed by Aung San,' Slim wrote. 'He was not the ambitious, unscrupulous guerrilla leader I had expected. He was certainly ambitious . . . but I judged him to be a genuine patriot and a well-balanced realist . . . The greatest impression he made on me was one of honesty . . . I had the idea that if he agreed to do something he would keep his word. I could do business with Aung San.'[11]

Slim saw the value of having Aung San and his troops on side. 'If they were not with us, as well as against the Japanese, we should end up by having to fight them too,' he recalled. 'I, therefore, recommended we should help Aung San, with arms and supplies, and try to get some tactical control of his forces to make them fit into the general plan.'[12] On 27 March 1945 Aung San's troops rebelled against the Japanese, and seven months later Japan formally surrendered.

Aung San, however, had not joined the British simply in order to welcome them back to Burma. When the Supreme Allied Commander in South East Asia, Lord Mountbatten, decided to accept Aung San's support against the Japanese, he knew that such support was not unconditional. Mountbatten, according to historian Martin Smith, 'recognized the rising tide of Asian nationalism and the inevitability of independence . . . He recognized it was only a question of time before the British would have to give way.'[13] Sure enough, as soon as the war was over, Aung San made it abundantly clear that he wanted independence, and threatened strikes and an armed uprising if there was no progress towards achieving it. His ambitions coincided conveniently with the defeat of Winston Churchill in a general election in Britain in 1945, and the election of the Labour Party under Clement Attlee. The new government was in a hurry to withdraw from its colonies and disband the British Empire.

Aung San's assassination in 1947, when his daughter Aung San Suu Kyi was just two years old, deprived him of the opportunity to see his dreams fulfilled and his country of an exceptionally able, wise young leader. He was just thirty-two. In 1948, U Nu was sworn in as Burma's first Prime Minister in his place, and served for just over a decade. Britain's Ambassador to Burma from 1953–1956, Lord Gore-Booth, recalls that U Nu was 'somewhat older than most of his Government, and this and his devout Buddhism made him sound like a solemn character. This was by no means so.' U Nu, writes Gore-Booth, 'had a unique smile compounded of saintliness and gaiety; he also had a certain political shrewdness which he used in day-to-day business and which made him for that period the undisputed leader of his country.'[14]

'Undisputed' may be too strong a term, for Burma's first decade of independence was one of fragile, turbulent parliamentary democracy. On the eve of independence, with the scars of the war still fresh, a civil war that would last decades broke out on several fronts. The communists rose up, and almost at the same time the Karen rebelled, after centuries of oppression at the hands of the Burmans. The spirit of Panglong, which promised a multi-ethnic federal democracy, was strained to breaking point. Despite having a Shan, Sao Shwe Thaike, as President, and a Karen, General Smith Dun, as head of the military, ethnic tensions boiled over. On Christmas Eve, 1948 eighty Karen Christians were massacred in Mergui, southern Tenasserim Division, and this was followed by mass killings of Karen civilians over the following weeks. On 31 January 1949 the armed wing of the Karen National Union (KNU), known at the time as the Karen National Defence Organisation (KNDO), took control of Insein Township, a suburb of Rangoon, to defend Karen communities against further attacks. Karen soldiers in the Tatmadaw defected en masse to join the uprising, and Smith Dun, although loyal to the national government, was replaced by Ne Win.[15] According to someone who was close to Ne Win and served in his regime, Ne Win orchestrated Smith Dun's removal, in part because of the Karen defections and in part because of an altogether more trivial grudge. Apparently, Ne Win had earlier tried to join a Masonic Lodge, but had been blackballed by the lodge master, a Karen called General Kya Doe. With Ne Win's promotion, Burma's decades-long nightmare began.

For the next nine years, what Sir Nicholas Fenn describes as Burma's 'charmingly inefficient parliamentary democracy' teetered on the brink of collapse as communists, Karens and other armed insurgents captured large parts of the country. While Patricia Gore-Booth, widow of the former British Ambassador, recalled a comfortable existence for diplomats, with 'cocktail parties which were free, easy and charming,' she noted that they were unable to drive out of the city, because it was surrounded by insurgents. And while Ne Win played golf, gambled and went to the races each weekend, it was clear, she said, that he had been 'very jealous of Aung San'.

Although U Saw, one of Aung San's principal political rivals, was found guilty of masterminding his assassination, with extensive evidence against him, there are lingering questions about what role, if any, Ne Win may have played. An extensive arms dump was found in the lake behind U Saw's home, and U Saw clearly expected to become Prime Minister. 'U Saw and his henchmen had enough military hardware to stage a revolution in Rangoon – which indeed may have been the plan. What were U Saw and his men actually up to?' asks Kin Oung, whose father, Major General Tun Hla Oung and father-in-law, Justice Thaung Sein, played key roles in bringing Aung San's assassins to justice.[16] However, in 1986 a bulletin published by the Karen National Union (KNU) carried an article which asked whether U Saw had been framed. 'Is there any truth to persisting rumours that General Ne Win, Prime Minister U Nu and others may have been involved?'[17]

It was no secret that Aung San and Ne Win had not been close. According to Martin Smith, one of the Thirty Comrades, Kyaw Zaw, has claimed that Aung San once seriously considered removing Ne Win from his position because 'his behaviour under the Japanese had led them to believe he had "fascist" tendencies'. Ne Win, described by Kyaw Zaw as 'double-faced' and a 'power-mad and evil king', only survived because of his 'cunning'.[18] Aung San and Ne Win often quarrelled, and Aung San's main objection to Ne Win was his 'immoral character . . . He was a gambler and a womanizer, which the strict moralist Aung San – and the rest of us as well – despised.'[19]

It is interesting that, according to Kin Oung, the first detailed telegram from the governor's office in Rangoon to London about the assassination noted that the gunmen were members of Ne Win's 4th Burma Rifles.[20] It is also interesting that an apparent attempt on U Saw's life had been made just ten months before Aung San's assassination. Kin Oung suggests that one theory is that 'Ne Win, with the mind of a race-goer, plotted that an attempt would be made on U Saw without taking his life. U Saw would then retaliate by taking revenge on Aung San – the two gunmen in the car that day wore the uniforms of Aung San's "private army" – by being convinced that he was behind the assassination attempt.'[21]

Whether or not Ne Win had any involvement in the assassination of Aung San, his jealousy of Burma's assassinated leader culminated in Ne Win seizing power in 1958. Although U Nu claimed he had invited the military to take charge, as a caretaker government to restore order, with the benefit of hindsight we can conclude that he had little choice.[22] Many believe Ne Win's first government did much to restore order to the chaos that was sweeping the country, and was a relatively benign dictatorship. Martin Morland, who served in the British Embassy in Rangoon from 1957 to 1960 and played tennis with Ne Win, says that Ne Win reversed U Nu's ban on beef (which U Nu had imposed, for religious reasons) and dealt with the 'pye-dogs' which were running wild, two policies which 'pleased diplomats'. Gore-Booth claims that Ne Win 'played a somewhat elusive part in Burmese public life, alternating between bursts of energy and an enjoyment of golf, racing and family life'.[23]

However, even if he restored order, there were early indications of what was to come. 'The caretaker government was sensitive to criticism and imprisoned numerous journalists for daring to critique its actions,' writes Fink. 'And much to civil servants' annoyance, battlefield commanders were brought in to replace or work alongside bureaucrats.'[24] Although originally intended to govern for just six months, Ne Win twice extended his term, but then 'pressure increased for an election to restore democracy'.[25] Ne Win complied, and fresh elections were held in February 1960. He hoped to influence the ballot and achieve a popular mandate for his continued rule, but instead the people overwhelmingly re-elected U Nu.

'It was democracy's last chance for some time to come,' writes Gore-Booth. 'But sadly, it was not taken.' U Nu's devout Buddhism consumed his attention, and the political turmoil escalated. 'Instead of reading accurately the lessons of what had happened and pursuing a stabilizing policy, U Nu set about fulfilling his conscientious dream of making Buddhism the state religion of the country. This effort, superfluous in a country in which Buddhism was the official religion in all but name, caused much disturbance and uncertainty.'[26] The predominantly Christian Kachins took up arms in revolt against the government, in part out of protest at the idea of Buddhism being imposed as the state religion.

Two years into the new U Nu government, Ne Win launched a coup d'état which set Burma on the course of military rule that has lasted to this day. The previous evening he had attended a ballet performance. He was seen congratulating the leading ballerina, and nothing seemed untoward. Yet at 8.50 a.m. on 2 March 1962 he announced on the radio that the military had taken power.[27]

Susan Fenn, wife of Sir Nicholas, was one of the first foreigners to become aware of the coup. In a nursing home having just given birth, she woke at 3 a.m. on 2 March to feed the baby. Hearing a low, rumbling sound through the open window, she looked out and saw an army jeep under the porch and guns in the bushes. The doorbell rang, and when she and the nurse opened it, they found 'a dozen rifles poking through the security grill'. The troops had come to arrest one of the other patients, Sao Sai Long, known as 'Shorty', the Shan *sawbwa* or *saopha* (local royal ruler, or 'king') of Kengtung. 'On an impulse, I offered the men the baby to hold,' recalls Susan Fenn. 'Immediately the guns were stacked against the wall and all attention focused on the smiling infant.' This deflected the tension for a while, but the soldiers had orders to carry out, and Shorty was carried down the stairs on a sedan chair. 'I asked if there was anything I could do for him, and he gave a regal wave, saying: "No thank you, my dear, this is just one of those things." And he was borne off into the night. At 9 a.m. his family came to the nursing home to settle the bill.' He was jailed for seven years.

When the telephone lines, which had been cut, were restored Susan Fenn called her husband. 'He was still asleep, but when he looked out of the window and saw the tanks, he was all attention. He rang the ambassador, and that is how the British embassy was the first embassy in Rangoon to report the coup,' she recalls.

U Nu had convened a meeting with ethnic leaders to discuss federalism and ethnic rights on 2 March 1962, and that provided the pretext for Ne Win's coup. 'Ne Win wanted to prevent what he feared was going to happen the next day. It was a pre-emptive move,' says Fenn. 'Ne Win believed U Nu was breaking up the union, and that he would allow that to happen "over my dead body". He was also undoubtedly impatient with the charming inefficiencies of U Nu's regime.' On the morning of the coup, Ne Win was quoted as saying: 'federalism is impossible – it will destroy the Union', and his chief spokesman cited federalism as the main reason for the coup.[28] U Nu, many members of his government, and ethnic leaders including Burma's first President, Sao Shwe Thaike were arrested and jailed. One of Sao Shwe Thaike's sons was killed, and he himself died in prison eight months later.

Burmese historian Aung Saw Oo believes Ne Win had been planning a coup for a long time. In 1956, Aung Saw Oo claims, Ne Win called the top generals together and told them that one day, the army would run the country. Two years later, that became a reality, but after losing the 1960 election his taste for power was not satisfied, and he wanted more.

President Sao Shwe Thaike's youngest son, Harn Yawnghwe, recalls the night of the coup vividly. He was fourteen at the time. 'The first thing I remember is bullets flying all over the place. Soldiers surrounded the house and opened fire. The shooting went on a long time. The walls of our house were eighteen inches thick. The upstairs was wood, the downstairs was brick. The bullets didn't hit us.'

Harn Yawnghwe was sharing a room with his seventeen-year-old brother, who was killed. 'My brother rolled out of bed when he heard shooting. He found the front door open, so he shut it. But then we couldn't find him. We heard shots, and then we found he had been killed. The military claimed we were resisting. The only thing I can think is that my brother had a spear, and that he must have gone out into the garden with it – and there they shot him, in the head and leg. We do not know why he was shot.' An officer ordered his troops to collect all the spent cartridges, but the next morning, at least one hundred cartridges were still lying around.

'The soldiers then shouted "Shan girls come out." In the house, it was just the family and our maids, but in the compound our ex-bodyguards had settled. They were all arrested. Then they shouted "This is the army." They searched the house, thinking that we had guns. My father and two brothers went out, and they took my father away. The soldiers pointed their guns at us, ordered us to put our hands up and told us to sit in a line on the front lawn.'

For the whole family, and especially for a fourteen-year-old, such scenes were 'traumatic,' says Harn Yawnghwe. 'Before that moment, you're somebody. Then, with the shooting and guns pointed at you, you become nothing. After the coup, people were afraid to be associated with us.' Today, the family home in Nyaung Shwe, Inle Lake, is a museum. In 2010 it was closed, shuttered, deserted and decaying. Even its status as a museum has been manipulated by the regime for political purposes, changing its focus from Shan culture, as it was initially set up, to a museum of Buddhism, stripped of ethnic associations.

Sao Shwe Thaike embodied the spirit of multi-ethnic Burma, and in jail he was placed in solitary confinement for refusing to retract his support for federalism. 'My father was a signatory of the Panglong Agreement. He was respected by everyone. He was not just a Shan, and he tried to maintain that role. He was more Shan during the Second World War – after the war he worked with Kachins and others and founded the Supreme Council of United Hill People. One of his bodyguards was a Burman and his private secretary was a Burman.'

Harn Yawnghwe's mother was also politically active, and the military wanted to arrest her too. Fortunately, she was in Britain at the time of the coup. Elected a Member of Parliament in 1960, her son describes her as 'very much Shan, and hated by the Burman army'. A year after the coup, when Ne Win called for peace talks with the Shan, the family fled to Thailand and have been in exile ever since. 'The Shan State Independence Army sent my brother to the dialogue. We left, because we didn't want to be held hostage.'

Another Shan family torn apart by the coup was that of Sao Kya Seng, the *saopha* of Hsipaw. Married to an Austrian woman, Inge Eberhard, whom he met when they were both students in the United States, Sao Kya Seng had attended Parliament in Rangoon the day before the coup, and had flown to Taunggyi to visit his dying sister. From Taunggyi he set out to return to Hsipaw, unaware of the events in Rangoon, but was stopped at a military roadblock. He was last seen being taken away by armed soldiers. His wife Inge was placed under house arrest, her bodyguards and drivers beaten with rifle butts and taken away. Now Inge Sargent, she recounts in her book *Twilight over Burma: My Life as a Shan Princess* her efforts to meet Ne Win to plead for information about her husband, and describes her eventual escape from Burma. Although she had Austrian citizenship, she required an exit permit to leave the country. Given her status as the wife of a prominent Shan leader and political prisoner, obtaining that was no easy task. To make life even harder, her children had been born in Burma and as such were regarded under Burmese law as Burmese citizens. They could only leave the country if she was able to convince Austria to give them citizenship. After considerable struggle she obtained all the necessary documents, and fled the country. Prior to her departure, she was informed by a source with high-level connections that her husband had been executed soon after his arrest.[29] Now based in Colorado, she continues to support the people of Burma almost half a century later. In 2008 she spoke enthusiastically about her charity, Burma Lifeline, and the work of the Burma Relief Centre that she supports. In 2014 I was able to visit the house in Hsipaw for the first time.

A hallmark of Ne Win's rule was an ingrained hostility to foreigners, and to non-Burman ethnic nationalities. But his racism was contradictory. He was himself part-Chinese, and yet fiercely anti-Chinese. He got round this by claiming to have royal blood. In a similar contradiction, he often travelled abroad, sometimes for months at a time. He made state visits to the United States, Australia, Japan, China and the Soviet Union, among other places. His visits to Switzerland to consult psychiatrists, and to Britain to enjoy the races at Ascot and tea with the Queen, were legendary – and yet, according to Gore-Booth, Ne Win lacked Aung San's 'self-confidence' and was 'naturally suspicious of foreigners'.[30]

Ne Win would visit Britain regularly, but even these visits were tinged with nationalism. In contrast to normal protocol, he would simply inform the British embassy that he would be visiting, and offers of assistance were bluntly refused. Sir Nicholas Fenn recalls one visit, a year after the coup, when Ne Win met the Foreign Secretary, Patrick Gordon Walker, to receive a collection of Burmese royal regalia which the British had taken in 1885. Fenn, who had left Rangoon to become the Foreign Secretary's assistant private secretary, was responsible for handing over the collection. The Foreign Secretary presented Ne Win with a ceremonial dagger, champagne was served, and then the General left, evidently delighted. 'In his mind, they were *his* regalia, and *he* brought them back to Rangoon in triumph,' says Fenn.

The hostility to foreigners and non-Burman ethnic minorities within Burma was abundantly clear. However, Ne Win was, according to Fenn, 'a contradictory and strange character', and as such his known xenophobia did not stop him pursuing non-Burman women. One of his several wives was June Rose Bellamy, daughter of an Australian bookmaker who had married a descendant of Burmese King Tharrawaddy, and he is rumoured to have tried to pursue former Miss Burma film star Louisa Benson, a Karen whose father was Portuguese. Nevertheless, a Burmese woman who cannot be named but whose father knew Ne Win recalls the period immediately after the coup: 'The atmosphere was terrible. We were the only family in our area who accepted foreign visitors. If you were visited by a foreigner, you had to give an account of what was said . . . We lived on rumour. We did not know who had disappeared.'

Soon, Ne Win's xenophobia took a new policy turn. Foreign business people, journalists and missionaries were expelled from the country, along with educational organisations such as the Ford, Fulbright and Asia Foundations, mission schools and hospitals were nationalised and the teaching of English was restricted. 'It was a mentality that wanted foreigners and foreign-ness to be banished,' says Fenn.

The Indian population was particularly targeted. One Indian man who grew up in Burma and now lives in the United States recalls the day when his tailoring business was taken over by the military. He was initially ordered to continue work, told he could not go home for lunch as was his normal practice, and instructed to hand over his profits. Shortly afterwards he was forced to leave the country. 'The Indians got the worst treatment,' confirms Fenn. 'Their rings were removed at the airport and if they could not get them off their fingers their fingers were chopped off. The brutality was really appalling. Some of these people had been born in Burma, Burma was their home, and some of them had never been to India before, so it was really crass.' Gore-Booth notes that 'a medical institute run by a gentle and respected Indian physician, Dr Suvi, was taken over one night and its director bundled into the next aeroplane for India.'[31] Men like scholar Gordon Luce, who had devoted much of his life to studying and writing about the country, were harassed. 'Foreign business was proceeded against with a blunt weapon,' concludes Gore-Booth. 'Life was made impossible for Gordon Luce and his wife and they had to leave the country: to make Burma uninhabitable for two such wise, patient people required real genius.' The effects on the country were devastating. 'The economy ran rapidly downhill and in a short time Burma, the country which stood above all things for self-sufficiency in rice, was suffering from a rice shortage.'[32] Fenn agrees. 'Burma was potentially the richest country in Asia, and it became one of the poorest nations on earth. That's an act of genius, and Ne Win was the genius who brought the nation to its knees.'

Ne Win established a Revolutionary Council, which nationalised all banks, industries and large shops, and demonetised 50 and 100 kyat notes. The military took over businesses, despite having little education or commercial management experience. Approximately 2,000 civil servants were replaced by soldiers, and with few opportunities left for them skilled professionals began to emigrate, starting a brain drain which has continued to this day.

As a person, Ne Win was 'cunning, shrewd and intelligent in some ways', according to Fenn, but also 'vain and latterly completely ignorant about his country'. His fierce temper ensured that no one on his staff ever contradicted him or told him bad news. His 'very short fuse', Fenn recalls, was on full display on Christmas Eve 1975 when he stormed over to the Inya Lake Hotel in Rangoon from his mansion on the opposite side of the lake, furious at the noise of the loud music keeping him awake. Accounts vary, but some claim he seized the drumsticks, kicked in the drums, beat up some of the musicians and declared the party over.

Four months after the coup, students at Rangoon University began to protest against Ne Win's regime. On 7 July 1962 they held a mass rally in the Student Union building and a demonstration outside. Soldiers and riot police stormed the campus, captured the Student Union building, and opened fire on the students. Aung Saw Oo witnessed some of the scenes. 'I heard automatic machine guns, and I saw the students covered in blood,' he recalls. It is believed that over one hundred students died, although officially the government declared the death toll to be fifteen.[33] Thant Myint-U describes what followed as 'the start of a decades-long and unfinished struggle between Burma's educated youth and the men in uniform'.[34] In the early hours of the next day the military took drastic action. 'An explosives team marched up to the whitewashed Student Union building, an icon of anticolonialism since the 1920s and home to speeches by Aung San, U Nu and U Thant, and blew it to pieces. Though there were many bloodier clashes to come, the scars of this particular incident lasted for a long time,' writes Thant Myint-U.[35] Aung Saw Oo believes there were students inside the building when it was blown up.

For a decade, Burma was ruled directly by the military's Revolutionary Council. A guiding ideology was devised, known as 'The Burmese Way to Socialism', and set out in a document that was both eccentric and Orwellian, 'The System of Correlation of Man and His Environment'. A strange blend of Marxism, extreme nationalism, totalitarianism and Buddhism, the ideology underpinning Ne Win's rule created a country which Smith describes as 'one of the most isolated and hermetically sealed countries in the world'. Foreign visitors, notes Smith, were few and tourists were only permitted visas for seven days.[36]

In 1972, Ne Win sought to solidify and legitimise his rule by resigning from the military, along with nineteen other senior officers, and establishing a civilian administration. This was, however, a superficial change. Most of the same people were in power, and the only difference was that they wore suits rather than military uniforms. The Burma Socialist Programme Party (BSPP) was established, and a new constitution drawn up, establishing a unitary state and one-party rule. In December 1973, a referendum was held on the new constitution. In polling stations, ballots were not placed in one box, but rather in one of two boxes – a white box for a 'yes' vote and a black box for a 'no' vote, making it possible for all to see how people voted. Officials watched intently as votes were cast, and if anyone attempted to place their ballot in the 'no' box, they would be encouraged to vote again, the right way.[37] It is therefore no surprise that the regime claimed 95 per cent turnout, and a 90 per cent vote in favour of the new constitution. In a referendum on another new constitution in 2008 history repeated itself, with just a few percentage points difference.

Six months after the referendum, major protests broke out. In May and June 1974, workers in state-owned factories went on strike, after the regime cut rations in half. More than 1,000 workers seized the dockyard, according to Khun Saing, a former political prisoner whose activism began in 1974 when he was a medical student. The regime's reaction, as always, was brutal. 'So many were gunned down,' recalls Khun Saing. 'Some were killed in factory compounds, some on the street. Navy boats recaptured the dockyard and many were killed. They were not challenging the government, they were just asking for the lowering of commodity prices and for salary rises. But Ne Win would not tolerate it. Many bodies disappeared. I was not into politics – but I started thinking about it then.' Aung Saw Oo, a third-year dental student at the time, confirms Khun Saing's account. He helped carry wounded workers to the university hospital and confirms that many died. 'Officially they said only sixty-four people died, but in reality there were many more than sixty-four,' he claims.

Another pivotal moment in Burma's turbulent political history occurred in December 1974, with the death of U Thant. A Burmese diplomat who served for a decade as Secretary General of the United Nations from 1961, just before Ne Win's coup, U Thant was loathed by Ne Win. Thant Myint-U, U Thant's grandson, claims Ne Win was convinced that U Thant and U Nu were 'conniving' against him, after U Nu had held a press conference at the UN in 1969. According to Thant Myint-U, U Nu 'launched a vitriolic attack on the Rangoon regime and called for revolution. Never before had a call for the overthrow of a UN member state government been made from inside the UN.' Although U Thant later reprimanded U Nu, Ne Win declared the then UN Secretary General an enemy of the state.[38]

Such was Ne Win's hostility to U Thant that when he died the normal arrangements for a state funeral were completely rejected. U Thant's body was flown back to Burma, but instead of being greeted with the pomp and ceremony that a Burmese who had served as UN Secretary General would normally expect, Ne Win gave orders that no state official should receive the coffin, and that U Thant would be buried like any ordinary person. The deputy education minister, U Aung Tin, who had been a former student of U Thant's, defied the orders and came to the airport. 'He was immediately sacked,' notes Thant Myint-U.[39] The people were incensed.

'We recognised U Thant as a world leader and were proud of him,' recalls Khun Saing. 'We thought the government would also respect him. But, as with Aung San, there was a personal history, a jealousy, by Ne Win. When U Thant's body was brought back, there was no recognition. So the students protested. We asked, "Why were there no senior officials to greet the body, why was there no commemoration?" The government planned to cremate his body – but we thought he should be given a memorial monument.'

U Thant's body was laid out in the old racetrack at Kyaikkasan, and almost immediately thousands of people came to pay respects and lay wreaths. Ne Win's anger increased, and he threatened U Thant's family with legal action for bringing the body back without permission.[40]

Eventually, the regime granted U Thant's family permission to hold a small private funeral on 5 December. It was, however, to be anything but private. Crowds of people thronged the streets and then, just before the body was to be cremated, outraged students took matters into their own hands. 'Students surrounded the area. They didn't accept the cremation. They seized the coffin, and then took it to the university campus. The whole street filled with thousands of students,' Khun Saing recalls. The coffin was placed on a platform in the Convocation Hall.

For seven days, demonstrations were held, anti-government speeches delivered, and the students protected U Thant's coffin. Work began on the construction of a mausoleum to U Thant, on the site where once the Student Union building had stood. Negotiations between the students, U Thant's family and the government began, and the regime offered a proper burial place near the southern part of the Shwedagon pagoda. 'The students did not accept this,' says Khun Saing, 'so they buried him at the Student Union compound, against the government's will.' At night two days later troops surrounded the campus, removed the body and buried it at the foot of the Shwedagon.

In the early hours of 11 December 1974, soldiers stormed Rangoon University. Perhaps as many as one hundred were killed. Almost 3,000 were arrested,[41] but Khun Saing says it may have been as many as 6,000. Although he had slept at the university every night since it started, that particular night Khun Saing went home, and escaped arrest. 'I was lucky,' he recalls.

Further protests took place in 1975 to commemorate the anniversary of the 1974 workers' strike. Khun Saing took part in a demonstration at the Shwedagon pagoda, but troops surrounded the students and arrested at least 200. Universities across Burma were closed down.

The students were not easily discouraged, however, and in March 1976 they demonstrated once again, this time throughout the country. The protests were held to mark the centenary of the birth of Thakin Kodaw Hmaing, a famous writer who had promoted peace talks between the regime and armed resistance groups in 1963. Ne Win had rejected the deal. 'Thakin Kodaw Hmaing was hated by Ne Win,' says Khun Saing. 'We wanted to make a memorial to him, so we marched from Rangoon University to his tomb. Thousands of people participated. We did this during the curfew period. I organised medical students, and we distributed pamphlets.' For this, at the end of April 1976, Khun Saing was arrested. He was held for eight days in a military compound, and was then moved to the notorious Insein Prison.

'I was put on trial in July 1976,' says Khun Saing. 'It was a one-day trial. Over seventy students were tried. The charges were read out, but there was no questioning. Then the sentence was passed: seven years.' Khun Saing was one of over one hundred in Rangoon alone to be arrested and sentenced to terms ranging from five to fifteen years. A prominent Chin student leader, Tin Maung Oo, was hanged.

Khun Saing served two of his seven years, and was then released early, in 1978, 'because the prisons were overcrowded'. During those two years, he went on hunger strike three times, in protest at hard labour duties and prison conditions. The first hunger strike was just three days into his sentence, and lasted three days. The second and third hunger strikes both lasted eleven days. As soon as he started his hunger strike, the authorities denied him water in retaliation. Sometimes students threw plastic bags of water into his cell, but during his third hunger strike he went without water for seven days. 'My mouth was totally dry, with no saliva. My gums were bleeding, my body temperature rising, and I felt weak and dizzy. There was no sugar in my blood. I was in a delirious state,' he describes. 'It was raining outside, so I tore up my longyi and threw it outside the cell to soak up the rainwater. Then I brought it back in to suck the water out. I did this again and again. I also collected water in the toilet pot to drink.'

For the next decade, Ne Win succeeded in retaining a tight grip on power. The country's isolation and economic collapse continued, and in 1987 the United Nations designated Burma a 'Least Developed Nation'. The country that had once been known as the 'rice bowl' of Asia was now ranked alongside some of the poorest countries in Africa. When Sir Nicholas Fenn returned as ambassador in 1982, he found that 'twenty years of utterly incompetent military rule had impoverished and dispirited the nation'. Yet while dissent remained under the surface, there were few visible outbreaks of protest. A plot by rivals within the regime was uncovered, and Ne Win's rule seemed secure. Until, that is, the dramatic events of 1988.

2

Cry Freedom

'It is infinitely difficult to begin when mere words must remove a great block of matter. But there is no other way if none of the material strength is on your side. And a shout in the mountains has been known to cause an avalanche.'

Aleksandr Solzhenitsyn

'RIGHT IN FRONT of Inya Lake, the army was already blocking us,' recalled Khin Ohmar. 'We were stuck. The police trucks started rolling towards us. We were holding each other, telling each other "Don't run, don't run." Then came the tear gas, and the riot police started beating us with batons. Of course we all ran.'

Khin Ohmar was a student at the Rangoon Arts and Sciences University, who joined the protests in 1988 just a few days after they began in mid-March. A brawl between students and local youth in the Sanda Win tea-shop in Rangoon sparked the uprising, but the fuse had been laid by a far more serious concern. Ne Win's decision the previous year to demonetise several Burmese kyat banknotes, and introduce new notes divisible by nine, his lucky number according to astrologers, wiped out people's savings overnight. 'People lost all their money,' recalls Victor Biak Lian, a Chin student at the time. 'I could not even buy a meal. I was in the middle of exams when the announcement came. Students who had usable money shared it with others, so we could buy food. That was the beginning of the 1988 uprising, because people completely lost trust in the government. Student anger was uncontrollable.'

The tea-shop brawl was started by the son of a BSPP official, in a dispute over music, and when the police came to the scene, they took no action against him. Protests in front of the police station were met with brutal force by the riot police, and a student named Phone Maw was killed.[1] His fellow students were outraged; the fuse had been lit.

Protests over the following few days culminated in what became known as the 'Red Bridge' incident, on 16 March. Originally called the White Bridge, near Inya Lake, it has been renamed in people's minds because of the bloodshed. According to Bertil Lintner, the police chased fleeing students into the lake and forced their heads under water, holding them there until they drowned. 'Clubs swished and bones cracked. There were groans and shrieks as students fell to the ground bleeding. Panic-stricken students trying to escape . . . were felled in droves . . . After about an hour, the orgy in violence was over. Sprawling corpses lay oozing in pools of blood all over the street.'[2]

Khin Ohmar's account of the event confirms Lintner's precisely. As they approached the bridge, the students saw the army and realised they were trapped as police trucks drove in from the back. When the police then began to advance towards the students, beating everyone in sight, some ran down side streets and others towards the lakeside, she recalls. 'I ran to a house by the roadside, and climbed over the gate. As a child I used to like climbing trees, even though my mother always told me not to because, she said, it was not something girls should do. I got into the compound. The house was our protection. We could witness everything happening in the street and on the bank of the lake.'

What Khin Ohmar saw next, from her vantage point behind the walls of the compound, was beyond anything she could have believed. 'People ran up the banks of the lake and were beaten,' she says. 'There was blood everywhere. Some people jumped into the lake, some were kicked into the lake. I saw a little boy in his white and green school uniform, maybe eleven or twelve years old, probably in the area by accident, being beaten up and dragged into a truck. I kept screaming. It was like hell.'

Her screams, however, drew the soldiers' attention. 'The soldiers saw us and ran towards us to get us. I ran to the back of the house, but the people in the house were very scared that they would be in trouble [for sheltering us]. There was another house behind, and the owner gave us a way to come into the house. It was a diplomat's residence, and an Indian-Burmese housekeeper gave us a small ladder to climb up and into the house. We hid there until it got dark, around 6.30 p.m.'

After dark and still in hiding, Khin Ohmar then heard the police saying 'search the houses'. She stayed silent. 'We heard people being beaten up, we heard screaming, and then we heard the trucks leaving one by one. Then it was dead quiet.' When she was confident that the police had gone, the housekeeper drove her and a few others to the corner of Inya Road and University Avenue, and from there she ran home. The scenes and sounds she had witnessed that terrible day, however, were to remain with her for ever. 'I was shaken – and that was just my first day [in the protests]. At home, I went to bed but I couldn't sleep. I thought to myself: "That's it." That was the day I determined that something had been done to us that was not right, that was brutal, and that had no reason. I felt I was in a war.'

Those who were not killed or, like Khin Ohmar, were fortunate enough to escape were arrested and taken to prison. Women prisoners were 'allegedly raped', according to Martin Smith. In one particularly horrific example of the regime's 'astonishingly severe' response to the protests, 120 students were crammed into a prison van made to hold less than half that number. The prison van was, Smith claims, 'deliberately driven around the city for two hours', and 41 of the students suffocated to death.[3]

Demonstrations of varying sizes continued throughout the following six months, and were met with further brutality. The universities were forced to close down on 18 March, but the students and others continued their action. Khin Ohmar's commitment deepened when she went secretly to Rangoon General Hospital, to visit students who had been injured. 'Two friends and I pretended we were medical students. We met some of those who were detained in the Rangoon General Hospital detention centre. One student, Soe Naing, had been shot at the same time as Phone Maw, but the doctors could not operate because the bullet was in his lung. He was tiny – but his legs were chained to the bed.' A clear look of bewilderment mixed with anger spread across her face as she recounted this experience. 'Where could he have run? I was outraged. What did he do wrong?' Soe Naing died two days later.

On 30 May, the universities re-opened, and the protests continued. The students had four demands: the release of all students arrested in

March, a list of all who had died in detention, the readmission of students expelled, and the formation of a students' union.[4] 'We wore white and black, as a symbol of sorrow', recalls Khin Ohmar. 'My friends and I took part in these first protests, and quietly mobilised people. By 16 June, [the movement] started to become really big. Students began gathering in cafes and recreation centres, and shouting: "What are we doing here? Our fellow students are in prison. Let us do something." Everybody already felt dissent and resentment, and these erupted like a volcano.'

Khin Ohmar helped lead a protest march from the recreation centre towards Convocation Road. She was invited to speak at a rally, and she focused her thoughts on the weaknesses of Burma's education system. 'After my talk, I said to the other students: "Let's work for the release of our brothers and sisters in prison." We went to the teachers in classes, and said: "What are you doing? Teaching? Teaching what? Stop – it is useless. Students, get out, come and join us."' With a smile, she added: 'I was very rebellious.'

Khin Ohmar's rebelliousness had not gone unnoticed by the authorities. Her brother worked as a government official, and military intelligence came to him with a photograph of her giving a speech, and a warning. 'They told him: "You stop your sister, or we will do what we have to do." I went home and had a shower, and then my brother came home. He told my mother everything, and she freaked out.'

On 7 July the regime released all the students who had been arrested, in a gesture aimed at defusing the tension. The students, however, seized the opportunity to strengthen the movement. Min Ko Naing, who had taken on the leadership of the students, issued a statement urging people to continue.[5] This was followed by invitations to several professional associations to reflect on how much they had suffered under Ne Win. The aim was clearly to broaden the movement beyond the student demonstrators.

Several national political figures began to emerge at this time in opposition to Ne Win's regime. Former Brigadier Aung Gyi, who had been one of Ne Win's closest allies in the early 1960s, had written an open letter to his former boss the previous year, warning of the dire consequences of his economic policy. Aung Gyi had travelled abroad for the first time in twenty-five years, and was shocked by the difference between Burma and neighbouring countries such as Thailand. In 1988, he wrote two more open letters, and a forty-page analysis of how Ne Win's regime had brought economic ruin on Burma. In one, dated 12 May 1988, Aung Gyi wrote: 'That the country has gone from bad to worse [26] years after the seizure of power is evident to anyone not living in a fool's paradise . . . The country has plunged to the bottom politically, economically and socially. The moral decay is the most deplorable.' In an attempt to sound conciliatory and respectful, he accepted his share of the blame, having served in the regime, and let Ne Win off the hook by blaming his advisors. 'All of us, including you and I, must bear responsibility for the present state of affairs . . . It is unfair that some people in and outside the country link Bogyoke's[6] name to, and hold you responsible for, whatever happens here . . . The habit among officials of concealing things from Bogyoke and only saying "done under Bogyoke's order" is intolerable.'[7]

Such open criticism of Ne Win's regime, even if carefully couched in terms that could be interpreted as constructive, was a shock. But it was in keeping with the public mood, which had become increasingly angry. By July, the country was descending into anarchy. Crowds unleashed their fury on suspected regime agents in horrific scenes. According to *Asiaweek*, outside the Rangoon Institute of Medicine a military intelligence official was spotted by the crowd of 200 students. 'Angrily, they set about him, pummelling him to the ground. When two truckloads of riot police arrived on the scene minutes later, the mob turned its hatred on them. One truck escaped, but the students hurled stones and whatever other objects they could lay their hands on at the second. Then they pushed it towards Rangoon General Hospital where they set light to it, burning to death those still alive inside.' In another incident, 'enraged students' attacked police who tried to take protest flags from the hands of demonstrators. They 'charged' at the police 'with sticks, knives and pieces of cement broken from the pavement'. In Myenigone district, an outraged crowd attacked policemen after a police truck had run over and killed three children. The crowd set upon the policemen, 'stamping their bodies to a pulp long after they were dead'. In Pegu, eighty kilometres north-east of Rangoon, demonstrators reportedly set fire to a dozen houses and ransacked a Ministry of Trade building.[8]

Rumours spread that the Tatmadaw soldiers shooting protestors were

Chins, and as a result a wave of anger was directed at Chin people. 'Posters went up accusing Chin soldiers of killing students, and calling for any Chin to be arrested and killed,' recalls Lian Sakhong, General Secretary of the Chin strike committee in Rangoon and a founder of the Chin National Union. 'One Sunday morning I went out to teach the adult Sunday school, and nobody showed up. We found out that no Chins would go out, because they were afraid, so the pastor, myself and two or three friends decided to launch a counter-propaganda campaign.' The false rumours stemmed from the fact that some of the troops were from the Chin Hills Battalion. After independence the different ethnic battalions were integrated into the Tatmadaw, mixing the troops together but retaining the historic names of each battalion. So although the Chin Hills Battalion were deployed in Rangoon, the soldiers themselves may not necessarily have been Chin.

The authorities imposed a curfew on 21 June, banning people from going outside between 6 p.m. and 6 a.m., in an attempt to control the crisis. Section 144 of the Criminal Procedure Code was invoked, banning public gatherings, speeches, marches and demonstrations.[9] Two days after this, however, Ne Win made an announcement that stunned everyone. He was resigning. To the astonishment of delegates at an emergency BSPP congress, the man who had ruled Burma for twenty-six years was not only stepping down, but apologising as well. He acknowledged that the recent events 'show a lack of trust in the government and the party', and he promised a referendum on whether to move to a multi-party system of government. 'If the choice is for a multi-party system, we must hold elections for a new parliament.' A further surprise came when Ne Win announced that not only would he go, but five other senior leaders, including the state President San Yu, would also step down. 'The nation, and possibly even more so the diplomatic community, was flabbergasted,' writes Bertil Lintner. 'Public outrage had forced an end to 26 years of one-party rule . . . Or had it?'[10]

Ne Win was nothing if not canny. Moreover, his promise of a referendum was followed immediately by a warning to demonstrators. 'I want the entire nation, the people, to know that if in future there are mob disturbances, if the army shoots, it hits – there is no firing into the air to scare.'[11] He meant it.

The students, however, were not appeased by Ne Win's resignation or by the pledge of a referendum on multi-party democracy. They were even more incensed when it was announced that Sein Lwin would take over as President. Sein Lwin, known as the 'Butcher of Rangoon', had presided over the White Bridge massacre in March. Ne Win is said to have described him as 'my necessary evil'.[12] He was the antithesis of reform, and his appointment provided further fuel to the protests.

At the end of July, Christopher Gunness, a BBC correspondent who had managed to get into Rangoon, broadcast an interview with a student who called for a nationwide demonstration on 8 August. The date was chosen deliberately, for its numerological significance, and at 8.08 a.m. on 8 August 1988 dock workers walked out into the streets. Thousands of other people joined them.

The previous day, Khin Ohmar came home from a meeting preparing for the '8888' protests and was confronted with her entire family. 'My mother had completely collapsed. The plan for 8 August had been announced, and there were already warnings of shootings. The family said: "You have to stop, you are killing your mother." She had a heart condition. But I said I would not change my mind. I would go on,' she recalls. In an act of desperation, her sisters urged her to lie, for the sake of their mother's health. 'They told me to tell my mother I was not going to take part in the protests, and then they would let me out by the window. I said no, I could not lie. My brother got angry, and he slapped me, beat me, and then dragged me into his car and drove me to his apartment, one block from City Hall. There was a movie theatre and a police station next door. He locked me in his flat.'

From the veranda of her brother's flat at 10 a.m. on 8 August 1988, Khin Ohmar watched the crowds gathering. The numbers swelled throughout the day. 'I tried to get out, but I couldn't. By night-time it got dark and I couldn't see the people on the streets, but I could hear them in front of City Hall. I felt so guilty for not being with my friends on the streets, and I felt angry because this was the day we had planned. I kept praying that there would be no shooting.'

The sound of army boots running down stairs, and orders being shouted from the police station, startled Khin Ohmar. It was 11 p.m. 'I rushed to the back window, and saw lots of police running out with guns.' Half an hour later, the crackdown began. 'Trucks loaded with troops roared out from behind City Hall,' writes Lintner. 'These were followed by more trucks as well as Bren-carriers, their machine-guns pointed straight in front of them . . . Two pistol shots rang out – and the sound of machine-gunfire reverberated in the dark between the buildings surrounding Bandoola Square. People fell in droves as they were hit. The streets turned red with blood.'[13]

The next morning, Khin Ohmar's brother's attention was diverted by his baby, and she found the key and slipped out. 'I went to the General Hospital. It was full of blood – everywhere. I was completely shocked.'

Despite the bloodshed, the demonstrations continued for a few days. Thousands were arrested; many were bayoneted to death. On 10 August the military turned its guns on medical staff from Rangoon General Hospital, who were tending the wounded. Five nurses were injured, three severely. An hour and a half later, soldiers returned and started firing directly into the hospital.[14]

Sein Lwin stepped down as President on 12 August, aware that public anger was intense. A week later, in an attempt to compromise with the protestors, a civilian President, Dr Maung Maung, was appointed. A lawyer and intellectual, he was regarded as more moderate than Sein Lwin, but in the eyes of the people he was too close to Ne Win and was dismissed as a puppet. His appointment did nothing to quell the protests, and on 22 August a nationwide strike was declared. 'The whole country ground to a halt,' says Lintner.[15]

Nita May, a Burmese publisher who was working as an information officer at the British embassy at the time, was in the United Kingdom during the summer of 1988, attending a training course. In August, she decided to return home. When she arrived, she found scenes of devastation. 'I saw a lot of trees blocking the roads – people were so scared that they blocked their own roads to stop army trucks. I went to the Rangoon General Hospital, and my husband told me that the army had shot nurses and doctors the previous day. I could see the bloodstains and smell the stench of blood.' In the subsequent days, she witnessed the army's actions herself. 'I was among the crowds at the demonstrations. I witnessed the scenes – the army shot, aiming at the crowds. The soldiers sat on their knees and shot at people. Sometimes I had to run for my life,' she recalls. On one occasion, a woman who had been shot gave Nita the bloodstained bullets as evidence.

Despite the horrific events of 8 August and the ensuing days, after Sein Lwin's resignation there was a brief period in which protests continued unhindered. 'We had about two weeks of freedom,' recalls Khin Ohmar. 'People from all walks of life joined in – monks, civil servants, workers, farmers, even police, navy, air force and army.' Lintner describes the extent of the diversity:

> There were the lawyers in their court robes, doctors and nurses in hospital white, bankers, businessmen, labourers, writers, artists, film actors, civil servants . . . housewives banging pots and pans . . . long processions of trishaw drivers, Buddhist monks in saffron robes, Muslims brandishing green banners, Christian clergymen chanting 'Jesus loves democracy' – and even fringe groups such as columns of blind people and demurely simpering transvestites demanding equal rights.[16]

These scenes are confirmed by foreign diplomats and their spouses who witnessed them.

The British ambassador at the time, Martin Morland, says the movement emerged gradually. 'People came out from their burrows to see how things were going on. Then there were constant marches in Rangoon and other large towns, with banners. The beggars marched. The gravediggers marched from the cemetery with banners that read: "We are waiting for you, Ne Win" – until villagers said it was bad luck, so they stopped. Some police and soldiers joined in too.'

Into this extraordinary scene stepped Aung San Suu Kyi, emerging 'suddenly and effectively' according to Morland. Until 26 August 1988 few Burmese had seen the daughter of Aung San, and almost no one expected she would be the leader they had longed for. She had, after all, lived most of her life outside Burma. Her mother had been Burma's ambassador to India after Aung San was assassinated, and Suu Kyi went to school in New Delhi, before studying at Oxford University. She worked for the UN in New York, before marrying Michael Aris, a British academic specialising in Tibet. The family settled in Oxford, and, apart from a period living in Bhutan and in Kyoto, Japan for research purposes, they remained there until 1988.

Aung San Suu Kyi had returned to Burma in April that year, after her mother had had a stroke. 'It was a quiet evening in Oxford like many others,' recalled her husband, Michael Aris. 'Our sons were already in bed and we were reading when the telephone rang. Suu picked up the phone to learn that her mother had suffered a severe stroke. She put the phone down and at once started to pack. I had a premonition that our lives would change for ever.'[17] Aris's premonition turned out to be completely true. The events of 8 August shocked her. On 12 September 1988 in an article for the *Independent*, she wrote: 'Moments of horror, anger and sheer disbelief are engendered in me by what is happening in Burma. Yet above all is the conviction that a movement which has arisen so spontaneously from the people's desire for full human rights must prevail.' Explaining her own decision to become involved, she continued:

> When I came to Burma last April I found that the mood of the people had changed and that the time for a popular anti-government movement was approaching. The massacre of peaceful demonstrators last August precipitated such a movement and decided me to come out in support of the people's aspirations. I have a responsibility towards my country, both as my father's daughter and by my desire to prevent further bloodshed and violence.[18]

The decision was not entirely unexpected, at least not for Aris. Prior to their marriage in 1972, Aung San Suu Kyi had written a letter from New York to Aris in Bhutan. Her letter read:

> I ask only one thing. That should my people need me, you would help me do my duty by them. Would you mind very much should such a situation ever arise? How probable it is I do not know, but the possibility is there. Sometimes I am beset by fears that circumstances and national considerations might tear us apart just when we are so happy in each other that separation would be a torment. And yet such fears are so futile and inconsequential: if we love and cherish each other as much as we can while we can, I am sure love and compassion will triumph in the end.[19]

In 1988, those words came to fruition. Her people did need her.

An estimated 500,000 people turned out to hear her speak at the Shwedagon pagoda on 26 August.[20] Jenny Morland, wife of the British ambassador, and Danielle White, wife of the British Council representative, were among them. 'Ambassadors did not go, at Aung San Suu Kyi's request,' recalls Tom White. 'She said the regime would manipulate it if foreign governments were seen to be supporting her.' Wives, however, could slip into the crowd more inconspicuously. Danielle White described the scene as a 'human sea' with 'everyone who could walk and who was fit enough'.

Conscious that the regime was already attacking her for being married to a foreigner and living abroad, Suu Kyi dealt with these points head-on. 'It is true that I have lived abroad. It is also true that I am married to a foreigner,' she admitted. 'These facts have never interfered and will never interfere with or lessen my love and devotion for my country by any measure or degree.' To the charge that she was ignorant of Burmese politics, she responded by evoking her history. 'The trouble is that I know too much. My family knows best how complicated and tricky Burmese politics can be and how much my father had to suffer on this account . . . The present crisis is the concern of the entire nation. I could not as my father's daughter remain indifferent.' In what became her rallying cry, she declared: 'This national crisis could in fact be called the second struggle for national independence.'[21]

In words designed to be conciliatory to the Tatmadaw, and perhaps even motivate soldiers to join the democracy movement, Suu Kyi declared her loyalty to the military. 'I feel a strong attachment for the armed forces,' she said. 'Not only were they built up by my father, as a child I was cared for by his soldiers . . . I would not therefore wish to see any splits or struggles between the army which my father built up and the people who love my father so much . . . May I appeal to the armed forces to become a force in which the people can place their trust and reliance. May the armed forces become one which will uphold the honour and dignity of our country.'[22]

The crowd was euphoric: for the first time perhaps since Aung San's assassination, they had found a leader who could inspire as much hope in them as he could. The fact that she was his daughter, and bore such a close resemblance to him, made the public response even more enthusiastic. 'There was no one else who would have had the bottle or the nerve to do what she did,' argues Morland. 'The other pro-democracy leaders did not have the image she had, as Aung San's daughter. It was perfect. She was very Burmese, and yet she was brought up in freedom. Nobody at that time could stay free. As soon as you stood up you would either be arrested, killed or forced to run away into exile.' Another former ambassador notes that 'she has a sense of destiny, a certain sense of obligation as the daughter of Aung San, which transcends normal patriotism'. Suu Kyi became, as another former Western diplomat described, 'a beacon' to people throughout the country.

The Shwedagon speech marked a turning point for the movement. Nita May attended the speech, and recalls: 'I knew from that moment that she was the one we had been looking for for many years. I would support her, no matter what.' Not only was it the start of Aung San Suu Kyi's leadership, it also galvanised other leaders to stand up. The next day, U Tin Oo, a former defence minister who had been dismissed and jailed by Ne Win, addressed an audience of 4,000. BSPP members resigned from the party in their thousands, in support of democracy.[23] On 30 August, the Foreign Ministry issued a statement calling for free and fair multi-party elections and admitting that BSPP policy had 'tarnished Burma's pride and prestige in international fora. We've lost face implementing policies which lack essence.'[24] The regime appeared to be collapsing. Press freedom flourished. 'There were a few weeks where everything could have changed,' recalls Danielle White. 'Everybody was in the streets.' When the housewives turned out banging their pots and pans, she joined them. 'It was a carnival atmosphere.'

In this atmosphere of freedom, however, there were grave concerns that it was bordering on anarchy. Local authorities had lost control almost completely, and in many areas Buddhist monks took charge. The Venerable U Uttara, for example, was in charge of Taunggyi, Shan State for one and a half months. 'I controlled the town, providing social services and security, because the police did not work any more, the soldiers stayed in their compound, there were many thieves and robbers, and young people were very scared,' he recalls. Local committees were established to handle daily issues such as food distribution and security, and inter-faith councils of Buddhist, Christian, Hindu and Muslim leaders were formed to provide rice to the most needy.[25] Even so, they were not able to keep the violence and disorder under control. Rumours abounded that the water had been poisoned. 'Public executions – mostly beheadings – of suspected DDSI agents became an almost daily occurrence in Rangoon,' writes Lintner.[26]

Much of the violence was an uncontrollable outpouring of sheer anger and bitterness and a desire for revenge after twenty-six years of brutal suppression. However, there is also evidence that the regime had sent in agents provocateurs. 'Prisoners were released to create chaos,' says Khin Ohmar. 'The whole bureaucracy collapsed. There were beheadings of 'spies', but it was hard to differentiate whether the person being beheaded was a spy, or whether the person carrying out the beheading was a spy. But the irony was there was no attempt by army patrols to stop this. We couldn't control people any more. We tried to stop the beheadings, but we could have been beheaded ourselves. It was not even human nature. It was a really ugly time.' The scenes, she says, were as shocking as Rwanda.

Other eyewitnesses confirm Khin Ohmar's account. Lian Sakhong recalls that after the prisons were opened, he saw 'heads stuck on poles' and heard rumours that the water supplies had been poisoned. 'It was chaos. The government mechanisms were totally broken.' Soe Myint, an international relations student at Rangoon University, believes that Burma's military intelligence infiltrated the demonstrations and deliberately created problems, although some of the worst violence resulted from public outrage. 'People were so angry, and for so many years they had not been able to do anything. So whenever they suspected someone of being a government agent, they just chased them and beat them up. It was the response of people who had been oppressed for decades.'

Morland agrees that the army 'promoted chaos', perhaps as a deliberate attempt to create a complete breakdown in order, to give the military the excuse to step in. He received reports from eyewitnesses claiming to have seen soldiers smashing up machines in a tobacco factory, and the German embassy reported soldiers looting a warehouse full of humanitarian aid supplies. Lintner details a case of a woman who was drugged before committing arson.[27]

On 9 September, former Prime Minister U Nu brazenly announced the formation of an 'interim' government, declaring that he was still the legitimate Prime Minister of Burma since he was deposed by an illegal coup. Aung Gyi and Aung San Suu Kyi gave his idea short shrift. Aung San

Suu Kyi said that 'the future of the people will be decided by the masses of the people'. The following day, the BSPP held an emergency congress and announced it would hold 'free, fair and multi-party elections'.[28] Eight days later, on 18 September 1988, the military seized direct power again. A State Law and Order Restoration Council (SLORC) was formed, led by General Saw Maung, with Than Shwe as his deputy.

Khin Ohmar was on her way back to Rangoon from Prome on the day of the 'coup'. 'At 5 p.m., it was not yet dark, and we arrived by bus. There were army checkpoints stopping cars and checking people as we entered Rangoon. We had not yet heard the announcement of the coup. We got out of the bus, and heard a radio announcement playing in a nearby teashop,' she recalls. She then saw tanks rolling into the city, and heard gunfire from her colleague's house on U Wisaya Road, where she spent the night. There was also shooting at south Okkalapa and near Shwedagon. Many were shot dead on the night of 18 September. A Western ambassador told Lintner that a group of schoolgirls, aged between thirteen and fourteen, were attacked and killed by troops in Kemmendine. 'It's so shameful what's happening, I have no words for it,' he said. 'It's just a small group of people who want to consolidate their power and are willing to shoot down school children and unarmed demonstrators to do so.' He added: 'It's not a coup – how can you stage a coup if you're running the damn place already?'[29]

As with earlier crackdowns on protests, the suppression of the demonstrations in late September was bloody. In Rangoon, observers estimate a death toll of between 500 and 1,000, mostly high school and university students. Diplomats described Rangoon as 'a city under hostile, foreign occupation'.[30]

Many activists fled out of Rangoon and from many other parts of the country to Burma's borders, to avoid arrest. Aung Htoo, now General Secretary of the exiled Burma Lawyers' Council, had to hide in the roof of a house for seven days before escaping through the jungle. 'The military were searching for me, house to house, and I had to camouflage myself, change my clothes, and trek through the jungle,' he says.

In the borderlands they regrouped, and some decided to take up arms against the regime. The All Burma Students' Democratic Front (ABSDF) was formed. 'It was the first students' army in the world to fight against a dictatorship,' says Soe Myint. 'But we were politically immature, and did not have a clear vision. All we thought about was to get training, take up arms and fight.'

Khin Ohmar stayed in Rangoon for as long as she could, trying to reorganise the remaining students into a movement, but the numbers and the willpower were depleted. 'One day I was going for a meeting, and military intelligence raided the place. They took away papers which had names of people and minutes of meetings, and so we had to meet at another place. We didn't go back to our homes any more.'

One night, Khin Ohmar and her colleagues from the All Burma Students' Democratic Movement Organisation (ABSDMO), led by Min Zeya, were staying in a friend's home when the army conducted a raid through the entire ward. 'We started hearing noises from the top of the street. We could see their green uniforms, their guns and their bayonets.'

Khin Ohmar and her fellow activists knew there were no hiding places left, and so they decided to escape to the border. They set out by boat in groups of three or four. Two students left first, but returned on 28 October 1988, as they were chased by the army. One of them was injured. Khin Ohmar followed with a few friends on 2 November, and behind her were the prominent student leaders Min Zeya and Htay Kywe. 'The boatmen were very kind. They didn't take a lot of money from us, and they took care of our security,' she recalls. 'We had to stop at Myeik, or Mergui, in Tenasserim. Some of our group were arrested. We had to hide in a Buddhist monastery for three days. Local people gave us food.' After another boat journey, Khin Ohmar and twenty others crossed into Thailand at Kawthaung, the southernmost point in Burma, 800 kilometres from Rangoon. Burmese navy boats were pursuing them, and drunken border-traders threatened them.

'When we left Rangoon, we had no idea what was ahead of us,' reflects Khin Ohmar. 'Some of my colleagues said I shouldn't go, it was too dangerous for women. But I told them it was my decision. "Either I go with you or I go alone," I said. "I got involved in this movement not because of you . . ."' They found their way to Three Pagodas Pass, on the border of Mon and Karen states, where they found refuge and began to make plans for armed struggle. 'We had nothing when we arrived in Thailand,' she recalls.

Meanwhile, back in Rangoon preparations were underway for the promised multi-party elections. Soon after the military took over direct power, Saw Maung invited political parties to register. On 27 September 1988 – barely a fortnight after the so-called 'coup' – the National League for Democracy (NLD) became the first party to register, with Aung San Suu Kyi, Tin Oo and Aung Gyi as its leaders. Three groups came together to form the NLD – intellectuals, students and former military officers. 'Aung San Suu Kyi was the cement that kept everyone together,' Morland believes. In addition, Student Union activists organised the Democratic Party for a New Society (DPNS). The regime disbanded the BSPP but created a new party in its place, the National Unity Party (NUP). In all, over 200 political parties were established, incentivised by subsidies from the regime in a deliberate strategy to create confusion and dilute the anti-regime vote.

The new regime, SLORC, immediately began a concerted propaganda war against the NLD, and a relentless attack aimed at discrediting Aung San Suu Kyi in particular. 'They've been trying that all the time with false propaganda about me – all sorts of nonsense,' she told *Asiaweek*. 'Things like I have four husbands, three husbands, two husbands. That I am a communist – although in some circles they say I am CIA. They have been trying to get prominent monks to say I have been insulting Buddha.' Just about the only true claim made was that she was married to a foreigner. 'But I've always admitted that. I'm not trying to hide that.'[31]

The charge of communism was perhaps the most dangerous. Burma had been dogged by a communist insurgency ever since independence, although it came to an end on 16 April 1989 due to what Lintner describes as 'an all-out mutiny within the rank-and-file of the Communist Party of Burma (CPB)'.[32] In the state newspaper, the *Working People's Daily*, the junta accused the CPB of placing 'hardcore cadres' in leadership positions of the student movement.[33] A letter from a leading CPB member and one of the Thirty Comrades, Kyaw Zaw, to Aung San Suu Kyi was found by military intelligence in her compound, and was used as evidence to support the claim that the NLD itself had communist links.[34] This charge was given further fuel when NLD Chairman Aung Gyi resigned in December 1988, after presenting a list of eight alleged communists in the NLD top leadership. He claimed that Thakin Tin Mya, a former CPB leader, was Aung San Suu Kyi's 'main adviser',[35] suggested that 'her crowd belongs to the communist group' and compared the NLD's encouragement of strikes and demonstrations to the behaviour of the communists in 1947. 'It's quite natural the army thinks their actions are like the communists. In that respect I agree with the army,' he said.[36]

The democracy movement dismissed such charges. In an interview with *Asiaweek*, student leader Min Ko Naing laughed at the suggestion that he was a communist. 'I am a student who believes that the country should have democratic ideals,' he said. 'Let me point out that this government labels anybody it is afraid of as a communist. None of us is communist.'[37] Aung San Suu Kyi herself said in her article in the *Independent* that such accusations are made by 'those who wish to discredit me'. While she acknowledged that veteran politicians 'of varying political colour' were assisting her, she said she had accepted their help 'only on the understanding that they are working for the democratic cause without expectation of political advantage or personal gain.'[38]

While throwing dirt at the opposition, the regime tried to paint itself in the best possible light, as the saviour of the nation. In a rare interview with Dominic Faulder of *Asiaweek*, Saw Maung said: 'I believe that I have saved the country from an abyss. The country has come back from an abyss, and I saved the country, for the good of the people, according to law.' He denied the 8 August 1988 massacre, claiming that 'we tried our best to be very controlled'. Soldiers fired four rubber bullets into the crowd, he claimed. 'Four, that's all. There were six people who were hurt. Six people. So we controlled the situation in this manner. But on the following day . . . the mob came to assault us. In defence, we fired. But we did it in a controlled manner, not in an irresponsible manner.'[39] If he believed that, he was even more deluded than people thought.

Saw Maung repeatedly promised fair elections. 'I give you my guarantee,' he told *Asiaweek*. 'I'll say one thing: Do you think that I'm assuming power today because I hunger for power? . . . In the armed forces we are not backed by a political party. In the next general election, none of us is going to stand for election.'[40] Kyaw Nyunt, member of the election commission, promised that 'there'll be no monkeying with the results'.[41]

These promises, however, sounded hollow when compared with the increasing harassment of the opposition. Aung San Suu Kyi faced growing threats to her personal security, but perhaps her closest encounter with death during this period came in Danubyu, on the Irrawaddy River fifty miles from Rangoon, on 5 April 1989. Touring the area with her supporters, she arrived in the town by boat towards the end of the day and walked towards the house where she was to spend the night. Surrounded by party colleagues and with a young man carrying the NLD flag in front, the group walked down the middle of the street. 'Then we saw the soldiers across the road, kneeling with their guns trained on us,' Aung San Suu Kyi recalled, in an interview with Alan Clements. As the tension mounted, a captain ordered Aung San Suu Kyi and her supporters to walk on the side of the road, not down the middle. He then told them that he would shoot even if they continued down the side of the road. Laughing as she recounted the experience, Suu Kyi said: 'Now that seemed highly unreasonable to me . . . I thought, if he's going to shoot us even if we walk at the side of the road, well, perhaps it is me they want to shoot. I thought, I might as well walk in the middle of the road.' Instructing her followers to stay back, Aung San Suu Kyi stepped forward and in an extraordinary act of defiance and courage, she walked, calmly and alone, towards the troops. Their guns remained trained on her, and the captain began the countdown. The soldiers were starting to shake – either at the thought of killing Aung San's daughter, or out of astonishment that she was disobeying orders and seemingly walking towards her own death. Seconds away from firing, a major rushed onto the scene and overruled the captain. He ordered the troops to lower their weapons, and a heated exchange between the two officers followed. Furious at being overruled and undermined, the captain tore off the insignia from his shoulder and threw it to the ground. 'We just walked through the soldiers who were kneeling there,' says Suu Kyi.[42] British Council Director Tom White saw her the next evening, when she returned to Rangoon. 'She said she was surprised at her own reaction,' he recalls.

White saw Suu Kyi regularly during that period. It was safer for her to communicate with him than directly with the British ambassador. On one occasion, the night before she was due to travel to the north of the country, she phoned White to ask if she could leave some private papers in his safe. 'She was afraid that the authorities would ransack her house while she was away.' He recalls her as a person not only of deep courage and intellect, but also 'very sociable, full of fun'. Suu Kyi appreciated 'the sheer absurdity of the mindset of the military'. Her inner steel, however, was very apparent as well. 'She could be very blunt and direct, and sometimes pretty cutting.'

Others who have known her confirm this description. 'She is not perfect, and some say she is too rigid,' says one former Western ambassador. 'But she has a great sense of humour. She was very much into word play, and very academic. She was an intriguing mix of oriental and Western – delightfully English about some tastes, particularly literature and music, and yet very proud of being Burmese.' The diplomat insists that when he first met her, he was 'reluctant to fall under the spell' but found her impossible to resist. 'She has an incredible combination of steely determination of principle coupled with incredible personal bravery. She has a magnetic combination of great presence, physical beauty and serenity.' Her devout Buddhism means she does not attach 'too much importance' to her own life, and this, combined with a recognition that she has had a privileged upbringing and has a duty to her country, shaped by her father's legacy, has made her the person she is, he believes.

Another former Western ambassador was similarly entranced. 'Suu is many things – a very sophisticated, highly educated person who operates easily across cultural boundaries, with a very good sense of humour, which you need. She is a devout Buddhist, and the great wheel of being, *karma*, is an important concept for her.'

A close family friend says that Suu Kyi's mother was a perfectionist, and that had rubbed off on her. 'She was very intelligent, very influenced by her father and mother, a brilliant cook, kept the family going, helped the kids with homework, shopped economically, learned to drive, did embroidery and learned to ride a horse. She was a paragon – but a nice one, with a lovely sense of humour. There was a core of steel underneath that beautiful exterior.'

This is borne out in an amusing account of how even the military intelligence assigned to follow her were sometimes nervous. Although she maintained good relations with them, on one occasion while touring a town, NLD workers asked the military intelligence to clear up the litter that had piled up during large public meetings. Warned that if they did not, Aung San Suu Kyi would 'get mad', the intelligence officers meekly went to work cleaning up the rubbish.

One of her former bodyguards confirms this. Phone Myint Tun joined the youth organisation known as 'Tri-color', using the yellow, green and red colours used by Aung San. The group, consisting of about twenty students, provided security for Aung San Suu Kyi in the first few years after 1988. 'One-to-one, Daw Suu was very kind and nice, but when we were working she could be very stern and strict. She left us with the impression that we had to take the job very seriously.'

Phone Myint Tun accompanied Aung San Suu Kyi on some of her travels outside Rangoon. He recalls one visit to Pathein, when the Tatmadaw divisional commander Nyi Aung sent a message warning her that if she went into the Irrawaddy Division, his troops would 'crush' her. 'She replied saying "Let's work together." When we went to Pathein, we were staying in a house and the military placed blockades in front of it so that no one could go in or leave,' Phone Myint Tun recounts. 'She went to speak to the soldier who was guarding us, and he told her that he was ordered not to allow us out. She ignored him, and just left. The soldiers did not shoot, but the commander came later and reprimanded them, asking why they let Aung San Suu Kyi leave!' Phone Myint Tun was jailed in 1991 for four years, but after his release he worked for Aung San Suu Kyi again for a year, serving as a contact point between her and political prisoners.

Another of Aung San Suu Kyi's security guards, Tri-color member Moe Myat Thu, recalls another occasion in 1989 where her steely determination was again on display. Students had gathered to commemorate the first anniversary of the massacre at Myaynigone, when many high school students had been shot dead by riot police during the 1988 protests. Aung San Suu Kyi spoke to the crowds outside the Sanchaung Township offices, and then went on to the NLD headquarters. Meanwhile, students had lined the streets in Myaynigone to present her with flowers. 'When we reached the Myaynigone junction, some students were waiting for us with flowers. But the area was surrounded by soldiers, and soon after her car had passed, soldiers began to arrest students. They then opened fire into the crowd,' says Moe Myat Thu. Aung San Suu Kyi's car was stopped at the traffic lights, but by the time the lights turned green and the car crossed the junction, the students had dispersed.

She had not heard the shooting, and so she asked where the students with the flowers had gone. We explained to her that the soldiers had fired two or three times. By this time we had driven past, and so she told the driver to turn around and go back. There were many soldiers, but she ordered the driver to stop and she got out for a short ceremony to honour the students. Many people were watching from afar, and a senior officer came over to her. 'Daw Suu,' he said, 'don't do like that.' After that two of our colleagues were arrested and taken away and after we drove away, the army fired into the crowd many times. When we stopped our car, soldiers shot over our car into the crowd, and she heard the gunshots very clearly.

What happened next is an example of her courage and determination. 'After fifty metres she ordered the driver to turn around and go back. He didn't want to, and she got very angry, tapping his seat and saying "Go back, go back." He went back, and we were surrounded by many police and soldiers who pointed their rifles at our car.' Aung San Suu Kyi and her close aides were taken to the Sanchaung Township SLORC office. 'Half an hour later a senior officer arrived. Aung San Suu Kyi and he talked politely, and she asked "What action do you plan to take?" They decided not to take any action, and we returned to the NLD headquarters.'

Moe Myat Thu lived in Aung San Suu Kyi's compound in Rangoon from 26 August 1988 until his arrest on 20 July 1989. He helped provide security at her Shwedagon pagoda speech and organised the NLD youth wing, and served two terms in jail as a result, during 1989–1992 and 1995–2001. 'After her speech at Shwedagon, on 26 August 1988 all around Rangoon there was unrest at night,' he recalls. 'We decided to stay at her compound to protect her. She thanked us very much.' He says her courage came not from an absence of fear but an ability to overcome fear. 'In some of her speeches she said that everybody has fear, but we have to do the right thing. She is a human being, and she has fear, but she decided that there were things that she had to do, she must do.'

Her critics say this core of steel has meant she has been too stubborn and principled, and should have compromised early on. A former Western ambassador who knew her, however, profoundly disagrees. 'She is very tough-minded, but that doesn't mean she can't compromise,' he says. 'I am not sure that much was being offered. What compromises was she asked to make? All politics ultimately is about choices, but you only make a choice when you have to. She was always in a position of weakness, because she was under house arrest of some sort. If you're under house arrest, it's a bit hard to be called upon to compromise.' In fact, dialogue has been her principal demand all along – it is the Generals who failed to compromise.

By the summer of 1989, Aung San Suu Kyi and U Tin Oo had come to be regarded by the SLORC as too much trouble. On 20 July, they were placed under house arrest. Soon afterwards, Suu Kyi began a hunger strike, demanding to be moved to Insein Prison along with several thousand of her detained party colleagues. Min Ko Naing had been arrested in March 1989, and Moe Thee Zun had escaped to the Thailand–Burma border.

The regime began to use virtually every conceivable tactic to ensure that it won a mandate in the elections in 1990. According to Dominic Faulder writing in the *Wall Street Journal Asia*, entire areas of key cities such as Rangoon, Mandalay, Prome and Taunggyi, deemed to be hostile to the regime, were simply levelled and inhabitants resettled to new 'satellite' towns. 'Western diplomats believe that up to 500,000 people may have been transplanted,' Faulder wrote. The country was closed off to foreign reporters, and draconian restrictions were imposed on those participating in the election. Faulder describes 'the usual tools of tyrants to thwart any real campaign', including a ban on any gathering of more than five people, censoring of campaign speeches in the media and no publication of a full list of candidates. In addition, 'candidates may not criticize the SLORC'.[43]

Despite the detention of key leaders', and severe harassment and restriction in the period leading to the election, polling day itself on 27 May 1990 was widely acknowledged to be free and fair. And even though key leaders such as Aung San Suu Kyi were unable to take part, the NLD won an extraordinary victory, gaining 82 per cent of the parliamentary seats. 'The SLORC was probably as taken aback as almost everybody else,' writes Lintner. 'It was utterly unprepared for an NLD victory of this magnitude.'[44] The regime had done all it could, bar rigging the ballot itself, to ensure victory for itself, and yet still it failed. It had massively underestimated the scale of support that Aung San Suu Kyi's party could command, even when handicapped, and had dramatically overlooked the depth of anger and hatred the people felt towards the military.

To the world's astonishment, the regime reneged on all its pre-election promises to honour the result. On Armed Forces Day the previous year, Saw Maung pledged that 'after the election, the . . . representatives elected by the people will form a government. . . . We, the Tatmadaw personnel, will go back to barracks.'[45] Just a few months later, he promised to 'transfer the power . . . If a government could be formed with a majority of votes, I will hand over. I agree with it.'[46] As far back as 22 September 1988 the military intelligence chief, Khin Nyunt, told foreign military attachés that 'the Tatmadaw would systematically transfer power to the party which comes into power after successfully holding the general elections.'[47] Yet in May 1990, when the result was not the one they intended, those promises were conveniently forgotten. The regime began using delaying tactics, claiming that first a National Convention would have to be held to draw up ground rules for a new constitution, and then the elected representatives could meet to draft the constitution. After that, the constitution would have to be put to the people in a referendum. Military rule would continue until that process was complete.

The NLD responded to the regime's delaying tactics by holding a special meeting at the Mahatma Gandhi Hall in Rangoon in July. The resulting statement, known as the Gandhi Hall Declaration, called for the convening of Parliament by 30 September. Elected MPs then began secret discussions about the formation of a parallel government. Such an idea alarmed the regime. The NLD Central Executive received a letter warning them not to proceed with forming a government. 'U Kyi Maung, the NLD Chairman, gave me a copy of the letter and asked me to translate it into English,' recalls Nita May. 'He said "If something happens to me", spread this news. It was a confidential letter, so if anyone searched my house I would be caught red-handed. I was so scared I could not sleep for the whole night.' Nita took the document to the embassy the next day, translated it, made copies and returned the original to U Kyi Maung. Soon afterwards, he and other elected MPs were arrested. Aung San Suu Kyi's cousin Dr Sein Win and a few other MPs escaped just in time, and fled to the Thailand–Burma border. There they formed a government in exile, known as the National Coalition Government of the Union of Burma (NCGUB).

Lian Uk, an elected MP and Vice-President of the Chin National League for Democracy (CNLD), escaped arrest three times. In one incident he went into an empty house and hid in the bedroom. When the owner returned, however, and found a strange man in her bedroom, she called the police, and Lian Uk went on the run again. In January 1991, the regime published his photograph in the newspapers, with a notice for his arrest. 'People came to me and said "This is you, isn't it?",' he recalls. '"No, no," I told them. "It's just someone who looks a bit like me."' After months in hiding, he escaped across the border to India.

Dr Thaung Htun, a medical doctor, was a democracy leader in Kyaunggon, in the Delta, who had to flee to escape arrest after the 1988 uprising. In December 1988 he arrived on the Thailand–Burma border, and immediately set to work treating students suffering from malaria. He was then elected to the ABSDF's Central Committee, and assigned to establish a foreign affairs office for ABSDF in Bangkok. In 1990, at the age of thirty-one and with 'no foreign experience at all', he was sent to Geneva to brief the UN Human Rights Commission, and was the democracy movement's UN specialist from then until the reform period that began in Burma in 2011. After the elections, he helped the NCGUB begin international advocacy from Bangkok, but at the end of a lobbying visit to New York in 1993 Thailand's National Security Council banned him, Dr Sein Win and three others from returning to Thailand. The NCGUB then established itself in the United States, starting with funding from the International Union of Bricklayers and Allied Craftworkers. In 1994, the UN General Assembly passed a resolution calling for dialogue between the regime, the democracy movement and the ethnic nationalities, and two years later the NCGUB opened a New York office.

Frustrated at the lack of international action following the regime's refusal to accept the election results, a small group of students decided to take extreme action. On 10 November 1990 Soe Myint and a few other ABSDF members hijacked a plane from Bangkok to Rangoon, and diverted it to Kolkata. 'After the election, media attention was gone. We decided to do something dramatic, to highlight the situation in Burma,' Soe Myint explains. It was, however, one of the most peaceful hijackings ever. 'We decided to do it without arms. Instead, we just used a "Laughing Buddha" statue. We put some soap and wire in it, and said it was a bomb. Later, we explained that we were Burmese student activists and that we would not harm the passengers.' On arrival in India, the hijackers were met with a surprisingly warm welcome. They were allowed to hold a press conference in the airport, to explain their action, before being arrested. At court the next day, they were covered in garlands, and after three months in jail they were released and granted asylum. Soe Myint transformed himself from student activist, soldier and hijacker into a journalist, working for the Democratic Voice of Burma (DVB) and Radio Free Asia (RFA), and then founding *Mizzima News*.

Inside Burma the struggle has continued in various forms. In 1992 Than Shwe replaced Saw Maung as head of the junta. In 1996, student protests broke out again, and as before were met with brutality. Like many previous protests, the 1996 uprising was sparked by a minor incident: an argument between three students and the owner of a food stall. 'Police reportedly interceded and manhandled the students,' *Time* magazine reported. 'Frustrated friends, unable to protest the beatings or even learn exactly what happened, started small rallies against the police.'[48] These culminated in a gathering of 2,000 students protesting against police brutality, demanding the right to form student unions, and demonstrating for democracy.

John Jackson, one of the founders of Burma Campaign UK, was in Rangoon at the time. Caught up in a protest by several thousand students at a junction in northern Rangoon late at night, he witnessed the brutal crackdown, an experience which was instrumental in his decision to focus on Burma full-time. 'Troops came down the streets with water cannons and charged the students,' he recalls. Jackson's family were Anglo-Burmese who had left Burma in 1957 due to the deteriorating political situation, and here, forty years on, he was seeing it for himself. In an article for the *Irrawaddy*, he describes what happened next:

I was lucky to get past the roadblocks which prevent most people from seeing what happens to peaceful demonstrators in Burma. I hailed a taxi driver who understood the importance of bearing witness to such events who took me on a special route around the blockades. My enduring image of that night was a lone student who stood up just as a water cannon was pointed at him and his sitting friends. He stood up to hold a student flag firm, while his body was blasted with a high-powered jet – it reminded me of the man who stood in front of a tank during the Tiananmen Square protests. At that point a rock was hurled at me by a riot policeman, missing my head by an inch. I ran for cover and had to spend that night with a group of other frightened 'visitors' to Burma, in an old tenement block, hiding from the riot police and military intelligence officers. From a fifth floor balcony, I laid low and heard the shouts and screams of the 'mopping up' operation.[49]

A few months before the 1996 protests, Aung San Suu Kyi and the democracy movement lost one of their closest friends. Leo Nichols, born in Rangoon in 1931 as the son of a Greek shipping family, had been Honorary Consul-General for Norway, Denmark, Finland and Switzerland. Arrested in April 1996 for possession of an unlicensed fax machine, he was sentenced to three years in jail. He used to visit Aung San Suu Kyi for breakfast every Friday after her release the previous year; consequently Michael Aris believed Nichols was jailed 'solely because of his loyal and courageous friendship for the leader of the movement for democracy and human rights in Burma, my wife Suu.'[50] He died after just two months in prison, reportedly after suffering a stroke and being denied proper medical treatment. As the obituary in the *Independent* put it, 'he was not a political man, but becomes another martyr for the cause of democracy in Burma.'[51]

In the midst of continuing brutality and thuggishness, the junta attempted an image re-make. In November 1996, it launched Visit Myanmar Year, a campaign designed to attract hundreds of thousands of tourists. Aung San Suu Kyi was clear what she thought. 'Our opinion is that this whole Visit Myanmar Year is intended solely to build up SLORC's image, and we cannot support it,' she told *Asiaweek*. 'The preparation of tourist sites and the beautifying of certain places for the benefit of tourists have resulted in the suffering of a lot of people.'[52] It was also predicted to bring in 100 million dollars for the regime.

The following year, in another purely cosmetic change made on the advice of a public relations firm, the SLORC abandoned its Orwellian name and renamed itself the State Peace and Development Council (SPDC).

Aung San Suu Kyi has never given up, despite spending most of the years since 1989 under house arrest. In 1991, she was awarded the Nobel Peace Prize but being under house arrest could not receive the award in person, so her sons accepted it on her behalf. The following year, Michael Aris issued a public statement expressing concern about his wife's well-being. 'I have reason to believe that the circumstances under which she is held now pose a grave threat to her life. The meagre personal funds she has used to maintain herself while her solitary detention continues are now almost exhausted . . . I am now very concerned that soon she will have no means at all of sustaining life . . . In a situation so dark and remote I fear it will be impossible to follow the course of events in the days ahead.'[53]

In 1995, she was released from six years of house arrest, and began to tour the country, defying bans restricting her to Rangoon. She reiterated her central message of dialogue with the Generals, telling *Asiaweek*: 'We would like to find common ground . . . we must be prepared to talk about everything . . . That is the essence of true dialogue: that we should not rule out anything.'[54] Once again the regime rejected the offer, and instead she was harassed and attacked by pro-regime thugs. On 2 September 1998, police blocked her car at Dala, a suburb of Rangoon. She remained in her car for nine days, defiantly refusing to turn back. Eventually, she was forced back, but immediately announced plans to travel to Mandalay by train. The day she intended to travel, the authorities closed the entire station.

Despite these restrictions on travel, for five years she had a certain degree of freedom in Rangoon, holding weekly public meetings at her home in University Avenue, where she would address crowds of thousands over the garden wall. One young British man visited her six or seven times during this period. 'I went to University Avenue to hear her speak, as she did every Saturday,' he recalls. 'There was a great crowd, and a large number of NLD people living in the compound.' A friend of his had recently interviewed her, so after one of these public meetings, he telephoned her. 'She invited me for tea. I took provisions – copies of the *Economist*, a radio and batteries, and I spent an hour with her. She gave over an incredible aura. She has real presence, charm, extraordinary serenity, but also awesome steel and will. She invited us to come again the next day, for lunch. From then on, I made a point of visiting as often as I could.'

Security was tight and he was watched closely. 'I was photographed, and my ID was taken when I went to visit. The military intelligence officers were at the end of the street, at the gate, and inside the gate.' The house, he recalls, was falling into disrepair. 'It was increasingly dilapidated, and needed several coats of paint. There was a problem of damp on the outer walls.' One of her requests was for films, because she held a film night every weekend for the NLD activists who lived with her. 'She liked quaint

English films, early classics. I remember *Breakfast at Tiffany's* was one. I also brought *Oliver Twist*, *Il Postino*, *Braveheart*, *Pride and Prejudice*, *Schindler's List*, *Gone with the Wind* and *Mr Bean*. I would try to slot in up-to-date films as well.' He noted that she had varied tastes in music, preferring classical, baroque and Gregorian chants, but admitting a fondness for Bob Marley and the rock group Grateful Dead, introduced to her by her sons. In addition to bringing her films, he would deliver messages from her to Michael Aris.

Conversation was wide-ranging, he recalls. 'We talked quite a lot about the situation in Burma, and how best to bring about pressure on the regime, from mobilising British politicians to pressure from other Asian countries, particularly the Japanese, Singaporeans and Thais. She was rather focused on the UN machinery.' Concern about her own role, however, was also highlighted, and she expressed a clear desire not to be a one-woman band. 'Everyone demanded to see her personally and party workers refused to settle for anyone else, which placed a massive burden and formidable responsibility on her,' recalls this visitor. Yet it was easy to understand why she was in such demand, given her speeches at public meetings, which both informed and inspired people. At one gathering in April 1996, according to a foreign visitor, she talked about the defeat of fascism in Europe in 1945, and the development of democracy in the Czech Republic. 'Throughout, she had the audience eating out of her hand. There was frequent laughter, nodding of heads, interspersed with bursts of enthusiastic applause.'

However, those who attended her public gatherings did so at significant risk. On one occasion in 1997, at least ten people were arrested, one of many signs of a tightening up. That same year, Aung San Suu Kyi's telephone was cut off, University Avenue closed and on-spec visits proved impossible. Her situation, said one foreign visitor, 'was physically and perhaps politically more isolated than on my previous visits'. According to one observer, while the previous year her compound was full of NLD workers playing football, and her assistant U Aye Win had talked openly in the garden, by 1997 he and many others were in prison and the compound deserted.

In 1999, Michael Aris died of cancer, and in an example of its cruelty and inhumanity the regime refused to allow him to visit Suu Kyi before he died. She was forced to choose between leaving the country to be with him, in the knowledge that the regime would never allow her back, or staying with her people. She stayed. A year later, she was again put under house arrest, this time for two years.

A further brief period of freedom followed when she was released in 2002. Again, she began to tour the country. Alarmed that her popularity remained undimmed, the regime orchestrated an attack on her at Depayin in Sagaing Division on 30 May 2003. Over a hundred of her supporters were beaten to death by thugs from the pro-regime militia, the Union Solidarity Development Association (USDA). Armed with iron bars, bamboo sticks and wooden bats, an estimated 3,000 thugs, some dressed as monks, lay in wait beside the road to ambush her convoy.[55] Her supporters were beaten, stabbed and knocked to the ground, where their heads were repeatedly smashed on the road until they cracked. Aung San Suu Kyi only narrowly escaped, protected by some of her brave young followers who linked hands and surrounded her car. It was a clear assassination attempt.

Aung San Suu Kyi returned to Rangoon, and was briefly detained in Insein Prison, before being returned to house arrest. Her telephone lines were cut once again, and she was more isolated than ever. Ironically, according to one young Burmese, it was the attack at Depayin and her subsequent detention that gained the attention of the new generation. 'In the past, if I was asked whether I liked the military government, I did not even know how to answer,' he said. 'I didn't know whether their rule was legitimate or not. But now, at least we know why we dislike the government so much. Aung San Suu Kyi had not made much impact on my growing up, but Depayin made her more visible. The younger generation is compelled to know more about her and what she is fighting for as a result.'

Six years later, following a sham trial, her house arrest was extended for a further eighteen months. Accused of breaking the terms of her house arrest after an American, John Yettaw, swam across Inya Lake and spent the night in her home, Aung San Suu Kyi was deliberately kept out of the way ahead of the regime's sham elections planned for 2010, and was only finally released when her term expired, conveniently, six days after the elections.

Meanwhile, what had happened to the student activists from 1988? Many were jailed and endured horrific torture. Those who fled to Burma's borders encountered new challenges. Mostly from the cities, they were unaccustomed to jungle life. 'I fell sick so easily,' recalls Khin Ohmar. 'I was stubborn and insisted on going, but in fact I had the least tolerance for the conditions.' She joined the ABSDF. 'We were so peaceful on the streets in 1988, and they killed us for nothing. So I wanted to join with the KNU, and take up arms,' she says. Her commitment to armed struggle, however, did not last long. 'When I got to the jungle, I came to realise I was not for armed struggle. It was out of anger and outrage. I realised I was not for violence.' Education, she believed, was a better weapon to fight the military regime and end the cycle of violence in the country, so she went to the United States to study for a degree. After gaining experience working for Human Rights Watch and Refugees International, she returned to Thailand to continue her work as an activist, and now leads the Burmese Women's Union, the Network for Democracy and Development, and the Burma Partnership, a network of activists throughout the Asia-Pacific region.[56]

Besides adjusting to jungle life, Burman students who fled to the ethnic areas from the cities had another challenge to deal with: the suspicion, and sometimes hostility, of the non-Burman ethnic peoples. Having suffered for decades at the hands of different Burman-dominated governments, many ethnic peoples were wary of the Burman students. 'When we got to the border, my eyes opened up to understand the suffering of the ethnic peoples,' says Khin Ohmar. 'It was painful. When somebody looks at you with hateful eyes, you feel it. But I learned why as I felt hatred towards the army itself.'

A Campaign of Brutality in the East

'I believe that even amid today's mortar bursts and whining bullets, there is still hope for a brighter tomorrow. I believe that wounded justice, lying prostrate on the blood-flowing streets of our nations, can be lifted from the dust of shame to reign supreme among the children of men. I have the audacity to believe that peoples everywhere can have three meals a day for their bodies, education and culture for their minds, and dignity, equality and freedom for their spirits.'

Martin Luther King Jr.

JUST BEFORE SUNSET, at the end of the school day, children lined up in straight rows in front of the flagpole. With extraordinary dignity, inspiring discipline and a perfect, modest, natural sense of pride in their culture, these young Karens sang their anthem as their flag was lowered. They were not singing the regime's national anthem for Burma, nor were they lowering the junta's flag – instead, with defiance but no sense of vengeance, they sang their own national anthem and raised the flag of their land which they call 'Kawthoolei'. They were internally displaced people, whose original villages had been either overrun or burned down by the Tatmadaw. This place, on the banks of the Moei River just opposite Thailand, was their place of sanctuary, one of the few remaining places where they could celebrate their culture. Even here, however, they were not safe.

As I stood in the heat and listened to them sing, it was a struggle to hold back the tears. My heart and mind swirled with a whole mix of emotions:

grief, in the knowledge of what these people had already been through, illustrated to me in the stories I had heard that day and on many previous visits; humility, in the knowledge that I doubt I would have the same grace and courage to stand to attention and quietly, gently, sing an anthem I knew would never be recognised legally, and lower a flag which meant nothing to the rest of the world; and fear, for what might yet still be inflicted upon them, despite their many years of suffering already endured. My emotions were stirred still further by the words of Rainbow, the schoolteacher – a young man I knew well. After translating the stories of new arrivals earlier in the day, Rainbow turned to me with a gentle smile and said: 'We don't fight the Burmans – we fight their policies.' After allowing that thought to sink in, he added, 'We can be friends with them. We can be brothers. Please pray for the regime. Pray for the regime more than you pray for the Karen people. Pray for them to change their policies, and change their hearts.'

Less than four months later, the Ler Per Her settlement was overrun by Burma Army troops and their accomplices, the Democratic Karen Buddhist Army (DKBA). Rainbow and thousands of others from Ler Per Her and the surrounding area were forced to flee – yet again. This time they had to get into boats and go across the river to Thailand. They had nowhere else to run. If they had stayed, it is a safe bet that many of the women would have been raped, and the men taken for forced labour.

I had been to Ler Per Her more than a dozen times, and heard many painful stories of people who had fled their villages. But in February 2009 there was an extra level of poignancy, made sharper with hindsight given the further misery inflicted upon them. I met one man who will always be in my memory. He had arrived just two days previously. In October 2008, Tatmadaw and DKBA troops had come to his village, and he had fled into the jungle. His home, along with most of the rest of the village, was burned down. After the attack, he returned to see whether he could salvage any property or livestock. As he approached the place where his house had stood, and walked across the ashes which were all that remained, his life changed for ever. The DKBA had laid a landmine, and he stepped on it.

This man then endured what most people in the developed world would count as an epic struggle for survival. 'My relatives carried me for an entire day, to the nearby town for medical treatment,' he told me calmly and quietly as we sat in a bamboo hut in Ler Per Her. 'I lost consciousness. After receiving medical treatment, I decided to come here, with my wife and four children. I travelled for two days through the jungle, using crutches.' I glanced at the stump of his leg which protruded from his longyi in front of me. 'I felt unable to stay in my own village. With only one leg, I cannot walk well, and so it is better to come here. I worry a lot about my future. I feel safe here, but I would like to go home when the situation is better. I really want all the people of Burma to have peace and freedom. If there is no peace and freedom, I cannot go home.'

When I heard the news about the attacks on Ler Per Her four months later, those words – 'I feel safe here' – echoed in my mind. Where can the Karen possibly feel safe? In 1997 and 1998, Tatmadaw soldiers attacked refugee camps in Thailand, burning homes and shooting people. Naw December, a Karen refugee now living in the United Kingdom, and her son were hit by mortar shells in Wang Ka camp. The Thai Army turned a blind eye to the attack.

Even those 3,000 people who fled to Thailand from Ler Per Her found only temporary respite, as within eight months they were harassed by the Thai authorities and forced to return to their occupied, heavily mined land. In February 2010, I was taken to the temporary camp on the Thai side of the border, opposite Ler Per Her, to meet some of those who had fled. Foreign activists and journalists were not allowed into the camp by the Thais, so we went at night, crossing paddy fields secretly. Each time a motorbike went past, we crouched down, silently, to avoid being caught in the headlights.

When we reached the camp, we had to creep through quietly, until we reached the bamboo huts. There, we heard the stories of some of those who had fled. One man, exactly my age, sat and talked by candlelight, surrounded by his wife and five children. As he talked, I noticed the stumps of his two legs, blown off by a landmine he had stepped on while in the jungle gathering vegetables. 'When I had two legs, I could earn money for the whole family and I could give my children money for snacks,' he told me. 'Now I cannot provide for them. It is not a normal life. It is hard to earn money. If I stay here, the Thais will not give me a chance to go out. I cannot do anything for the children now. I have no legs, no rations, and I have to stay in camp and share my wife's rations.' Despite his injuries, the

Thai authorities continued to harass him, urging him to return to Burma. 'Inside Burma I had to flee the Burma Army many times. I did portering for the Burma Army many times,' he said. Then he looked into my eyes and said words which sum up the plight of the Karen: 'Run and run and run until now – this is my life.'[1]

Since 1949, the Karens have been fighting an armed struggle for basic human rights, a degree of autonomy, and more recently a battle for existence. 'They will try to wipe us out,' KNU Vice-President David Thackerbaw once told me. 'Their plan is to eliminate the Karen as a people.'

Although there would be Karens whose first choice, if asked, would be an independent state, the official policy of the KNU – as with almost all the ethnic nationalities in Burma – is autonomy within a federal, democratic union. The Karens' struggle today is with the regime which has sought, at least in part if not in whole, to eradicate them. However, the roots of the struggle go much deeper. The Karens, earlier settlers in Burma than the Burmans, had faced centuries of oppression at the hands of Burman kings. When the British colonised Burma, accompanied by missionaries, the Karens believed they had found their liberators. In turn, the British favoured the Karen, and provided opportunities in education and government service. By 1939 Karen troops outnumbered Burmans in the British Burma Army by a ratio of three to one.[2] Their loyalty to the British colonial rulers drew further Burman wrath. In the Second World War, while the Burmans sided with the Japanese, the Karen fought loyally alongside the Allies, in return for vague promises of independence, or at least autonomy and protection, after the war.

There are still Karens alive today who remember British rule – and have not forgotten the promises that were made and broken. In 2010, I met an elderly man in Mae La refugee camp whose son-in-law had been killed two and a half years previously. Twice, the villages he lived in were attacked by the Burma Army, and burned down, and he had been forced to work a porter. On one occasion, his cousin was beaten and left blinded by Tatmadaw soldiers. This elderly man had fought in the Second World War, under the command of a Captain Wilson. 'I kept my army ID card but when the village was burned [by the Burma Army], it was all burned – nothing left but ashes. I worked for the British because we were suffering under the Japanese, and I thought that if I worked for the British I expected something better,' he said. 'To my British friends, I say I am still expecting [help]. May you have mercy on us, one way or another, and help us.'³

The KNU's chairman, Saw Tamlabaw, fought with the British in the infamous Force 136. His daughter, Zipporah Sein, was elected the KNU's first woman General Secretary in 2008, and the Karen struggle is all she has ever known. She is now the KNU's Vice-President and one of its chief negotiators in the ceasefire talks. 'I came from a revolutionary family because my father has been involved with the Karen revolution since it started,' she told me.

The plain truth is, the British made false promises during the Second World War, on which they completely reneged once Burma became independent. Cut adrift, the Karen decided to soldier on alone in their struggle for recognition. In August 1946, unhappy with the lack of a coherent British response, a Karen 'Goodwill Mission' led by Sydney Loo Nee, Saw Than Din and Saw Ba U Gyi went to London.⁴ They returned to Burma empty-handed and betrayed, and within a few months of Burma's independence, following unprovoked attacks by Burmans on Karen communities, their armed struggle began.

On 12 August 1950 the Karens suffered their first major setback when their leader, Saw Ba U Gyi – their equivalent of Aung San in terms of inspiration – was killed by the Tatmadaw, along with his chief lieutenant Saw Sankey. Saw Ba U Gyi, born in Pathein in 1905, had studied at Cambridge University and qualified as a barrister before returning to Burma to work as a civil servant. In his leadership of the KNU, he established what became their enduring motto, known as the 'Four Principles': 'surrender is out of the question; we shall retain our arms; the recognition of the Karen state must be complete; we shall decide our own political destiny'.⁵

The Karen struggle then continued through the following decades, until today. Consumed with numerous internal divisions between left and right, it regained strength in the 1960s under the leadership of General Bo Mya, who dominated the KNU for the best part of four decades. Born in the Papun hills in 1926, Bo Mya was a Second World War veteran who fought with Force 136. He became a Seventh Day Adventist under the influence of his wife, and developed a staunchly anti-communist position. Supported by Thailand until the 1990s, Bo Mya, along with Generals Hla Htoo, Taw Hla,

Tamla Baw and others rebuilt the KNU and provided a robust resistance to the Burma Army for many years. In the early 1990s, after students from the pro-democracy uprising of 1988 and Members of Parliament elected in 1990 fled to Karen State, the KNU headquarters at Manerplaw became in many eyes the alternative power-base to Rangoon. Bo Mya welcomed the students and NLD members, and an alliance among different ethnic nationalities and the Burman-dominated democracy movement began to develop. By 1994, however, Manerplaw was under threat and the regime's divide-and-rule tactics were, once again, bearing fruit.

U Thazana, a Karen Buddhist monk, arrived in Manerplaw in 1989. He was the cousin of KNU Forestry Minister Padoh Aung San, who defected to the regime in 1998. Over the following years, U Thazana gathered several hundred followers and began to construct a pagoda at the confluence of the Salween and Moei rivers. The KNU's armed wing, the KNLA, objected, suspecting that it could be used by the Tatmadaw to launch attacks on them. Tensions between Christian and Buddhist Karen mounted.[6]

In 1994, tensions boiled over when a group of disaffected Buddhist soldiers from the KNLA deserted and joined U Thazana. On 21 December 1994, U Thazana established the Democratic Karen Buddhist Organisation (DKBO), and the DKBA, its armed wing, was formed a few days later.[7] The regime's agents provoked disaffection within the KNU, deliberately exacerbating the split, and the Tatmadaw provided the DKBA with military and logistical support.

Divide-and-rule policy, says Zoya Phan, daughter of the assassinated KNU General Secretary Padoh Mahn Sha Lah Phan, is the regime's 'most effective tactic'. Yet the KNU leadership in 1994 could have taken more action to prevent a split. 'We did have weaknesses in the leadership, and we need to learn from that experience and correct mistakes,' argues Zoya. One key problem was that while the front-line KNLA troops were predominantly Buddhist and Animist, the leadership was overwhelmingly Christian. Indeed, the KNU had emerged from the Karen National Association, established in 1881 by Karen Baptists. From the beginning of the Karen struggle, Christian individuals and organisations played key roles in developing expressions of Karen culture, ethnicity and politics. A perception arose that foreign donors, often Christian themselves, gave gifts to the Christians in the KNU which were not shared among the Buddhists and Animists. These may not have been entirely fair perceptions, but the KNU leadership were not proactive in reassuring their critics and minimising any potential for religious tensions. The regime took advantage of this, and deliberately exacerbated the divide.

Zoya's father was sent to negotiate with those who were forming the DKBA, the armed wing, but it was too late. As an Animist he was well positioned to mediate between the Christian and Buddhist communities, but the DKBA refused to listen. Instead, they arrested him and held him captive for over a week. 'The DKBA was aggressive. My father was almost killed there,' she recalls.

Since the fall of Manerplaw in 1995, the KNU has steadily lost ground and now retains barely a foothold in its old territory. With the significant advance of the Burma Army has come dramatic displacement of Karen civilians, desperate to flee the military's abuses.

In February 2007, I visited a camp for internally displaced people (IDPs) just inside Karen State. It had only been established less than a year before, and already accommodated 3,000 people. I met one woman who had walked for over a month to reach this camp, having fled her village after it had been attacked and burned down by the Tatmadaw. Seven villagers had been shot dead. She told me how three years previously, her husband had gone to the nearby town to buy food. He was caught by Burma Army soldiers, who tied his hands, dragged him through the jungle, tied him to a tree upside down, gouged out his eyes and then drowned him.[8] As soon as I finished hearing her story, I met another woman. She came from the same village. Her fifteen-year-old son had been arrested by the Burma Army, tied to a tree and tortured. He was then beheaded. A third woman told of her husband's death in 2006. He had been on his way home from his farm, when soldiers caught him and carried him through the village. The soldiers then tore out his eyes, cut off his lips and chopped off both ears. Then they let him go, and he died alone in the forest.

These are by no means isolated incidents – and in recent years, the Tatmadaw has developed a shoot-on-sight policy. 'When the Burma Army sees people, they don't arrest them any more. They shoot,' one man told me. 'They even kill children and babies.' Another man, who had been severely tortured, said that at least 1,000 troops from thirteen Tatmadaw battalions occupied the area in which he lived. 'They come hunting people,' he remarked. 'Whatever they see in the jungle, they steal, burn and destroy. They steal pots, clothes, everything from people's homes. I dare not return to my village. There is no hope, no place for me for the future.'[9]

Rape is used as a weapon of war by the Burma Army, and is widespread and systematic – and not limited to women. On 27 December 2008 the body of a seven-year-old girl was found near her home in Ma Oo Bin village, Kyauk Kyi Township in Nyaunglebin District, northern Karen State. She had been raped and shot dead. Villagers reported seeing a soldier from the Burma Army's Light Infantry (LI) 350 entering the village shortly beforehand. They heard the girl's screams – and then rifle shots.[10] The military campaign against the Karens was particularly intense between 2006 and 2010. In the worst offensive for a decade, within the space of just a few weeks in 2006, over 15,000 civilians were displaced, and at least twenty-seven Burma Army battalions were poised to destroy hundreds of villages in Papun District. As the Karen Human Rights Group described, these were 'attacks against undefended villages with the objective of flushing villagers out of the hills to bring them under direct military control so they can be used to support the Burma Army with food and labour'. The group added: 'Please note that this is not an offensive against Karen resistance forces, and there has been very little combat.'[11] On 27 March 2006, a nine-year-old Karen girl, whose name is Naw Eh Ywa Paw, which means 'The Flower that Loves God', was shot. She survived, but her father and grandmother did not.

The Free Burma Rangers, a humanitarian aid group working in the conflict zones of eastern Burma, described the events surrounding the attack in which Naw Eh Ywa Paw was shot. 'The people had fled the attacking Burma Army who were sweeping the entire area . . . They did not know the Burma Army was waiting for them . . . The shock of having a line of troops open fire at point-blank range must have been tremendous,' the group reported. One of the survivors said: 'The Burma Army waited in a prepared position to kill villagers. They waited until they were only ten yards away and opened fire on a man carrying his mother, as well as the families and children behind him. What kind of people, what kind of system, can do this?' Another observer summed up the situation: 'The Burma Army soldiers shot at the families who were slowly climbing up toward them . . . This was not a case of startled soldiers shooting wildly at people by mistake. This was not a case of soldiers shooting at a large group of people from hundreds of yards away. On a different occasion, Burma Army soldiers shot at a father, carrying his sick grandmother, and walking with his nine-year-old daughter, from point-blank range. And they continued to fire at the other people as they ran away . . .'

Such attacks expose the lie that this is simply a counter-insurgency campaign. Children, grandmothers and teenaged girls do not count as insurgents – and raping and mutilating them, or shooting them at point-blank range when they are fleeing, are not legitimate tools of counter-insurgency. As the Free Burma Rangers conclude, 'these attacks reflect the ongoing effort of the Burma Army to break the will of the people and control them. The murder of porters and the laying of landmines to terrorize and block food to a civilian population are two of the tactics used in the strategy of the Burma Army to dominate, assimilate and exploit the ethnic people of Burma . . . What is clear is that the Burma Army is slowly attempting to expand its control, that people are under great danger and there is already a shortage of food.'[12]

The attacks continued since 2006, at least until a fragile ceasefire was agreed in 2012 – and periodically since then. Two years later, more than 30,000 Karens were displaced in the north of the state alone. Villages were mortared and shelled. The Free Burma Rangers claim that those who flee are 'hunted and shelled like animals' with the Tatmadaw 'seeking out villages and pockets of IDPs and destroying homes, food and property'.[13]

Many of the places I have visited are now under the Tatmadaw's control. In 2009, I attended the sixtieth anniversary of the start of the Karen struggle, at the headquarters of the KNLA's Seventh Brigade. I was struck by the extraordinary pride and dignity which the Karen displayed, despite being beleaguered and bombarded by the regime. Disciplined military parades were followed by beautiful traditional dancing and singing, in a celebration of Karen culture expressing a quiet determination to fight on to the bitter end. Surrounded on three sides by Burma Army troops, this tiny enclave was almost all that remained of 'Kawthoolei', a Karen homeland controlled by the Karen. Within six months, it had been overrun, a small remnant of KNLA soldiers driven back into the jungle to fight as guerrillas, the civilians fleeing to Thailand, and the very existence of Kawthoolei in peril. Padoh Mahn Sha Lah Phan was buried at the Seventh Brigade headquarters, and his elder daughter was married there. Now, his children cannot even return to visit their father's grave or the site of his daughter's wedding.

While the Karen have suffered perhaps the most severe offensive over the past decade, the other ethnic groups in eastern Burma, particularly the Karenni and the Shan, have endured similar atrocities. The Karenni, sometimes known as the Kayah or the Red Karen, have been fighting a struggle for survival for as long as their ethnic cousins, the Karen. Historically the Karenni, who number no more than 250,000 today, were never part of Burma. Until the twentieth century, the Karenni inhabited five different sub-states, each ruled by a king known as a 'Saophya'. In 1835 the Burmese king ordered his troops to attack Karenni, but they were expelled by Karenni forces. Diplomatic relations were established between the Karenni rulers and the British, and in 1875 Britain and the Burmese King Mindon both recognised Karenni independence. During colonial rule, the Karenni States were never incorporated into British Burma, but upon independence in 1947 the Karenni found themselves forced to become part of Burma. To resist this, they formed the Karenni National Organization (KNO) and a series of demonstrations were held. At 4 a.m. on 9 August 1948, Burmese military police attacked the KNO headquarters, and the Karenni launched their armed struggle. In 1955, the organisation which today is the major Karenni resistance group, the Karenni National Progressive Party (KNPP), was formed.

Today, Karenni State is one vast concentration camp. At least three-quarters of the population live under the Burmese military's control in relocation camps, where they are used constantly as a source of forced labour. Moe Bu was just ten years old when her entire village, Teetankarloe in Dee Moe Soe Township, was forced to relocate. 'We were surrounded by Burmese soldiers, and we could not go out of the relocation camp,' she recalls. 'We had no school, no clinic, nothing. We could not go out to work in the fields. We just had to stay in our houses.'

One seventeen-year-old Karenni woman told me she fled to Thailand from a relocation camp because she 'was tired of having to undertake forced portering'. A forty-eight-year-old Karenni Buddhist man, from Loikaw Township, said his entire village of over 1,000 people was forcibly relocated in May 2002. Villagers were forced to cut down trees and bamboo to provide materials to build houses for the military, and to carry packs of rice. At 8 p.m. one night, soldiers came to the relocation site, arrested all the villagers and took them to the headquarters of Light Infantry Battalion (LIB) 250, where they were beaten and forced to work as porters. They were also forced to dig trenches for the army, working from 8 a.m. until 4 p.m. with only a half-hour break. They had to provide their own food, and were forced to speak Burmese. They were tied together by their hands in groups of three or four. During the year he spent in the Nwar La Poe relocation camp, he claims he heard reports of rape, including a case in August 2003 when five girls were raped by seven soldiers.

Villagers are typically ordered to move to relocation camps with just a few days' notice, according to the former KNPP General Secretary Rimond Htoo. 'They can only take what they can carry on their backs. They live in a space within a fence, controlled by the army.' On 25 December 2003, for example, the commander of the Tatmadaw's 55th Division held a meeting in Maw Chi, in which he ordered villagers to move to a relocation site at Mahntahlaying within ten days. Anyone failing to move would be shot. Three days later, however, troops came to villages and ordered people to move immediately. Some escaped, and over 3,000 ended up hiding in the jungle. Those who went to Mahntahlaying were forced to repair the road and provide their own food. Those who escaped remained constantly on the move. 'They have to run, in order to stay alive,' said a Karenni spokesman. 'They are fed up with moving all the time. They have no homes, no health care, no food and no education. If this is not ethnic cleansing, what is?'[14]

In the relocation camps, villagers are forbidden from going out without permission. There is little education and no adequate health care. Those who attempt to flee the relocation sites and are caught face dire consequences. On a visit to the Karenni refugee camps near Mae Hong Son, Thailand, in 2004, I met a twenty-four-year-old woman who told me how her family escaped, along with twenty other families. One family, however, was caught. The soldiers tied the father to a tree and beat him to death with a rice pounder. They killed the rest of the family as well.

After two years in a relocation camp, Moe Bu and her family were allowed to return to their village. However, there they faced regular attacks from the Tatmadaw. On one occasion when she was thirteen years old, her school in Pruso Township was attacked, although Burma Army soldiers made sure they took their own children away from the school in advance.

'They came with a truck and took all their children away, and half an hour later a bomb exploded in the school. All I could see was smoke, and people running around crying. Almost every day was like that, hearing gunfire, shooting, bombs,' she recalls.

When she was thirteen, Moe Bu's mother died and she had to look after her younger brothers herself. Three years later, her father decided the situation was too dangerous, and sent her to the refugee camps on the Thai border for safety. Escorted by Karenni resistance soldiers, Moe Bu walked for three months through the jungle. 'We walked at night and slept during the day,' she recalls. 'To avoid landmines we had to follow the Karenni soldiers, and only step where they stepped. When we were close to the border, we had to walk through the river, because there are landmines everywhere. The Karenni soldiers saved my life. They believe in freedom, that is why they are fighting the Burma Army.'

As in the rest of Burma, torture is widespread in Karenni State. A thirty-one-year-old man fled to Thailand in February 2004, having endured severe torture. In June 2003, he was held captive by Tatmadaw soldiers, and tied up and tortured for ten days. On one particular day, from 11 a.m. until 6 p.m., soldiers rolled a log up and down his legs, sometimes stamping on the log with their boots. That same night, he was subjected to water torture. He was forced to lie down while soldiers poured large quantities of water into his mouth until his stomach swelled, and then they stamped on his stomach. They then smothered his mouth with a cloth, and continued to roll a log up and down his legs. He was unable to walk for five months as a result. 'I thought I was going to die,' he told me.[15]

On several occasions, the Karenni have engaged in peace talks with the regime, but each time the regime has reneged on its promises. Rimond Htoo joined the KNPP in 1975, and between 1991 and 2007 at least nine rounds of talks were held. On 1 March 1995 a ceasefire was signed, but three months later, on 30 June, the regime broke the agreement. According to Rimond Htoo, the sixteen-point agreement included an end to portering, an end to extortion and no increase in Tatmadaw troop presence in Karenni State. 'But before the ceasefire, there were ten SPDC battalions, after three months it had increased to twenty battalions. The SPDC also increased their outposts,' recalls Rimond Htoo. A statement issued on 28 June 1995 by Aung Than Lay, the Karenni 'prime minister', claimed that on 15 June the Burma Army started rounding up porters and demanding portering fees, and two days later two battalions crossed into KNPP-designated areas. 'KNPP desires peace. It does not want a resumption of hostilities. It deems SLORC hostile activities highly deplorable,' Aung Than Lay wrote. 'Should SLORC continue breaking the ceasefire agreement, and should it refuse to withdraw the troops it has moved into KNPP areas, it will be SLORC, and not KNPP, that will have to assume the responsibility for the outbreak of hostilities.' He ended with an appeal: 'Karenni is a small nation under siege. It has been fighting for survival for decades, and will continue doing so in spite of the heavy odds against it. If SLORC should use its military might to attack Karenni – which KNPP believe it will – KNPP expects and requests all sympathetic and democratic forces the world over to extend humanitarian assistance to the Karenni people.' Two days later, fierce fighting broke out. The Karenni reported that Tatmadaw troops numbering between 4,000 and 5,000 were 'poised for an all-out onslaught on Karenni bases.'

On a visit to Karenni refugees in 2004, the poignancy of the situation was highlighted by orphans singing. Translated, the words of their song were:

> My home, my home,
> When shall I see my home again?
> My home, my home,
> I never forget my home.
> I don't know about tomorrow
> It may bring poverty and hunger
> But the one who feeds the sparrows
> Will not forget me.
> My home, my home,
> When shall I see my home again?
> My home, my home,
> I never forget my home.

Their suffering is underlined in many children's drawings over the years, depicting the scenes they have witnessed. It is almost impossible, and cruel, for children to speak about their experiences, but they are often willing to draw. In 2006, for example, my sister, a violinist, visited and played the theme tune to the movie *Schindler's List*, the story of Oskar Schindler, who rescued thousands of Jews during the Holocaust. She did not tell the children the story behind the music, but asked them to draw whatever images came to mind as she played. The images were graphic and horrifying: soldiers killing, torturing, raping and burning.

The Shan, ethnically related to the Thais, are the largest non-Burman ethnic nationality in Burma, and played a leading role in the Panglong Agreement. In 1957, the Shan princes, dissatisfied with the constitutional arrangements and concerned that the central government was intruding too much in Shan territory, decided they wanted to exercise their right to secede from the Union of Burma, a right granted to them in the Panglong Agreement and the constitution. U Nu, however, had other ideas, and General Ne Win was implacably opposed to any form of federalism or autonomy for the ethnic nationalities, let alone secession. Ne Win banned the teaching of the Shan language in schools, and although peace talks were held in 1963, no deal was reached. Sao Shwe Thaike's wife Sao Hearn Kham, an elected MP herself, escaped through the jungle to the Thailand–Burma border, where she was appointed head of the Shan State War Council. She formed the Shan State Army (SSA), drawing together all the Shan groups and, as her son Harn Yawnghwe says, 'dropping the word "independence"'. The uprising began.

Over the course of four decades, the Shan people have endured horrific abuse from the Burma Army. According to Dr Chris Beyrer of the Johns Hopkins Bloomberg School of Public Health, Shan State is perhaps 'the most profoundly affected region', more than Karen and Karenni, because the Shans are a larger, better resourced and more disciplined fighting force and a more prevalent ethnic group in Burma. They occupy a fifth of the country. 'There is a particular animosity between the Burmans and the Shan, and much more widespread use of rape,' he explains. In the past, the Shan have been involved with the drugs trade, which has not helped their image. 'Their link to narcotics has meant they have had much less support from the international community.'

Harn Yawnghwe agrees. 'The Burmans see the Shans as more of a threat than other ethnic groups,' he argues. 'To be a Buddhist, in their eyes, is to be "civilized", and so the Shans are seen as more "civilized", while the other ethnic groups are seen as "uncivilized". The Shans had a set of rulers, as did the Burmans, so they were seen as competitors. The Burmans felt more threatened by the Shans than they did by others. It wasn't hatred, it was competition.' The mother of King Thibaw, the last Burmese king, was a Shan from Hsipaw, and Sao Shwe Thaike's uncle was raised by King Mindon. These relations soon turned into rivalries.

At the beginning of the struggle, according to Harn Yawnghwe, the Shan armed forces were 'really cohesive and coherent'. The movement was led by university graduates who were idealistic and educated. However, after those leaders died, the movement began to fragment. Factions emerged with deep involvement in the drugs trade, led by the warlord Khun Sa, or attached to communism. Over the years, several factions split and signed ceasefire deals with the regime. Today, the largest remaining fighting force is the Shan State Army (South), led by Colonel Yawd Serk, who had served in Khun Sa's Mong Tai Army. 'It has some legitimacy and is seen as a beacon of Shan nationalism,' says Harn Yawnghwe. 'Yawd Serk is the only one continuing the struggle.'

In 2002, I hiked through the jungle for six hours, up and down mountains and across rivers, to reach Yawd Serk's base in Shan State. We deliberately avoided paths, because we wished to go undetected along the border. So we hacked our way through the undergrowth, regularly slipping and sliding because the soil was loose and muddy. It gave me just a glimpse of life as an internally displaced person on the run. Although I experienced those conditions for only a few hours, and other people helped carry my baggage, I could empathise more easily with the internally displaced peoples after that journey than I could before. As I struggled up and down the mountains, frequently losing my footing, I imagined doing that day after day, with little food, struggling children and stumbling, frail elderly relatives in tow, with your life's possessions on your back, and with soldiers hunting you down. The words from a Shan student spoken to his foreign teacher, Bernice Koehler Johnson, and quoted in her book *The Shan: Refugees Without a Camp*, highlight this image: 'In Burma, we must be afraid all the time, Teacher. We must run, run, run until our legs break.'[16]

The SSA-South base protected a camp for internally displaced peoples who had fled their villages. There I heard stories which were eerily familiar to me from my visits to the Karen and Karenni. One boy, aged fourteen when I met him, had walked for one and a half months to reach the comparative safety of the camp. He had been taken as a porter at the age of twelve, and forced to carry a 25-kilogram sack of rice for two days. He witnessed soldiers shoot a man from his village, beat five other porters with sticks and rifles, and burn down his village. His parents had been killed by the Tatmadaw.

In April 1998, the Shan Human Rights Foundation published a report called 'Dispossessed', which claimed that 80,000 Shans had fled into Thailand in the previous two years. During that period, from 1996 to 1998, over 1,400 villages in central Shan State had been forcibly relocated, and over 300,000 people driven at gunpoint out of their homes. In one township alone, over 300 people were killed. In one relocation site, 664 villagers were executed.[17]

Rape is widespread and systematic in Shan State, and the Shan Women's Action Network (SWAN) has been pioneering in its documentation of the abuses. In 2001, its report 'License to Rape', detailing 173 incidents involving 625 girls and women, between 1996 and 2001, brought the issue to world attention for the first time, prompting an investigation by the US State Department. According to the report, at least 83 per cent of rapes were carried out by officers, usually in front of their soldiers; 61 per cent were gang rapes; and in 25 per cent of the cases, the victims were killed. Some of the cases involved little children. A ten-year-old and a twelve-year-old were raped and killed. Most shockingly, a five-year-old girl was raped, after her 'arms and legs had been tied spread-eagled to a bed'.[18] Local military officers threatened to 'cut out the tongues and slit the throats' of villagers who dared to speak out to the Red Cross when they visited Shan State in 2003.[19]

These are not simply stories in a report. On that first visit to Shan State, I met twelve women who had been raped, and others who knew of rape cases. One woman told me that one of her friends had been raped by Burma Army soldiers, and then stabbed to death with bamboo spikes. Another woman claimed that she and her two daughters had been gang-raped by over fifty soldiers. After their unimaginable ordeal, she found the bodies of her two daughters, aged fifteen and eighteen at the time, both with their dresses pulled up over them. The elder daughter had been gagged and suffocated, while the younger one had been shot in the waist and forehead.

'I still have a vivid image of the bodies of my daughters wrapped in plastic sheets,' she said.

In 2009, another offensive against Shan civilians began. On 29 July, Tatmadaw soldiers burned 62 houses in Ho Lom village, and more than 100 in Tard Mawk. At least 10,000 civilians were forced from their homes. According to Chris Beyrer and Richard Sollom in the *Washington Post*, more than a quarter of all Shan families had been forcibly relocated in 2005, in 24 per cent of families at least one person had been taken for forced labour, and in 9 per cent of households at least one person had been injured by a landmine. These, the authors argue, are some 'of the highest rates ever documented'.[20] A statement from the Shan Human Rights Foundation confirmed these attacks, and claimed that 'over one hundred villagers, both men and women, have been arrested and tortured. At least three villagers have been killed. One woman was shot while trying to retrieve her possessions from her burning house, and her body thrown into a pit latrine. Another woman was gang-raped in front of her husband by an officer and three of his troops.'[21]

In addition to these shocking stories, the regime is engaged in a more subtle campaign to eradicate Shan history and culture. Some of the Shan princes' palaces have been allowed to fall into decay, or have been destroyed altogether. On 9 November 1991 the palace at Kengtung, described as 'the grandest of the Shan palaces' and built in 1903 by Prince Kawn Kiao Intalang, was demolished, following a direct order from the regime. In its place, the regime built a modern hotel. While Shan State includes the famous Inle Lake and hill towns such as Maymyo and Lashio, popular with tourists, it is worth noting that 'the vast majority of Shan State is off limits to foreigners', according to SWAN.[22]

Colonel Yawd Serk has described his homeland as 'under Burmese occupation'. According to SWAN, over 150 Tatmadaw infantry battalions are deployed in Shan State – almost one-third of the Burma Army.[23] Yawd Serk fought an armed struggle because 'we have no other choice – it is just for survival'. The Shan, he told me, want peace, but for decades the regime was unwilling to negotiate. 'In recent years, whenever the ethnic groups have proposed talks, the junta has responded with force,' he said. As for him and his troops, 'though we are in military uniform, we are civilians and we long to live in peace'. He called for international pressure on the regime to allow international observers and reporters complete, un-hindered access to all parts of Burma. 'If the junta forbids reporters to enter, to investigate drugs, rape and human rights violations, then it is clear that they are involved,' he concluded.[24]

On 2 December 2011, years of fighting came to an end, at least for now, when Yawd Serk and the SSA-South signed a ceasefire with the regime. Preliminary talks were also held with the KNU and other ethnic groups in a possible effort by President Thein Sein to establish, even if initially piecemeal, a peace throughout the country. On 1 March 2012, in a speech to parliament, Thein Sein made a clear pledge to make ending the conflict in the ethnic areas his priority, and to recognise equal rights for the ethnic people. In a rare and significant shift in rhetoric, Thein Sein appeared to abandon the regime's traditional description of the ethnic groups as 'insurgents', 'terrorists' and 'rebels' and instead declared: 'We all have to work so our ethnic youths who held guns stand tall holding laptops . . . The expectation of ethnic groups is to get equal rights for all. Equal standards are also the wish of our government.'[25] Such a change of language, and a recognition of the ethnic people's desire for equal rights, is very welcome. The real test of peace, however, will be whether the military's abuses of civilians cease, because hitherto even an absence of war in some parts of the country has not meant a genuine freedom from fear, as the experience of the other major ethnic group along the Thailand–Burma border, the Mon, has shown.

The Mon are generally recognised, according to Martin Smith, as 'the earliest inhabitants of modern Burma'.[26] Although a minority in Burma today, the Mon were once the dominant ethnic group in what is now Burma. The Shwedagon pagoda in Rangoon, the most important Buddhist symbol in the country, was built by the Mons, and Burmese culture is heavily influenced by Mon culture. Lower Burma was ruled by Mon kings from 1287 until 1539, but their influence extended beyond Burma to much of mainland South East Asia during the first millenium, for more than a thousand years.

The Mon took up arms at the same time as the Karen, in 1948, but a decade later the Mon People's Front (MPF) surrendered to Rangoon. The very next day, however, Nai Shwe Kyin, sometimes known as Ba Lwin, established the New Mon State Party (NMSP) to continue the struggle for autonomy and self-determination. In 1995, after almost fifty years of fighting, the NMSP signed a ceasefire agreement with the SPDC, and agreed to attend the regime's constitution-drafting National Convention.

Despite signing a ceasefire, however, there is no real peace in Mon State. The Tatmadaw continues to perpetrate human rights violations. The Human Rights Foundation of Monland regularly reports incidents of forced labour, particularly for road and bridge construction projects. Many villages are required to provide three weeks' forced labour every month, disrupting crop production cycles. In some places villagers are prohibited from tending their crops, in case they support the resistance. Land confiscation is common, and sexual violence is widespread. A report shockingly titled 'Catwalk to the Barracks', by the Women and Child Rights Project in southern Burma and the Human Rights Foundation of Monland, documents sexual violence by Tatmadaw soldiers against fifty women and girls aged between fourteen and fifty. Young women are forcibly conscripted to serve local battalions as 'comfort women' or, more accurately, as 'sex slaves', and schoolgirls are forced to parade on a catwalk for the entertainment of soldiers. 'Nowhere Else to Go', a subsequent report by the same organisation, documented the trafficking of women and children from nineteen townships across Burma, including Mon State, into the sex trade. The report detailed forty separate incidents, involving seventy-one victims.

As a result of the continuing violations and the regime's failure to provide a satisfactory political solution, the NMSP has become one of the most outspoken of the ceasefire groups. In 2005, the NMSP downgraded its status at the National Convention from full participant to observer, out of frustration at the lack of meaningful dialogue in the constitution-drafting process. Tensions with the regime were heightened further when the NMSP refused to sign a statement criticising the United States for proposing a resolution on Burma at the UN Security Council. Trading privileges provided to the NMSP as part of the ceasefire deal were withdrawn. One Mon leader told me when I visited their office in Sangkhlaburi that most Mons have no trust in the new constitution. The NMSP, he added, retains its arms 'not because we want to fight, but because we have to be ready to defend our lives. If the NMSP gives up its arms, it should only do so to the United Nations, not to the SPDC.'[27]

In the face of this horrific suffering in eastern Burma stand an extraordinary number of people with truly remarkable courage and initiative. Charm Tong is one of the most prominent. Born in the conflict areas of Shan State, she was sent to Thailand by her parents at the age of six, to be raised in an orphanage run by nuns. 'The villages were attacked all the time and we had to move all the time, and so my parents decided to send me to the border so that I could go to school and be safe,' she says.

At the age of sixteen, Charm Tong began her activism, as an intern at the Shan Human Rights Foundation (SHRF). She saw a newsletter, published by the Shan Herald Agency for News (SHAN), and decided to learn more about human rights documentation. She completed an internship at the Alternative ASEAN Network on Burma (ALTSEAN), and then co-founded the Shan Women's Action Network (SWAN), to work on education, health care, income generation, women's empowerment as well as international advocacy. Her motivation came from her own experiences. 'I became an activist because of what I witnessed in the war in Burma, the attacks by the Burma Army, being separated from my family and growing up on the border,' she says. 'Every day you witness and see how people suffer. It is not new to hear about rape and forced labour. I always consider myself a very lucky person, because at least I am safe and could get basic education. Many young people today don't receive any basic education.'

Within a year of beginning her activist work, she was thrown onto the international stage when she testified at the United Nations Commission on Human Rights – in front of the regime's ambassador. Undaunted, she presented evidence of the regime's crimes. 'It is good that the regime was there,' she says. 'They should know that the world actually knows what is happening, and that we are trying to bring the voices of the people to the international community.'

Two years later, at the age of twenty, Charm Tong decided to try to give other young people the opportunity for education. She founded the School for Shan State Nationalities Youth, and since 2001 at least 260 young people from Shan State have been trained and sent back to work in or for their communities, as teachers, medics, journalists, women's activists and cross-border relief workers. Every year, the school receives at least one hundred applicants, and accepts thirty.

In 2005, Charm Tong went to Washington, DC where she met President

George W. Bush in the Oval Office of the White House. Those who had initiated the meeting expected it to last no longer than ten minutes – a brief exchange of views, an opportunity for Charm Tong to impress on the President the urgency of the crisis in Burma, and a photograph which would help raise headlines. Instead, the President spent almost an hour with Charm Tong. 'The meeting with President Bush was an encouraging sign,' she says with typical modesty and understatement. 'He was very concerned and asked many questions about the situation of the people in Burma, and about what the United States and the international community could do. It was a message of solidarity with the people of Burma, a sign that the world has not forgotten.'

Charm Tong, a recipient of numerous international awards including the Reebok Human Rights Award, has been nominated for the Nobel Peace Prize, named one of *Time* magazine's Asian Heroes and listed by *Marie Claire* magazine as a 'Woman of the World'. She continues travelling around the world to brief politicians, travelling to London in 2006 to testify at a hearing in the House of Commons and meet the then Foreign Secretary Jack Straw, the Leader of the Opposition at the time, now Prime Minister, David Cameron, and the Shadow Foreign Secretary William Hague. But despite – or perhaps because of – her international profile, she continues to be harassed by the regime. However, she is dismissive of their tactics. 'It's very common for them to burden any groups that speak out about the crimes against humanity that they have committed. For us, it is very important that we continue to speak the truth.' She points to the development of pro-democracy and ethnic civil society groups operating along Burma's borders, working on women's rights, environmental concerns, media and broader human rights issues, and campaigning against the regime's dam projects, oil and gas pipelines and military offensives. In addition, they are not only campaigning against the regime, but offering positive alternative development ideas. 'They are more organised, they are providing services for the community, and they are working together . . . These have been built up over the past twenty years. You could see there were none before,' she points out. 'We are empowering our people, so that in the future when there is change in Burma it doesn't mean that any democratic government can just go and build the dams or take all the natural resources, without consultation.' Charm Tong is also adamant that those who dismiss the border-based organisations as 'exiled' groups do not understand the situation properly. 'We are working inside Burma. There's no inside or outside Burma, everyone is working for change in Burma. We may be physically based outside, but we have our networks and people who work inside.' The border-based groups, she adds, serve as a vital channel for information and documentation of the situation inside Burma.

Karen activists like Ka Hsaw Wa have also helped motivate people and draw the suffering of eastern Burma to the world's attention. Ka Hsaw Wa was born in Rangoon, and became involved in the student uprising in 1988. He was arrested and tortured, and that experience, he says, was the origin of his work today. 'After I was tortured, I was angry and wanted to do something against the authorities who wrongfully tortured me,' he recalls. Aware that he could easily be arrested again, he fled from Rangoon to the Karen jungles. 'My first intention was to join the KNU, or KNLA, but when I visited many villages and talked to many people, I saw many horrible things and talked to villagers about the human rights violations. It made me think that I should expose these violations to the international community.' Teaming up with a Canadian activist called Kevin Heppner, he helped establish the Karen Human Rights Group, and began documenting the destruction of villages, the suffering of the Karen people and the environmental degradation. In the course of his work he met and married an American human rights lawyer, Katie Redford, and the couple then founded a new organisation, EarthRights International, in 1995, to focus on areas 'where protection of human rights and the environment is intrinsically connected', marshalling – as their slogan puts it – 'the power of law and the power of people in defense of human rights and the environment'. Today the organisation documents human rights and environmental abuses, conducts international advocacy campaigns, trains and mobilises ethnic peoples to be involved in documentation and campaigning, and litigates in US courts on behalf of victims of human rights abuses. EarthRights established a remarkable school in Thailand in 1999, to train people from different ethnic nationalities, equipping them with the skills to document human rights abuses and provide leadership to their communities.

EarthRights is perhaps best known for its involvement in the ground-breaking case against the US oil company Unocal. A group of villagers from Karen State, with the advice and support of EarthRights lawyers, particularly Katie Redford, sued Unocal for complicity in forced labour, rape and murder committed by the Burma Army in the area surrounding the Yadana gas pipeline built by a consortium led by Unocal, and the French oil company Total. The lawyers used the US Alien Torts Act, and built the case around the fact that Unocal had hired the Burma Army to provide security for the pipeline. Most lawyers believed the case would not succeed, but in 2005, after a ten-year legal battle, Unocal settled out of court, the first time in history that a company has settled this kind of case. The story is told in a film, *Total Denial*.

Zoya Phan has similarly brought hope to her people. The daughter of Padoh Mahn Sha Lah Phan, the KNU General Secretary assassinated in 2008, Zoya was born in Manerplaw, the Karen headquarters, in 1980. Both her parents were involved in the Karen resistance, but Zoya recalls her life until 1995 as 'relatively peaceful'. When he was not engaged in political activities, her father tended his flower garden, and her mother looked after their chickens. Zoya, her sister Bwa Bwa and her brothers Slone and Say Say played on the riverbanks. Her life changed, however, when the Burma Army attacked Manerplaw and she and her family had to flee. 'The Burma Army attacked our area with mortar bombs and air strikes,' she recalls. 'When the bombs dropped, the ground would shake and as children we were so scared.' The family escaped to the jungle, where they survived with little food, shelter or medical care. 'We could only carry a few things on our backs. We walked through the jungle for weeks until we arrived in Thailand.'

For five years, Zoya lived in various refugee camps along the Thailand–Burma border, where she studied English and gained some education. Although refugees were better off than many inside Burma, as they received food, rations, shelter and schooling, the restrictions they faced were frustrating. 'Life in the refugee camp was very difficult,' she told me. 'Thousands of people were put together in a small land, behind barbed wire, where we were not allowed to go out from the camp. It was like a prison camp.'

In Mae La refugee camp, the school motto, as Zoya recounts in her book *Little Daughter*, was 'to learn, to live, to serve'.[28] In 2000, she gained a rare opportunity to continue her studies in Bangkok, but as a refugee she had to travel to the Thai capital without any identification. 'I had to be smuggled out of the camp,' she writes.[29] Sponsored by the Open Society Institute, Zoya pursued her studies at the St Theresa Institute of Technology, an international school linked to Bradford University in the United Kingdom. There, Zoya learned how to use a computer, how ASEAN works, and how to dodge the Thai police. Studying business administration and adjusting to city life, however, was demanding. She writes in her book: 'It was so alien to me. I didn't understand many of the most basic concepts. I had no idea about the practices of international business. As to the relative benefits of Kimberly-Clark's logo versus that of Toyota or Tesco – I was completely lost. What was a logo? What was a superstore? Who were Tesco, Toyota and the rest?'[30]

During her studies in Bangkok, Zoya did an internship at a Thai telecommunications company, Telecomasia, and was on the verge of being offered a corporate career. Three things, however, happened which changed the course of her life for ever. Her mother, whose health had been poor for some time, became seriously ill, with liver failure and a heart condition. She returned to the border, to look after her mother, and then decided to make a visit inside Karen State. She wanted, she recalls, 'to get into those areas that the media and human rights workers were seldom able to visit'.[31] She went with her father's blessing, and his hammock and mosquito net. On that visit, she met people who were terrified of imminent attack, suffering from cholera, chronic diarrhoea and malaria, and who had no opportunities for health care or education at all. 'They were so poor and destitute that even the clothes they stood up in were in shreds,' she recalls. 'They had nothing; *nothing*. No pots and pans; no blankets; precious little to eat.' It was this situation, she explains, that began to turn her away from 'a soft, moneyed and easy future' and back to her people and their struggle.[32]

Her mother died in 2004, and Zoya accepted a place at the University of East Anglia in the United Kingdom to study for a Masters in Development and Politics. Ten months after starting her course, she attended a demonstration in London, and her activist's life was born. 'All my life I had been a victim,' she writes, 'but today I had felt what it was like to fight back.'[33] Within a few weeks she was doing interviews on the BBC, leading protests outside the Burmese embassy and 10 Downing Street, and addressing audiences around the country. Recruited to the staff of Burma Campaign UK, she became one of the most prominent faces of the movement in exile.

In 2006, I was in Kunming, returning from a visit to the China–Burma border. I opened my emails, and found a note from someone working for the Conservative Party, saying that they wanted to invite a Burmese speaker to address the party conference that year. They said the person needed to be based in the United Kingdom, or nearby. In my mind, there was only one candidate: Zoya. A few months later, dressed in a traditional Karen outfit, and speaking immediately before the Shadow Foreign Secretary William Hague, she stood on the platform of the conference hall in Bournemouth and brought the audience of several thousand to their feet. With extraordinary poise and charm, she told her story.

> When I was just fourteen years old, the soldiers came to my village. They opened fire. There was no warning. The mortar bombs exploded. We fled for our lives, but many people were killed. My family ran, carrying what we could on our backs. We left everything, and our home, behind. I still remember the smell of the black smoke as our village was destroyed. At the same time, and as we hid in the jungle, homeless and afraid, a British trade delegation dined in Rangoon, making business deals with the military dictatorship that had just slaughtered my people.

But it was her challenge to Britain that drew the strongest applause, and that caused eyes to water and minds to ponder. 'How many more generations will have to suffer while the world looks the other way?' she asked.

> As a democracy activist from Burma, I am confused by the response of the international community. How can any government's foreign policy not make human rights a priority. What is more important than the basic rights for all of us to live in peace without fear? How can governments stand by while in Burma innocent children are shot, girls as young as five years old are raped by the soldiers, and while a thousand political prisoners are tortured and facing cruelty every day . . .? Why has it taken sixteen years for the United Nations Security Council to even discuss Burma?

She concluded with these words: 'Promoting human rights and democracy is not imperialist, it is not a cultural issue, it is everyone's business. I believe it should be a priority for every country. The opportunity to speak to you today has given me hope. I hope that your party will help my people in their struggle for human rights, democracy and freedom in Burma.'

There was barely a dry eye in the hall, and Zoya was surrounded by delegates at the end offering help and extending goodwill. So powerful was her address that she was invited back the following year, to speak just before the President of Rwanda, and she gave an equally moving speech. But seeing how gracious, articulate and yet defiant she was, few would have known what had happened the evening prior to that first conference address in Bournemouth. Thousands of conference delegates' passes had not been processed, and there was a backlog awaiting police security approval. When Zoya arrived the previous evening, I took her to collect her conference pass. Hers was one of the many that had not been approved, but worse – she was an asylum seeker at the time. Despite being a guest speaker at the Conservative Party Conference, due to address the hall the next day, she was subjected to a frustrating and humiliating interrogation by the British police. They were just doing their job, and they were not unkind, but it brought home to me the struggles Zoya herself was fighting on many levels. She was becoming an international voice for her people, she was adjusting to life in an entirely foreign land, she was still grieving the loss of her mother and concerned for her father's safety, and she was stateless. Those factors made her performance at the conference the next day all the more extraordinary. She admits herself that life at that time, for 'a person from the jungle', was 'very challenging'.

Since then, Zoya has been granted asylum in the United Kingdom, and travels throughout Europe raising awareness. Her father's assassination in 2008 came as a shock, but not a surprise. 'He knew that the regime had a plan. He was on a hit list. We knew for many years that the regime was trying to destroy the Karen leaders,' she told me. Zoya herself has survived three attempts on her own life. After her father's death, Zoya, her two brothers and her sister established The Phan Foundation in their parents' memory. 'We wanted to carry on what they were doing – fighting poverty, promoting Karen culture and helping Karen activists and organisations to develop.' Her motivation to continue comes from a combination of factors. 'Seeing the suffering, hearing the stories makes us want to do more,' she explains. 'In addition, the encouragement of friends around the world, giving support, political activism and solidarity with our struggle, helps us keep going. There is no way we would give up – we know we have many friends who support us.'

Dr Cynthia Maung is another light in the darkness of eastern Burma. A Karen doctor who fled Rangoon in 1988, she established an emergency clinic in Mae Sot on the Thailand–Burma border to treat the students who fled the crackdown, expecting it all to be over within a few months. More than twenty years on, she has established the Mae Tao Clinic and the Back Pack Health Worker training programme.

Dr Chris Beyrer has worked closely with her for some years, and describes her work as 'extraordinary'. Although the project 'started as emergency care for the students in 1988' the woman who is now internationally known as 'Dr Cynthia' recognised very quickly that 'what people needed was more than an emergency stop-gap,' says Dr Beyrer. The clinic now provides a range of services, including reproductive health, dental care, malaria treatment, eye surgery, prosthetics and rehabilitation for victims of landmine injuries, an immunisation programme and a variety of public health and primary care education and training initiatives. 'The need just keeps growing,' says Dr Beyrer. 'People come from all over Burma for treatment, because the Burmese health system is privatised, in a country where people have been divested of income and cannot afford care.' The clinic now provides health care to a population of approximately 150,000, including refugees and migrant workers in Thailand, internally displaced people from Karen State, and people from deeper inside Burma who travel for days to her clinic.

In addition to the clinic, Dr Cynthia has established at least seventy-five Back Pack Health Worker teams, working in the conflict zones of eastern Burma. The teams are given a year's intensive training, and then travel back to their communities to provide basic medical care for their people. They do vital work. 'There is a lot of loss of life among the internally displaced peoples, from completely treatable diseases,' says Dr Beyrer. 'So we are training people from ethnic groups because no one else can get in and out of there.' They estimate that at least 170,000 people inside Burma are reached by the teams – people who would otherwise receive no help at all. But the teams operate at great personal risk. Since 2001, seven of her back-pack medics have died, mostly as a result of stepping on landmines. One medic was beaten to death by the regime's border guards.

As well as providing basic health care in the jungle, the Back Pack Health Workers have also documented crucial data on health issues in eastern Burma. Published in a report called 'Chronic Emergency: Health and Human Rights in Eastern Burma', the Back Pack Health Worker teams argue that Burma's health indicators are among the worst in the region, and in eastern Burma the situation is comparable to the humanitarian crises in Sierra Leone, the Democratic Republic of Congo and Cambodia soon after Pol Pot's demise. A new report published in 2010, called 'Diagnosis Critical', claims that over 40 per cent of children under the age of five are acutely malnourished, and that 60 per cent of deaths of children under five are from preventable and treatable diseases. One in fourteen women is infected with malaria, one of the highest rates in the world. The maternal mortality rate in eastern Burma is three times the national average. In 2007, a report published by the University of California and Johns Hopkins School of Public Health added further evidence of a desperate crisis. 'The Gathering Storm: Infectious Diseases and Human Rights in Burma' documented the spread of malaria, tuberculosis and HIV/AIDS, concluding that they are at their highest along Burma's frontiers.

Dr Cynthia's work has been widely recognised – she has been nominated for the Nobel Peace Prize and was awarded the Ramon Magsaysay prize. Yet, as Dr Beyrer points out, she is herself a refugee. 'She is illegal in Thailand,' he says. The challenges this causes her are constant. In recent years, due to the United Nations resettlement programme, emigration has been added to the list of challenges she faces. 'Close to half her best people have gone abroad,' says Dr Beyrer. 'She is having to train new people. But she has shown tremendous capacity.'

Her staff are mostly Karen, but some come from other parts of Burma. Many are, like Dr Cynthia, refugees. One doctor previously worked in Myitkyina, capital of Kachin State. He had to flee, after a foreigner made an unannounced visit to the city hospital, and found it in dire conditions. According to Dr Beyrer, 'there were patients sharing beds, no bandages, no antibiotics, disposable gloves for one-off use used multiple times.' The doctor had shown him around – but was later charged with sedition for doing so.

Dr Cynthia is one of the regime's most hated opponents. Describing her as an 'absconder, an insurgent and an opium-smuggling terrorist', the regime said that any attempt to deny this is 'as futile as covering the rotting carcass of an elephant with a goat hide'.[34] For hundreds of thousands of people, inside Burma and on the border, she is a ray of hope.

Another organisation which provides real hope is the Free Burma Rangers. In 1993, David Eubank, a former American soldier who had served in both the US Army Rangers and Special Forces, met the Wa people's Foreign Minister in Thailand. Eubank, the son of missionaries in Thailand, had studied at Fuller Seminary in the United States and become a missionary himself. Inspired by the story of William Marcus Young, the first missionary to the Wa people, he responded to the Wa Foreign Minister's request for help, and was told by one of their leaders that as a former soldier he was 'the type of missionary we need'.[35] He made several subsequent visits to the Wa, traditional headhunters, who he says were 'feeling very disaffected from the rest of Burma'. In 1996, he went to Rangoon, and had a meeting with Aung San Suu Kyi which changed his life. Aung San Suu Kyi, a devout Buddhist, told this American missionary that she reads the Bible every day and that her favourite verse is John 8: 32 – 'You will know the truth, and the truth will set you free.' She then issued a request, even a challenge, to him: saying that she knew he was a Christian, and that Christians pray, she asked him to mobilise Christians around the world to pray for Burma. As a result of the direct request of Burma's democracy leader and Nobel Peace Prize Laureate, David Eubank established the Global Day of Prayer for Burma – an annual event on the second Sunday of March around the world. She also pricked his conscience about the need to build unity among the peoples of Burma. Eubank's mission was born.

A year later, Eubank became aware of a major offensive by the Burma Army against the Karen and responded immediately by going to the border. Thousands of Karen were fleeing attacks, and the humanitarian crisis was desperate. Joined by a few Karen volunteers, he established the Free Burma Rangers as a relief team to bring, as their motto puts it, 'help, hope and love' to the people in the conflict zones of eastern Burma. Since 1997, the Free Burma Rangers have trained 110 multi-ethnic relief teams, drawing together Karen, Karenni, Shan and Pa-O and, more recently, people from northern and western Burma – the Kachin, Chin and Arakanese (or Rakhine). At least fifty-five full-time Free Burma Ranger teams are currently active, consisting of people from eleven ethnic groups, and have conducted over 350 relief missions into the conflict zones, each one usually lasting one or two months, on average treating 2,000 patients per mission. Each team consists of a medic, a videographer and photographer to document human rights abuses, and a pastor or counsellor. Although the ethos of the Free Burma Rangers is overtly Christian, the teams are multi-faith and include Buddhists and Animists. 'We are held together by a bond of love and a common purpose of freedom, justice and reconciliation in Burma,' says Eubank.

Besides delivering much-needed emergency relief, the Free Burma Rangers document atrocities and issue detailed reports, often with photographs and maps. Equipped with satellite communications, their reports are now able to reach the desktops of human rights groups, journalists and politicians around the world, direct from the jungle, within hours of an incident occurring. The reports are always shocking. In May 2009, for example, the Free Burma Rangers spoke to a Karen man who had been tortured, accused of planting a landmine which destroyed a bulldozer. He was given a choice – destroy all the village's food crops, burn down the village or pay for the bulldozer, a sum of 3 million kyats or 2,400 dollars. 'Then a pistol was held against the side of his head and shot twice on both sides and then up to six times in front of him. He was then tied to a durian tree and, thinking he was going to be killed, he asked to see his wife and children,' the report claimed. 'When they saw his condition, they began crying before being sent away by the Burma Army soldiers. Hot water was then poured on his legs and head and his back was beaten with a gun. He was also smashed in the mouth with a gun by troops whom he said were drunk. The torture began at 1 p.m. and continued until nightfall when he was released.'[36] Another report includes an interview with a Karen man who had witnessed his father being tortured by Burma Army soldiers. 'The soldiers started kicking, punching and hitting him with a branch of wood,' the man told the Free Burma Rangers. 'His face was smashed; his neck and chest were badly hit; and his penis was burned and sliced. They also put the knife in his mouth and twisted . . . He was taken away by soldiers and I was ordered to go back home. Within a few minutes I heard two gunshots. I knew that he had been killed.'[37]

Free Burma Ranger teams take significant risks in order to reach people who need help in Burma's conflict zones, and several have given their lives. Saw Mu, known as 'Mr Happy', for example, stepped on a landmine and died on 5 May 2006. Saw Lee Reh Kyaw was captured by the Burma Army while delivering aid to Karenni villagers. He was tortured and interrogated for two days and then, on 10 April 2007, he was executed. Shining Moon died on 20 May 2008 from acute malaria. Disease, landmines and the Burma Army are some of the dangers the Free Burma Ranger teams face on a daily basis. Writing about Saw Lee Reh Kyaw, David Eubank said: 'He was a wonderful man who smiled at everything; he is missed by us all. He was killed doing what he believed in: bringing help to people under oppression. His death is tragic, but not in vain. He has made a mark of love and service that made a difference in the lives of those he helped, and in all of our lives.'

I have travelled with the Free Burma Rangers, attended some of their training and witnessed their extraordinary courage, grace, humility and compassion. They are among the real heroes of Burma's struggle. Men like Eliya, known to his friends as 'Mad Dog', provide an example of true love in action to people in the comfortable free world. A medic, trainer, cook, singer, artist and champion kick boxer, Eliya is, say his friends, 'almost always smiling'. He was one of the first Karens to join the Free Burma Rangers, when Eubank met him in 1997. Eubank recalls the encounter:

Over ten thousand people were fleeing into Thailand during the 1997 Burma Army offensive. The border road we were on was clogged with families carrying all they had. I pulled my truck over to the side of the road and as I stepped out, a man emerged from the jungle. He was in full camouflage fatigues, with a hand grenade on his harness and a M16 in his hand. He had a warm and open smile and a bright red earring in one ear. He looked like a pirate. 'Hello,' he said in English. 'My name is Eliya and I am a medic. Can I help you?' Eliya immediately began to help Eubank unload packs of medical supplies from his truck, and then stopped some of his fellow Karens who were fleeing. 'You can run away tomorrow,' he told them, 'but now is the time to help your people.'

Since 1997, Eliya has helped treat thousands of people, including landmine victims. On one visit, the Free Burma Rangers met a seventeen-year-old boy, Saw Sa Lu, who had stepped on a landmine. 'His lower leg was shredded,' Eubank recalls. 'The bone shattered and was only connected by a strip of skin to his upper leg. Eliya immediately took charge of the situation, organised our other medics, and began to work on the boy . . . He controlled the bleeding from the stump, put in intravenous [drips] and began to clamp and suture off blood vessels and arteries. He comforted the boy, and prepared him for travel. Saw Sa Lu's life was saved.'

In one of the most remarkable examples of Eliya's commitment to his people, Eubank describes an incident that occurred in a village at the end of one three-month mission in northern Karen State. 'A steady stream of families fleeing attacks far to the north were trickling into this village,' he says. 'We had no medicines left so we treated them the best we could as we waited for the re-supply.' As they waited, Eubank was told that Eliya had gone to treat one of the children who was sick. 'The boy had sores all over his face and had both mucus and pus draining out of his nose . . . He had not changed his clothes or bathed in days. He was dirty, sick and scared. Eliya was talking to him gently and trying to calm him down.' The boy had been playing with a ballpoint pen, and had pushed it up his nose, where the tip had broken off and stuck in his nasal passage. 'I will try to get it out,' Eliya said. He tried to remove the pen tip with forceps, but after an hour he had made no progress. Eubank describes what happened next: 'He looked at the boy and the parents and said "There is no other way" and smiled. He then bent over and put his mouth over the boy's nose and began to suck the mucus and pus out . . . He kept sucking, hoping that the pen tip would come out too. In the end, the pen tip was removed . . . I looked at the whole scene and was amazed and grateful for Eliya's love and commitment.'

Eliya is perhaps best known within the Free Burma Rangers for an occasion when a team was being pursued by the Burma Army. Accompanying ninety-six people who were fleeing a forced relocation site, with grandmothers, small children and babies, the situation was extremely dangerous. 'The Burma Army was chasing us and had us surrounded by five battalions,' recalls Eubank. Everyone was hiding, and silently trying to work out a plan of escape. As they crouched on the ground, Eliya came along.

> He was bent over slightly with a broad grin on his face. Still smiling, he leaned over to me and very softly sang, 'Don't worry about tomorrow, just really good today, the Lord is right beside you to guide you all the way; have faith, hope and charity, that is how to live successfully; how do I know? The Bible tells me so.' Then he continued up the line of people on the ground, smiling and encouraging them in a soft voice. Everyone he passed smiled back at him and the whole mood on the jungle floor shifted. By prayer, the skill of the Karen soldiers and Eliya's and others' can-do attitude, we were eventually able to get out of that situation and take all of the ninety-six people to safety.[38]

But Eliya is not by any means the only inspirational Free Burma Ranger. Doh Say, a Karen who grew up in Karenni, now spends almost the entire year in Karenni State, having established a mobile medical clinic. In 1991, he joined the KNPP and became a soldier, but a year later, on the front line, he was shot. After a miraculous recovery, he decided to devote his life to working for his people. The risks he takes today are immense, working in very demanding conditions. But he shows a remarkable lack of concern for his own hardship, recognising the scale of suffering of his own people. 'It is good for us to live in the same conditions as the villagers,' he says. 'We wake up every hour with the cold, but it is better to do this than to sleep deeply, as we have to be ready to move at any moment . . . I always have to hang my hammock low for four reasons: more chance of being below the line of bullets, less possibility of being hit by shell blast as it spreads out, it is warmer near to the ground, and it is less far to fall if it breaks!'[39]

An email which Doh Say sent to me in 2005 sums up his spirit: 'I will try my best to follow what God asks us to do and will never give up in fighting against the dictators who are oppressing the entire people of Burma in many forms for many years already. I will also always try to find a way to help the oppressed . . . My big present to the oppressed people is [to be] "free from fear" . . . I will try my best until my last day.'

The Free Burma Rangers have also made a significant contribution to deepening unity between the ethnic nationalities. Since 1997, Eubank and his team have organised ethnic unity seminars, bringing together all the major groups, including ceasefire groups. 'Disunity starts with a lack of faith in each individual, that what they are doing is good enough. If you don't have faith then you grab everything you can see, and it makes you more selfish and insecure. From that comes jealousy when you see other people getting things. And beyond that, disunity is caused by unequal resources, and by disagreement on the way forward: one person wants to go right, another wants to go left,' he says. Competing political and religious ideas, and tribal identities, also contribute to a lack of unity. The common enemy, the Burma Army, is not enough to unite people, Eubank believes, without a common vision of what Burma might look like after the military regime falls. As a result of the ethnic unity seminars run by Free Burma Rangers, he adds, there is 'more respect and more understanding'.

Building on the Free Burma Rangers' efforts, several agreements have been signed between the different people groups in Burma in support of federal democracy. In 1992, the Manerplaw Agreement was signed by the two major ethnic alliances, the Democratic Alliance of Burma (DAB) and the National Democratic Front (NDF), along with the NCGUB and the exiled NLD. Four years later, the NLD expressed its support for autonomy for the ethnic nationalities and the 'Panglong spirit'. In 1997, at a conference convened by the Free Burma Rangers, ethnic nationalities signed the Mae Tha Raw Hta Agreement, in which they declared that they 'unanimously agree to establish a genuine federal union'. On 14 December 1998 the exiled NLD, exiled MPs and the ethnic groups signed the Thoo Mweh Klo Agreement, again pledging support for a federal democracy.

In November 2010, an alliance of ethnic armed groups – ceasefire and non-ceasefire – was formed, calling itself the Committee for the Emergence of a Federal Union. Three months later, it was dissolved and replaced with a broader alliance, the United Nationalities Federal Council, consisting of most of the ethnic groups except the Shan State Army. Its objectives were clear: to form a united front in support of a political settlement for the ethnic nationalities.

For Karenni leader Rimond Htoo, unity among the ethnic nationalities is crucial. 'We cannot fight on our own. We need to join hands with other ethnic nationalities, and we need encouragement from the international community,' he told me. He also emphasised that their struggle now is for a free – and federal – Burma. 'At the beginning of the revolution, our fight was for independence. Everyone was for independence – the Shan, Karen, Karenni. But now, all the ethnics are together and we are focusing on federal union. We are not going to split up the union. The regime always says we are separatists, but this is not true. Federalism is the only way for peace in Burma.'

In 2011, President Thein Sein began to change the regime's rhetoric about the ethnic people and move towards ceasefire negotiations. In a speech to Parliament on 30 March 2011, he promised to 'give top priority to national unity' to overcome 'the hell of untold miseries' brought about by decades of war.[40] Subsequent months proved confusing, as he dropped previous demands for ethnic groups to surrender and form part of a Border Guard Force (BGF) under the Burma Army's control, and offered peace talks, while at the same time breaking long-standing ceasefires with two major ethnic groups, launching new offensives against civilians in Kachin and northern Shan states. Nevertheless, although a new war was waged in these areas, by the beginning of 2012 there were preliminary ceasefire agreements with several key ethnic groups, including the KNU and the SSA-South. The peace process is fragile, and hinges on the establishment of a longer-term nationwide, inclusive political process that addresses the political desires and needs of the ethnic groups. Without a political agreement, a ceasefire is simply an absence of fighting and no guarantee of genuine peace.

The situation in eastern Burma has been one of the world's worst humanitarian crises, and one of its least known. Since 1996, over 3,700 villages in eastern Burma have been destroyed[41] – a scale comparable to Darfur. Over half a million people are internally displaced. Pascal Khoo Thwe has described what is happening as 'Pol Pot in slow motion'. Amnesty International,[42] Human Rights Watch, and leading international jurists call it 'crimes against humanity', and the UN's special rapporteur on human rights in Burma has called for these to be investigated.

A Silent Cry in the North

'All we do know . . . is that evil labours with vast power and perpetual success – in vain: preparing always the soil for unexpected good to sprout in.'

J.R.R. Tolkein, 1944

HALF AN HOUR after entering the hotel to meet a man who had come especially from Myitkyina, the capital of Kachin State, to talk to me, I received a message from my Kachin hosts. 'We have just received news that the Burma Army's Northern Region commander and Kachin State commander are passing through town. They will be having lunch in this hotel. Do not under any circumstances leave the room you are now in until we let you know,' they said. I had already been smuggled into the hotel through the back door, having been brought there in a car with darkened windows. Now, I was sitting two floors above two of the most senior officers in Burma's military regime. I was tempted to go and join them for lunch, as a conversation with them would have been most interesting, but I knew the consequences for my hosts if my presence was discovered, so I remained hidden in the room. A little later, I glanced out of the window. The courtyard was swarming with Tatmadaw troops, their guns glistening in the midday sunshine.

This was how it was even though the Kachin Independence Organisation (KIO), the main resistance group for the Kachin ethnic people, had a ceasefire with the regime at the time, and under the terms of the ceasefire agreement they were in control of this area. The KIO had signed a ceasefire with the regime in 1994, which brought an end to armed conflict, mass displacement, destruction of villages and widespread killings and enabled the KIO to engage in business and establish some semblance of fledgling civil society. Yet the peace was always fragile and the atmosphere was one of fear. The Tatmadaw came back and forth through KIO-controlled areas, as I discovered that morning, and while my Kachin friends were glad to have me with them, they were terrified about what might happen if my presence became known. Human rights violations, as I shall describe in this chapter, continued even during this supposed time of peace – rape, forced labour, religious discrimination and land confiscation in particular. And for many years, the Kachins' silence on these abuses had been bought by the regime. The Kachin were afraid to report what was happening to the international community, out of fear that it might jeopardise the ceasefire.

All that ended in June 2011, when the regime broke the seventeen-year ceasefire and launched a major offensive against the Kachin. At least 60,000 Kachin civilians were displaced from their villages, fleeing to temporary camps around the KIO headquarters close to the border with China. Horrific stories of rape, forced labour, torture and killings emerged. Several churches were attacked, priests and pastors beaten, and in at least one case soldiers opened fire on a worshipping congregation. Several reports alleging the use of some form of chemical weapon began to appear, and while these are so far unverified, they are consistent with similar reports over the years from other ethnic states. The KIO's Vice Chief of Staff, General Gun Maw, compared it to 'a foreign invasion'.[1]

Just over six months after the new offensive began, I travelled back to Kachin State, now a war zone, to visit the camps for the displaced people. The conditions were dire – overcrowded urban camps, set up in old warehouses and factories, were full of people sleeping on thin mats on cold concrete floors, with minimal rations. Aid from the international community was almost non-existent – a few aid agencies were providing some support, and the United Nations had brought one small convoy of trucks with basic supplies for no more than 800 families, but the people were primarily reliant on their own Kachin community for help. An impressive group of young Kachin activists established an umbrella organisation, Relief Action Network for IDP and Refugee (RANIR), to coordinate humanitarian efforts, primarily around Laiza, and another organisation known as Wunpawng

Ninghtoi, meaning 'Light for the People', was set up to help internally displaced people in camps further south, around Mai Ja Yang.

Of the twenty internally displaced people I met, almost 70 per cent told stories of direct killings of civilians. A twelve-year-old boy described how his mother was shot dead as she tried to gather her possessions and lock up her house; a woman with her eight-year-old son recalled how her husband had been shot dead in his paddy field; a woman with three children told me that her husband's arms and legs had been chopped off before he was shot by Burma Army soldiers. Another woman recalled how she had hidden from the soldiers under a bed for two entire days, without food or water. She was pregnant at the time. She could hear bullets fly over her, and a Burma Army officer telling his troops, 'If you see someone, kill them.' I met a man who had been shot but had survived. He showed me the bullet. Another man told me: 'My grandfather fought in the Second World War, and he said even the Japanese were not as cruel as the Burma Army.'

Few foreign journalists or activists have visited Kachin areas, particularly those controlled by the KIO, and as a result the Kachin feel their plight is unknown. 'We have been crying for a long time for someone like you to help us,' one Kachin pastor told me on my first visit, during the ceasefire. 'We felt we had been forgotten. We felt alone.'

Annexed by the British in 1885, the Kachin Hills were self-governing until the 1930s.[2] The Kachin are a predominantly Christian people, converted at the turn of the twentieth century by American Baptist missionaries. They number perhaps one million, and fall into six sub-groups – Jinghpaw, Lisu, Maru, Lashi, Atsi and Rawang.[3] Dr Ola Hanson, the first missionary, transcribed the dominant language, Jinghpaw, into written form. According to a UN Development Programme report in 2005,[4] Kachin State has a population of 1.3 million, approximately 2.5 per cent of Burma's population, but only 500,000 are Kachins (the remaining population may be Burmans, Shans and other ethnic peoples). A further 175,000 Kachins live in northern Shan State and 32,000 in Mandalay Division, while 120,000 Kachins inhabit a semi-autonomous zone across the border in China. Several thousand are in India and some have fled as refugees to Europe and the United States.

Like the Karens, Chins and other ethnic groups in Burma, the Kachins fought bravely alongside the Allies, and particularly the Americans led by

'Vinegar' Joe Stilwell, against the Japanese in the Second World War. Prior to independence they participated in the Panglong Conference and signed the Panglong Agreement, but in the 1950s some Kachins began to agitate for genuine autonomy. In 1961 Prime Minister U Nu, a devout Buddhist, proposed making Buddhism the state religion, and the overwhelmingly Christian Kachin population rebelled. On 5 February 1961 Zau Seng founded the KIO, and when General Ne Win seized power in a coup the following year, suspending the constitution and abandoning the principles of federalism and equal rights set out in the Panglong Agreement, armed struggle ensued for thirty-two years.

Chit Myaing, who served as a senior member of Ne Win's regime, believes U Nu's decision to declare Buddhism the state religion was a mistake. 'I personally believe that was not really necessary,' he told *Burma Debate*. 'I am a Buddhist and even though I was in the military, I was very much involved with religious affairs.' But, he argues, 'We did not require a state religion . . . I was in Kachin State for one year as brigade commander. I never had any problem with the Kachins. When U Nu, as Prime Minister, was about to declare Buddhism as the State religion, the army appealed to him not to do that, but he said he had no way of turning back because that was his commitment made during the elections.'[5]

During the three decades of conflict with the Tatmadaw, the Kachin people were subjected to the regime's notorious 'Four Cuts' policy, aimed at trying to end access to food, funding, recruits and intelligence for the KIO and its armed wing, the Kachin Independence Army (KIA). The KIO claimed that by 1994, one-third of the Kachin population was internally displaced, while the Burma Ethnic Research Group estimates that there were 64,000 Kachin IDPs in 1994, with at least 100,000 having been displaced since the 1960s.[6] According to the KIO, 658 villages were destroyed between 1961 and 1993, while the Tatmadaw's intense campaign in April 1991, known as 'Operation Scupper' and 'Operation One Hundred Outposts' resulted in the forcible relocation of twenty-eight villages.[7] From 20 March to 25 May 1991, 324 villages in Kutkai District were destroyed.[8] Perhaps as many as 100,000 civilians are believed to have died during the thirty-two years of war.[9] 'Both sides, the regime and us, lost, but the people were the worst losers,' says KIO's Deputy Foreign Affairs spokesman James Lum Dau.

On several occasions in the 1970s and again in 1980–1981, the KIO attempted to negotiate a peace agreement with the regime, but to no avail. However, in 1989 Lieutenant General Khin Nyunt, head of the regime's military intelligence and Secretary-1, initiated a process of piecemeal ceasefire deals with different armed groups. Typical of its divide-and-rule strategy, the regime refused to negotiate a nationwide ceasefire, but instead entered into individual agreements with particular groups. By 1995, ceasefire deals had been reached with twenty-five armed groups. The KIO entered into talks in 1992, and by 1994 an agreement had been reached, mediated by the General Secretary of the Kachin Baptist Convention, Reverend Saboi Jum, his brother, an influential businessman called Khun Myat, and a former Burmese ambassador, an ethnic Kachin, U La Wom.[10] The KIO's respected chairman, Brang Seng, died the same year.

The KIO were the only ceasefire group to have a written agreement – all the other groups simply had 'an understanding', according to a regime spokesman.[11] The KIO's agreement, which is not public, was believed to include the following points: to make a nationwide ceasefire; to announce a general amnesty; to have a tripartite dialogue; to conduct development activities in Kachin State; and that the KIO will maintain its arms until its demands are reflected in a new constitution.[12] The first three points were not enacted by the regime, and a new constitution was introduced which falls far short of the KIO's demands. Development was perhaps the only point that has been turned into action – with dire environmental consequences, to which we will return later in this chapter. Under the ceasefire terms, the KIO – and its 6,000-strong KIA – were given control of a 15,000-square-mile (39,000-square-kilometre) territory, and a population of 300,000,[13] although its territory consists of pockets of land, mostly in rural areas, unconnected to each other, and a long stretch of land along the border with China. Most of the urban areas in Kachin State remained under SPDC control.[14] The KIO expanded its interests in jade and logging.[15]

These benefits, however, presented a false facade. Although the KIO had some space to organise, the Kachin could develop civil society, and people were not being killed in large numbers, one only had to scratch the surface to know everything was far from well in Kachin State, even during the ceasefire.

In April 2009 I went inside Kachin State, and met a twenty-one-year-old

Kachin woman studying at Bible school.[16] With quiet, calm dignity, she offered to tell me her story. In December 2008, she had been taking part in an evangelistic programme organised by her Bible school, sharing songs and Christian teachings with fellow Christians among the Kachin. All the participants wore a particular uniform. On 26 December, she attended the events in Myitkyina, and the following day she learned that one of her family members was sick, so she was worried and decided to return to her home village. She took the 3 p.m. train from Myitkyina and as the train approached her village she looked at her watch and it was 6 p.m. The train was not scheduled to stop in her village, but it slowed down, and so she jumped off the train just outside the village. Two soldiers jumped from the next carriage. She describes what happened next:

When I jumped, I felt very dizzy. I couldn't see around me properly. The two soldiers who also jumped from the train came over to me, and asked what was wrong. They pretended to take care of me. I told them I felt dizzy, and I sat down for a while beside the railway line. The soldiers asked me how I felt. The big soldier started to massage my head. After a few minutes I felt OK. I said: 'Don't touch me, I am OK.' Then I asked the soldiers where my luggage was. I had previously asked the passenger next to me, before jumping, to put my luggage down from the train. But I couldn't remember where she had put it. The soldiers were very nice and helpful, and they pointed behind the train and said my luggage was there. They tried to touch me again, and I told them not to touch me. The big soldier said: 'We are patriotic', and I believed them – I thought they were good people. But it was getting dark, so I decided to go home without my luggage and collect it in the morning.

At that point, the younger soldier grabbed the young woman and the larger soldier pushed her to the ground, beside the railway line. 'He raped me,' she said, retaining an extraordinary dignity as she continued her testimony. 'Then he squeezed my neck, trying to strangle me. I struggled as much as I could. The soldiers said they had a knife and would kill me. Finally, I lost consciousness as a result of being strangled. I do not remember what happened next.'

At 10.30 p.m. she regained consciousness, only to find she was lying in a bush, in the mud. 'The soldiers must have assumed I was dead, and thrown me into the bush. My skirt and underwear were gone. I was half-naked,' she recalled.

I didn't know where I was. I covered my lower part with part of my [evangelistic] campaign uniform, and walked along the railway line. Along the way I met an old man from the village, and asked him for help. 'I'm in trouble, please help me,' I said. He thought I was crazy – I was barefoot, half-naked, walking slowly due to the pain of the rape. But he heard the sound of suffering in my voice and had sympathy. He instructed me on how to go home. I walked home alone. A little later I met the local administrative council Secretary, and he took me home the rest of the way. My whole body was muddy.

At this point she realised she had nothing. 'The soldiers had taken my rings, wallet, watch and registration card. When I got home, I went to wash the mud off. The water was very cold, and I couldn't clean all the mud away. Some mud was on my head and back, and I couldn't clean it off. As I was washing, my elder sister came out with a torch and asked: "Who is there?" I said: "It is me. Don't shine the torch light on me." Then I went to sleep. My elder sister asked me so many times what had happened, but I felt shy. I just told her I had lost my luggage, and I asked her to go and look for it.'

Early the next morning, her sister went to look for her luggage – and found her underwear, longyi and other clothing spread about. The young Bible school student recalls:

She collected it up, and brought it home. She asked again and again what had happened, but I couldn't tell. I felt so shy. My elder sister and neighbours kept asking, but I felt angry, upset, frustrated and shy. Finally, I decided to tell my case to the clerk of the local administrative council. On 28 December, I went with my sister to look for the two soldiers. Around 2 p.m., I found them and identified them. My family, and the local authorities, asked one of them if he had raped me, but he denied it. He said as we had accused him, we

would be accused of damaging his reputation. But I remembered him
– he had a bad tooth, and that helped me recognise him.

As if her ordeal had not been enough, her trauma continued as she decided
to seek justice. Having come face to face with her attackers, she was
summoned by the local Light Infantry Battalion commander to meet him.
The village elder, the church pastor, her two elder sisters and the president
of the local administrative council accompanied her. 'We told him that
the soldier had raped me, but he said no, it was not possible, he has a kind
attitude,' she recalled.

> So we then went to the township police station, and submitted a case.
> But while we were there, I felt uncomfortable. My neck swelled up
> and I vomited. The soldiers denied putting a knife in my mouth, but
> that is what they had done. I went to hospital for medical checks, and
> then went home. My family did not have enough money for medical
> treatment, but [again] I went to hospital for further checks. The
> next day, [local Tatmadaw officials] ordered us to meet them at the
> [military] base, and although my health was not good, I obeyed his
> order. He told me that this case should be kept quiet. He said because
> I am a student, I face many stresses in my theological education and
> so this case should be resolved in a proper way. He gave 100,000 kyats
> for the costs of medical checks. He said he had given instructions to
> other officers to solve the case as quickly as possible.

Even then, however, her trial was not over. While one officer tried to
hush up the case and buy her off with money, another officer, a major,
summoned her to the base and forced her to identify her attackers from
a line-up of soldiers. 'I pointed at the right one. But then he ordered the
soldiers to change uniform. They changed clothes three times. First they
wore their rank and insignia, then they changed into the uniform of a
private soldier, and then they changed into civilian clothing. Each time,
I was still able to point out the right person, but then I lost consciousness.
I remember nothing more.'

A week later, a village elder was ordered to go to the base, where he was
confronted with a barrage of irrelevant questions designed to annoy and

harass. A few days after that, while the young woman was in hospital, a captain came to question her. He summoned her again for questioning six days later. She recalls:

> He asked me so many questions including how many chapters are there in the Bible! On 22 January, he questioned me from midnight until 2 a.m. He was smoking a cigarette the whole time and he asked so many questions. He would light a cigarette, and sit silently smoking it until it was finished, and would then ask another question. Most questions were unrelated to the case. At 2 a.m. he asked me if I was hungry, but I could not eat anything that night. I was sick and very uncomfortable. The next day the questioning continued. I was sick again.

Yet another captain was appointed to lead the investigation – which was clearly a sham and an excuse for prevaricating. To add insult to injury, he summoned the young woman for another identity parade – only this time, she could not see the soldiers. Instead, he ordered the soldiers to sing a military song, and asked her to identify the rapist by listening to his singing voice. 'I told him I am a student, I have no money, no time, I cannot come for questioning very often. Then he said the case was finished.'

The grotesqueness of the charade which she had to endure, on top of the trauma of rape, is astounding. 'I have been through three different military courts and investigations, and until today there has been no action, no compensation, no sympathy. All I received is 100,000 kyats for medical care, and a rice bag and cooking oil sent to my family by the district head of strategy. My family has not used the rice or oil. I spent over a month in hospital. The military are protecting the soldier who raped me. I have heard that he has raped so many girls, but no action has ever been taken against him,' she concludes. 'Every woman should be careful. My experience should be an example for other girls. I want justice to be done.'

Hers is by no means an isolated case in Kachin State. On 27 July 2008 a fifteen-year-old schoolgirl was gang-raped, severely mutilated and murdered. Nhkum Hkawn Din was attacked near Nam Sai village in Bhamo District, on her way to bring rice to her brother who was working in a paddy field. At 9 p.m. she was reported missing, and three days later her naked body was found, just two hundred metres from an army checkpoint. Her clothes, slippers and rice basket were also found. A local witness claimed to have seen Tatmadaw soldiers follow Nhkum Hkawn Din, and after her body was found other witnesses testified that they had seen soldiers leaving the area after the time she had disappeared. According to her family, her skull had been completely crushed, her eyes gouged out, her throat cut, she had been stabbed several times and all her facial features had been 'obliterated'. The local authorities refused to take any action.[17]

In February 2007 four Kachin girls were gang-raped by Tatmadaw soldiers in Putao Township. However, when they reported the case and it gained international attention, the girls were jailed – and the perpetrators went free. Eventually, the girls were released and escaped to Thailand. I met two of them in a secret location one year after their ordeal. Unsurprisingly, they were totally traumatised. Unable to make eye contact, they kept their heads bowed as they sat, wept and struggled to tell some of their story. It was too much to ask them to relive each moment, and so I simply reassured them that they didn't need to, and told them that I was there to help in any way I could. But inside my mind I wrestled with anger and frustration at the tormenting question: how could any regime, as a matter of policy, tear apart the lives of young women, not only physically but mentally and emotionally, in this way?

For throughout Burma, wherever the Tatmadaw is present, rape is a common occurrence. And in Kachin State, the Tatmadaw presence has increased significantly. Even during the ceasefire, according to the Kachin Development Networking Group (KDNG), between 1992 and 2006 the number of Tatmadaw battalions in Kachin State increased from twenty-six to forty-one.[18] The Transnational Institute concurred, claiming that 'ceasefire groups complain that the number of Burma Army battalions around their areas increased after the ceasefire'. The report quotes a Kachin development worker: 'There have been many constructions of military compounds and bases. No one could disagree that there are now more SPDC military bases inside Kachin territory than before ceasefire time.'[19] If the regime was serious about peace-making, why would it increase its presence in the ceasefire areas? Indeed, during the ceasefire the Tatmadaw continued to carry out sporadic attacks on the KIA, as it did on 21 March 2001, when it tortured and killed nine KIA soldiers and two civilians,[20] and on 2 January 2006, when it killed five KIA soldiers[21] and burned their bodies.[22] In November 2007 the SPDC raided a KIA outpost near the KIO headquarters at Laiza, and arrested six KIA soldiers.[23] As one Kachin activist concluded, 'the ceasefire [was] one-sided. It [was] not peace-making or peace-building, and there [was] political deadlock. There is no improvement politically.'[24] Since the regime broke the ceasefire, the number of Burma Army battalions in Kachin and northern Shan States has risen to at least 150, a dramatic increase in an already heavily militarised area.

Just as rape accompanies the military presence in Kachin State, so does forced labour. Villagers, particularly those living near a Tatmadaw base, are regularly required to provide a 'labour contribution'. Villagers are ordered to dig bunkers, build barracks and fences around army camps, clean towns and villages or even build entire army camps. They face heavy fines, or jail, if they are unable or unwilling to help. .

Forced labour is often demanded on Sundays, deliberately, because the Kachins are predominantly Christian and their faith is integral to their identity and culture. The church, as one senior pastor told me, is at the centre of Kachin society and provides a structure 'upon which our identity, our lifestyle, are based'.[25] Although Christians in Burma, including Kachin State, can generally worship on Sundays, there is a subtle – and sometimes less subtle – hostility towards them from the regime. 'I want to tell the world that the Burma Army discriminates against us,' a woman in a camp for internally displaced people told me in January 2012. 'We never loot or destroy or disrespect Buddhist pagodas, but they do this with our churches. There is a lot of religious discrimination. We always pray for freedom for the Kachin. We ask you to pray for freedom, especially for the next generation.' A Catholic priest said: 'They do not honour churches. They stay in the churches, [using them as army bases], and they destroy statues, open fire at churches.'

During the ceasefire, religious persecution in Kachin State was, according to one pastor, 'not harsh or aggressive' in comparison with the situation in Chin State, but nevertheless there was even then a clear undercurrent of discrimination. One Kachin pastor told me that 'there is no religious freedom' in Kachin State, because although on the surface

Sunday services can be held, churches are subjected to a variety of other forms of restriction, discrimination and harassment. 'The SPDC hates Kachins and Chins because we are Christians,' one Kachin pastor told me. Another said: 'The regime wants Burman Buddhism to dominate. They want all people to be Buddhist. So they discriminate against the rights of other religions.'[26] Christians, concluded a third pastor, 'are forced to accept Buddhist traditions, to recite Buddhist scriptures – it is a clever strategy, a sort of [subtle] forcible conversion.'[27]

In the ceasefire period, this took insidious forms. The local authorities, for example, regularly hold staff meetings and training days for government employees on Sundays, in the full knowledge that for the Kachin Christians, Sunday is a day of rest and worship. Christians in government service, including schoolteachers and doctors, are therefore forced to make a choice: to attend these meetings, and miss their Sunday church services, or refuse to attend the government meetings but risk being sacked. Those who are sacked are typically replaced with Buddhists.

Obtaining permission to build new churches, or renovate or extend existing churches, or hold church gatherings other than a Sunday service can be extremely difficult. In 2003, the Kachin Baptist Convention asked the SPDC for permission to hold its convention, which normally takes place every three years. Permission was delayed for several months, until it was finally granted – but the convention had to take place in a different location. Such delays are deliberately intended to disrupt and hinder church activities without completely preventing them.

In 2006, a church in Bhamo received a letter from local authorities ordering them to stop the construction of a new church building. Although they had received verbal permission from General Khin Nyunt when he had been in power, it appears that approval had been rescinded when he was purged. A new order had been issued by the Ministry of Religious Affairs prohibiting the construction of new churches or mosques. In contrast, there are no restrictions on the construction of new Buddhist monasteries, and the previous year a new monastery was built in Kachin State, and Christian villagers were forced at gunpoint to contribute construction materials for it.

In October 2005, the Burma Army's northern commander, Brigadier General Ohn Myint, gave a speech at the Second Quarterly Executive

Meeting of the Kachin State Peace and Development Council, in Myitkyina Township Hall, in the presence of other senior local officials. He left no one in any doubt of how the regime views Kachin Christians. He focused on an order to every village to display a signboard with the village name and population statistics. Then he announced:

> No village has done this yet. Instead we see only the religious symbols of the cross. Some of these religious symbols are made of concrete, rocks and bricks. A big cross with a crucified Christ was built on the top of the highest hill (2,885 feet) in Myitkyina town, just five miles from the town centre. Even though there was a big religious celebration at the hill, it is surprising that the Kachin State SPDC officials were not informed. They cannot build Kachin cultural symbols and religious symbols of the cross everywhere in Kachin State . . . We must not allow church buildings everywhere without legal permission.

The implication is that the Kachins' religious faith makes them disloyal to the state, accusing them of following 'a colonial legacy'. He equally attacked any hopes of autonomy that the Kachin may have. 'We must rebuild the spirit of union of Myanmar . . . . We cannot in any means accept separation of the states. As long as there is the Union of Myanmar, there must not be any separation. It is absolutely unacceptable if there were separation of the states from the union. Therefore we must try to diminish such ideas.'

General Ohn Myint was, in addition, determined to counter the activities of the democracy movement in Kachin State. 'We must be prepared to know everything,' he told government officials, 'so that we can crush them and root them out.' He said that the SPDC must hold mass public gatherings to show their strength. 'We should not just read out our speeches, but persuasively tell the people in order to make them believe what we are doing is right.' Government officials, he added, must follow orders. 'Responsible officials of all state departments must obey the law – you must either lead or be led, and those who cannot lead or be led will be punished.'[28]

Land confiscation is widespread, and sometimes impacts on religious freedom. In 2002, a prayer mountain belonging to the church at Daw

Hpum Yang, very close to the KIO headquarters in Laiza on the Myitkyina–Bhamo road, was seized by the Tatmadaw and occupied. A cross and prayer room at the top of the mountain were destroyed, and it is believed that Russian-made rockets were installed, targeting the KIO. Villagers were then forced to build a landing strip on the mountain, and it is reported that both Senior General Than Shwe and the then Prime Minister Soe Win visited on several occasions.

On Christmas Eve 2005, residents of a village in Putao district were ordered to relocate, and to destroy the church they had constructed. Earlier that year, farmland in another area, including a forty-acre fruit farm, growing oranges and mangos, belonging to a church pastor, was occupied by Light Infantry Battalion 438.[29]

Religious discrimination, land confiscation and environmental degradation, the three major challenges for the Kachin during the ceasefire, are all interrelated. The regime, its businesses, and Chinese-owned businesses have all been active in plundering the land in Kachin State, for teak and other natural resources. Deforestation is widespread, and none of the forests have been replaced. Dam construction is a concern too, as it leads to displacement of villages, and the regime plans several dams along the Mali Hka, N'Mai Hka and Irrawaddy rivers. Gold mining has had a particularly devastating effect, causing not just environmental disaster but widespread displacement. 'After the mining is finished, the land is destroyed, mercury pollutes the rivers, there are no trees – but then the people are told they can return to their land,' one Kachin told me. 'When you look at the policy from above, it looks like development. But when you look closely, you see that it equals land confiscation and displacement.'

Perhaps one of the starkest examples of this phenomenon is the Hukong Valley, and particularly the Yuzana Company, a corporation with close links to Senior General Than Shwe. The company is engaged in rubber, physic nut, teak, tapioca and sugar-cane plantations, and has confiscated large areas of land in the Hukong Valley, without providing any compensation to the local people. In June 2007 a Kachin man organised a petition, with 1,300 signatures, calling for thirty-six acres of wet paddy rice farmland to be returned to them. He sent the petition to Than Shwe, and copied it to various government ministries, and when he did, he was arrested, detained, interrogated and harassed. He escaped, and went into hiding.

Remarkably, he came out of hiding and met with the local authorities, and secured agreement for the return of some land to local farmers – a rare and miraculous outcome in Burma.[30]

Public opinion may be taken into account in more development projects in the future, if President Thein Sein's decision to suspend the Myitsone Dam is anything to go by. In September 2011, after months of petitions and protests led primarily by the Kachin, Thein Sein announced the suspension of the $3.6 billion hydroelectric dam scheduled for completion in 2019.[31] Although he has suspended the project only until the end of his term of office, in 2015, the decision surprised many, not least because of the anger it caused China, the other major investor in the dam. Taking public opinion into account, however, is unlikely to be the only explanation for the decision – a desire to distance Burma from China, and win favour in Washington, DC, Delhi and Brussels, is likely to have been a consideration as well. The test will be what happens after 2015.

Another major social challenge for the Kachins is the trafficking of women. Although this is not perpetrated directly by the regime, it is a consequence of the regime's mismanagement of the economy and its failure to invest in education and job creation. Moreover, the regime has completely failed to tackle the issue. As a result, women disappear 'almost every day', according to Kachin sources. Since 2006, over 138 cases of trafficking have been documented, mostly involving women aged between fifteen and thirty. But many, many more cases go unreported.

Women are typically lured with the promise of a better job in China, where wages are higher than local salaries in Kachin State. Once in China, however, they are often taken thousands of miles, to the far north – Beijing, Hunan, Shandong and Manchuria – where they are either sold into prostitution, or traded as 'wives' to Chinese men. Often they are sold on by their buyers many times.

Those who are sold into the sex trade are often subjected to violent exploitation and grotesque treatment. In one case, albeit an extreme one, a thirteen-year-old girl, who was eventually rescued, reported having been forced to have sex with dogs. Another reported being gang-raped by ten men, before her owner then decided he did not like her and ordered her to repay the money he had paid for her. When she told him she was unable to refund the money without a job, he arranged a job for her where she stayed twenty-eight days. She claimed she was gang-raped every night. Finally, unable to endure it any more, she escaped, but was chased by her captors with dogs. She fled into the forest, where she wandered for five days without food or water, before reaching a town. She found the police station, and was rescued and returned to Kachin State.

Most cases involve women, but in some instances children have been abducted and trafficked as well. At the end of 2008, a five-year-old boy from Laiza disappeared, and in Myitkyina a baby was abducted and sold. In 2009, an eleven-year-old boy was taken to Yinjiang, in Yunnan Province, China, three hours from the border, where potential purchasers came to examine him. They checked his height but found he was taller than their requirements, and so he was left, un-sold, in Yinjiang. Having no idea where he was, he sat crying until he was found by a woman who helped him return to Burma.

Kachin groups working to help women who have been trafficked say that the Chinese authorities are very cooperative, and help rescue women and children. If a victim of trafficking is able to make a telephone call, the number can be traced and the Chinese police can often locate them. In many cases, the women are held captive and not allowed out, but sometimes they are able to go outside for a walk and are occasionally recognised by police or local people as being foreign.

Returning rescued women to Burma, however, is expensive, and the Chinese authorities are now saying they will only rescue victims of trafficking if the travel expenses involved can be recovered. This can require up to 10,000 renminbi (1,500 dollars). The women usually do not have any clothing, so they need money for food and clothes as well.

The regime is doing little to stop this trade, and in some cases actively denies that it is happening. In 2007, a woman was rescued and returned to Myitkyina, where she identified the trafficker and filed a lawsuit against him. In an ultimate injustice, the trafficker reportedly won the court case and the woman was jailed for a month for violating immigration laws, including crossing the border illegally. After her release from prison she had to move to another location due to the risks she faced in Myitkyina. The wife of the Tatmadaw commander in Kachin State, who serves as chair of the Kachin State Women's Affairs Organisation, was informed, but she denied that the case was true.[32]

As if rape, forced labour, land confiscation, religious discrimination, environmental degradation and human trafficking were not enough, Kachin State has become a centre for drug trafficking and addiction in Burma. There is widespread belief among the Kachins that drugs are deliberately promoted by the regime. Government agents are allegedly involved in distributing drugs, and only Burman drug users are arrested. Kachin students at Myitkyina University openly use drugs, without any penalty, and it is claimed that the police only arrest dealers if they stop dealing. 'It is part of a deliberate policy to destroy Kachin young people through drug abuse,' one person told me. 'If they cannot destroy us militarily, they try to do so using drugs.'

As a result of the drug trade, prostitution and trafficking of women, HIV/AIDS has spread through Kachin State in a dramatic way. In 2008, the biggest hospital in the KIO-controlled town of Laiza reported over 1,000 HIV/AIDS patients, most of them intravenous drug users. In Mai Ja Yang, the second major KIO-controlled town, eight out of ten intravenous drug users are HIV positive, according to Health Unlimited. Médecins Sans Frontières claim that AIDS-related illnesses killed 25,000 people in Burma in 2007, and that at least 240,000 people are infected with the virus.[33]

In April 2009, I made another visit to KIO-controlled areas in Kachin State. On the day I arrived, 28 April, I was told that senior KIO officials had been summoned to Myitkyina for a meeting with regime officials. The following day, they returned and invited me to meet them. They told me that the regime had issued an ultimatum, to them and to all other ceasefire groups: to become a border guard force, under the auspices of the Tatmadaw, and with a remit restricted to a ten-kilometre zone along the China border. Under the proposal, the KIO and its armed wing, the KIA, would surrender their troops and arms to the SPDC.

When I met them, the KIO and KIA leaders were adamant that this deal was unacceptable. 'Asking us to disarm without solving the political situation is cheating us,' said one very senior leader. 'They didn't discuss a political solution, but demanded the submission of our arms to be under their control. They wanted us to surrender not only our arms but also our troops. It's like a joke.' In an extraordinary understatement, he added: 'This demand shows that the regime is not pure-hearted.'

The ceasefire agreement signed in 1994 stipulates that the KIO and

KIA would retain their arms until a constitutional agreement is reached. The KIO has consistently expressed its view that the new constitution introduced in 2008 is not satisfactory. A senior KIA officer warned me that the regime's ultimatum could break the ceasefire. 'If the political situation is solved properly, then we don't want to retain our arms. But we have been waiting for a real federal union for a long time. The SPDC is destroying the essence of federal union. Even though we try to speak about a union, they do not . . . The government is creating a situation to force us back to war. We do not want war, but they may force us into that situation.' Two years later, that prediction was proven all too prescient.

Just four months after my visit in 2009, further south along the China–Burma border, the regime did to another ethnic group precisely what the Kachins predicted might happen to them. After the Kokang, an ethnic Chinese group who had had a ceasefire with the regime for twenty years, rejected the idea of becoming a border guard force, the Tatmadaw launched a brutal military offensive, causing the largest refugee flow from Burma in years. The Kokang, or Myanmar National Democracy Alliance Army (MNDAA), had grown out of the old Communist Party of Burma, and the leaders were involved in the drugs trade, establishing a heroin refinery in their region. The regime used this as one reason for the attack, issuing arrest warrants against the Kokang leaders, even though for twenty years a ceasefire had prevailed and the regime was itself complicit with the drugs trade.

At least 30,000 people fled into China in August 2009, prompting Chinese authorities to open seven refugee camps and provide food, drinking water, shelter and first aid.[34] In a three-day conflict, the Burma Army gained control of Kokang territory and forced rebel forces led by Peng Jiasheng to flee into China. The SPDC installed a new leadership in the Kokang region, led by regime loyalist Bai Souqian. At least 500 people were reported killed.[35]

The KIA and the Wa, another ethnic group in the area, were on high alert. The United Wa State Army (UWSA), one of the largest and best equipped armed groups in Burma, with an estimated 20,000 troops, expected they would be the next target, and were poised for battle.[36] The KIA's chief of staff, Major General Gunhtang Gam Shawng, ordered his troops to shoot at Burma Army soldiers if they entered KIA territory.[37]

China was unusually outspoken, summoning the Burmese ambassador to Beijing to explain the regime's actions. China was particularly angry about instability on its borders and threats to ethnic Chinese people and business interests in the area. A Chinese foreign ministry spokesman said China had 'made representations about harm caused to the rights of Chinese citizens in Myanmar, restated China's position, demanded Myanmar rapidly investigate, punish law-breakers and report the results to China.' The regime should 'take prompt measures, earnestly protect the legal rights of Chinese citizens in Myanmar, and make sure similar incidents do not happen again.'[38]

The attacks on the Kokang, and the continued abuses in Kachin State, demonstrate how fragile the ceasefire agreements are and how little they mean in reality. Since 2008 relations between the KIO and the regime have continued to deteriorate. On 7 October 2009, KIO Chairman Zawng Hra sent a letter to Senior General Than Shwe, noting that the junta had conceived a plan 'to liquidate our organisation'. In extraordinarily measured, but equally brave terms, he continued: 'Accordingly, we feel it proper to bring to your attention all the facts that pertain to our status.' Emphasising the KIO's commitment to peace, he reminded Than Shwe that 'on nine occasions' the KIO had explained its position to the regime, as to why it could not accept the proposal to become a border guard force. Such an idea was 'quite unrealistic' until a mutually acceptable political settlement had been reached.[39] The regime responded by cutting off all communications with the KIA,[40] describing the KIO and its armed wing as 'insurgents', a phrase that had not been used since the ceasefire.[41] A KIO liaison office was raided by the Tatmadaw, and a new political party that had been set up by a former senior KIO leader to contest the regime's elections was refused registration. Two other Kachin parties were also rejected, and fifteen pro-KIO independent candidates were disqualified. Some villages under KIO control were not allowed to take part in the poll.[42] Pressure on the Kachin mounted, until the mortars finally started to fire in June 2011. After seventeen years of fragile peace, the Kachin were back at war. 'We do not want to hold arms – we are not a warlike people. We just want our political rights,' Zawng Hra told me. 'When we asked for political negotiation, the response of the government was war.'[43]

On 28 July, Aung San Suu Kyi wrote an open letter to President Thein

Sein and four armed groups – the KIO, as well as the Karen National Union, New Mon State Party and Shan State Army – calling for 'immediate ceasefires and a peaceful resolution of the conflicts' and offering herself as a mediator.[44] For five months, there was little sign of a response from the regime. However, in December 2011 the KIO received an official letter from Naypyidaw, requesting formal peace talks. A month later, the two sides met in Ruili, China, for two days. I was with the KIO in Laiza at the time, and followed the talks closely. The KIO took a clear and firm position: this time round, they were not interested in offers of economic development and cessation of hostilities. For seventeen years they had abided by a ceasefire agreement, in the hope that the key promise – a political process leading to a political solution – would be fulfilled. They had waited in vain, and were not prepared to return to such an unsatisfactory ceasefire agreement. They want peace, but they want it to be genuine and secure, and that can only be achieved if a ceasefire is accompanied by a political process. Ultimately, they told me, they want the 'spirit of Panglong' to prevail – the establishment of a federal democracy in which they and other ethnic nationalities have a degree of autonomy and equal rights, within the Union of Burma. 'We are committed to a federal Burma,' a senior KIO leader emphasised to me. 'We do not want to secede from the Union.'[45]

A Cross to Bear in the West

'We are not to simply bandage the wounds of victims beneath the wheels of injustice, we are to drive a spoke into the wheel itself.'

Dietrich Bonhoeffer

IN 1993, PASTOR ZANG KHO LET was arrested and interrogated by the Tatmadaw. When his answers failed to satisfy his interrogators, they cut open his mouth to his neck. They did this, they said, 'so you will no longer preach'.[1]

While such barbaric punishments for religious activity are the extreme, the Chin people in western Burma are suffering inhumane treatment at the hands of the regime, on three counts: ethnicity, religion and politics. The regime's attitude to non-Burman and non-Buddhist ethnic and religious groups is shaped by a fascist mentality which has echoes of Adolf Hitler and the Nazis. In Burmese, this is summed up in the phrase 'Amyo, Batha, Thathana', which means 'one race, one language, one religion'. As a non-Burman ethnic group the Chin face discrimination. As a non-Buddhist religious group – indeed, an overwhelmingly Christian population whose faith is integral to their identity and culture – they face religious persecution. And as a group with several pro-democracy organisations, some of them armed, the regime regards the Chin as opponents. To compound their plight, Chin State is the poorest, most remote and least developed part of the country, with almost non-existent health care provision and few natural resources. There is no high school education beyond the age of fifteen, and there are no universities in Chin State. According to Chin sources, for a population of approximately one million, there are an estimated 184 nursery schools, 1,167 primary schools, 83 middle schools and just 25 high schools.[2]

The Chin consist of various subgroups, clans and tribes and a multiplicity of different dialects. Originating in the Tibeto-Burman group, the Chin are believed to have come to Burma from western China and eastern Tibet. The groups considered to be Chin are too numerous to mention, but include the Asho, Cho, Khuami, Laimi, Mizo or Lushai, Zomi, Kuki and Mara.[3] Their lands straddle the borders between Burma, India and Bangladesh, so that the Chins in Burma are closely related to the Mizo people in Mizoram State, India. Although each group within the Chin has their own dialect and specific culture, according to Lian Sakhong, in his book *In Search of Chin Identity*, the factor that unites them, and makes them all 'Chin', is a common adherence to a myth about their origin, expressed in folk songs and folklore. 'The common proper name of the "Chin" is inseparably intertwined with "the myth of common descent" and the "myth of origin",' Sakhong writes. 'According to the origination myth, the Chin people emerged into this world from the bowels of the earth or a cave or a rock called "Chinlung".'[4]

Until the British invaded the Chin Hills in a series of battles with the local inhabitants in the late nineteenth century, the Chin had been entirely self-governing. 'None of the surrounding powers, such as the Bengali Indian or Burman, ever conquered the Chinram,'[5] writes Lian Sakhong.[6] For this reason, the Chin were never converted to any of the major religions that surrounded their land – Buddhism, Hinduism or Islam. Instead, they followed their own traditional beliefs, known as *phunglam* or 'ways of life'.[7] This was a monotheistic tradition, based around a belief in a Supreme Being, souls and life after death.[8] It was perhaps for these reasons that when the Christian missionaries came, the Chins embraced Christianity virtually 'en masse'.

Although it is believed that the first contact the Chins had with the British was in 1760, when the British East India Company occupied the Chittagong region of what is now Bangladesh, the first recorded encounter came in 1824, when Chin villagers killed some British traders who entered Chin territory to collect bamboo and timber and refused to pay taxes to the local people.[9] In the following years, the Chins made a series of raids on British territory, leading to an operation in 1860 known as the 'Great Kuki Invasion', in which fifteen villages in Tripura, modern-day India, were destroyed, 185 British people were killed and about one hundred captives taken.[10] In Lian Sakhong's words, 'The British could not tolerate the challenge to their sovereignty involved in this harassment, killing and capture of their subjects.'[11] A series of battles followed, in an operation which one British soldier claimed was intended not to 'exterminate these frontier tribes, but convert them into our allies'.[12] The Chin proved to be fierce and skilful fighters, regularly blocking the British troops' routes and launching frequent ambushes.[13] Sir George White, one of the leaders of the British forces, described the Chin as the 'most difficult enemy to see or hit that I have ever fought'.[14] By 1896, the British had occupied the Chin territories,[15] as well as the rest of Burma, adopting 'a policy of pacification through permanent occupation'.[16] The Chin Hills Regulation was promulgated, establishing a basic colonial administration for the entire Chin territory.[17] The Chin, however, had not been defeated by the military might of the British forces, but rather by famine because they had been unable to cultivate their land due to the war, and the British had burned many villages and rice barns.[18] Famine, the burning of villages and the destruction of rice barns were to become regular features of Chin life a century later, under the rule of the Tatmadaw.

Christian missionaries had first arrived in Burma in the sixteenth century, when Jesuits accompanied the Portuguese traveller and mercenary Philip de Brito y Nicote, who was employed by the Arakanese King Min Razagyi.[19] De Brito and an Arakanese convert from Buddhism to Christianity, Nat Shin Naung, were subsequently crucified as heretics by the King of Ava, Maha Dhamma Raja, who saw Nat Shin Naung's conversion as an insult to Buddhism.[20] Italian priests came to Burma in 1720, and in 1783 Father Sangermano arrived, and subsequently published one of the earliest histories of Burma.[21] In 1807, the first Protestant missionaries arrived, sent by the London Missionary Society, but it was Adoniram Judson and his wife Ann, the first American Baptists, who made the most significant and long-lasting impact.[22] They arrived in 1813, and among their contributions were the translation of the Bible and the compilation of a Burmese–English dictionary still in use today.[23] It was Judson's successors who ventured into the Chin Hills, led initially by the Reverend Arthur Carson and his wife Laura in 1899.[24]

Although in much of Burma the British colonialists did not welcome, and at times disapproved of, missionary activity, in the case of the Chin Hills the missionaries were invited by the British. According to Lian Sakhong, the primary objective of the British was 'the pacification' of the Chins, and they believed the missionaries might help this. One source claims that the British concluded that 'if most of the Chin became Christians there would be a fairly good chance that they might welcome all other changes'.[25] The British were proven right, and the Carsons were soon followed by a medical missionary, Dr E.H. East.[26]

The Chin, however, did not welcome the missionaries or embrace Christianity immediately, or without a struggle. As a result of their war with the British, famine and disease were rife, and the colonial occupation caused a breakdown in the traditional structures of authority in Chin society. 'Crisis in life and conversion to Christianity . . . were more or less linked with each other,' Sakhong concludes.[27] Thuam Hang, the first Zomi convert, for example, accepted Christianity only after a miserable struggle over 'great loss of economic and social status'.[28] His eldest son suffered from a disease that was not just physically painful but caused him to become a social outcast. His other son had what was described as 'tuberculosis of the spine'. Both appeared to be cured, the first by a medical operation conducted by Dr East, the second seemingly as a result of prayer. 'The Chin people now view such a story as the "mighty work of God" in their history,' notes Sakhong.[29] Thuam Hang was baptised by Dr East in 1906.[30]

In the early years, Chin converts to Christianity faced persecution from within their own community. Chins regarded conversion as a betrayal of their own traditional culture and beliefs. Tsong Kham, for example, the first convert from the Bualkhua people, was beaten by three men armed with bamboo rods, each one ordered to give him fifteen strokes. In the midst of the beatings, he asked them to pause, and he prayed for strength to endure the torture. He repeated the words prayed by Jesus Christ on the cross, and by St Stephen: 'Count it not against them, Father, for they do not understand.' According to Sakhong, Tsong Kham then urged his torturers to resume their work. The village chief, who had ordered the punishment, was 'filled with superstitious awe', writes Laura Carson, and 'no man dared to strike again'.[31]

Gradually, however, the Chins began to accept Christianity, in part because of its parallels with their own traditional beliefs, and in part because of the contribution of missionaries to developing their own society. In particular, the missionaries' emphasis on education, the development of a written language which previously did not exist, medical provision and the unification of the disparate tribal groups inhabiting the Chin Hills into one common Chin identity made Christianity increasingly attractive to the Chins. Over the past century, Christianity has become 'inseparable' from Chin identity, and as a result, as Sakhong concludes, it has also 'played a very important role in the people's social and political lives, not just their religious lives'.[32]

Of all the Christian groups in Burma facing varying degrees of restriction, discrimination and persecution, the Chins experience religious intolerance in its starkest forms. A common Chin practice, as an expression of their faith and their culture, is to construct crosses on hillsides and mountaintops. In recent years, however, the Tatmadaw has torn almost all the crosses down. In many instances, Chin Christian villagers have themselves been forced at gunpoint to destroy their crosses, and to build Buddhist pagodas in their place. Not only are they forced to tear down the symbols of their own faith, which is so associated with their cultural identity, but they are forced to contribute labour and resources for the construction of symbols of Buddhism, the religion of their oppressors. According to Salai Bawi Lian Maung, the 'destruction of crosses started around the early 1990s with the rapid increase in army battalions established across Chin State'. Since that time, he adds, 'almost every cross in all nine townships in Chin State has been destroyed by the regime . . . Many of them have been replaced by Buddhist pagodas and statues of Buddhist monks.'[33]

In 1994, for example, a local Roman Catholic Church in Tonzang Township, northern Chin State, built a cross, and the local authorities ordered its destruction. The church refused, and so at midnight on 16 May the township authorities and local police burned the cross.[34] The following year, a cross built on Mount Rung in Hakha, the state capital, was torn down, and when the Hakha Baptist Church attempted to rebuild the cross they were ordered not to. A few years later, a statue of a Buddhist monk was built in its place.[35] On 5 January 1999, Chin Christians built a large memorial cross on a hilltop west of Thantlang, to celebrate the centenary of the arrival of Christianity among the Chins. That same night, the authorities ordered its destruction, and forced the people who had erected it to pull it down. When they refused, the police destroyed it themselves, and arrested six pastors.[36] Three years later, a thirty-foot cross that had been built in Matupi, southern Chin State, in 1984 was ordered to be destroyed,[37] and in 2005 a fifty-foot cross on the top of Mount Boi, believed to be the only remaining cross in Chin State, was torn down.[38] It is believed that this cross was removed on the orders of a senior Tatmadaw officer, and according to Salai Bawi Lian Mang, 'after destroying the cross, troops from Light Infantry Battalion 304 hoisted a Burmese flag as a sign of victory against Christianity in Chin State'.[39]

In the place of crosses, the regime have built numerous pagodas, often forcing Chin Christian villagers to contribute labour, money and construction materials. The Chin say that for the regime the construction of pagodas is a symbol of control and occupation, so they have a political as well as religious significance. A large pagoda has been built on the third highest mountain in the country, Mount Victoria, and a cross that was destroyed on Mount Rung has been replaced with a large Buddha statue and pagoda.

It is not only crosses which the Tatmadaw destroys in Chin areas. Churches are not secure either. In 1998, several churches were destroyed on SPDC orders, and in 2000, Captain Khin Maung Myint ordered the destruction of a church in Min Tha village, Tamlu Township, in Magwe Division, next to Chin State. The following year he forced villagers to destroy two other churches in the same township. Construction of church buildings in Tiddim Township was ordered to cease in 2000, and all Christian schools in Tamu Township were forced to close.[40] According to one pastor, 'it is totally impossible to build a church' now.[41] Printing the Bible in Chin State is forbidden, and so Bibles are printed in India and smuggled in. In 2000, it was reported that 16,000 Bibles were seized by the Burma Army and burned.

The regime has attempted to forcibly convert Chin Christians to Buddhism, in various ways. In some places, Christians are offered induce- ments such as rice if they become Buddhists, and families are offered educational opportunities for their children if they convert. Many children from Chin Christian families have been sent to Buddhist monasteries for schooling, but once there the children are forced to participate in Buddhist worship and in many instances their heads are shaved and they are forced to become novice Buddhist monks. The same practice is occurring in Kachin State.

Pastors and church workers who are perceived as being either too active, too influential or too resistant to the regime face grave danger. The Chin Human Rights Organisation claims that in some instances, pastors have been 'abducted, tortured and even killed' by the Tatmadaw.[42] 'The Burmese army restricted all kinds of Christian activities,' Salai Ram Lian Hmung concluded, while participating in a protest against the destruction of the cross at Matupi. 'They don't even allow us to print the Bible in the country. The Burmese military are destroying our religion and our culture, and trying to assimilate the entire Chin population into the mainstream Burmese culture . . . We have to do something about it.'[43]

Christians, particularly from the Chin community, in other parts of Burma also face religious discrimination and persecution. In a town in Magwe Division, pro-regime Buddhist monks issued an order prohibiting the practice of Christianity in the town. In Rangoon, there have been periodic crackdowns on unregistered churches. In early 2009, it was reported that at least one hundred churches were ordered to close down, and some sources claimed that as many as 80 per cent of the churches in the city would be affected. At least fifty pastors were rounded up and forced to sign at least five documents promising to end their church services, and were warned that they would be jailed if they disobeyed the order. The crackdown did not affect historic churches which owned long-established buildings; instead it was targeted at newer denominations that met in private apartments, offices or other private property. 'Christians are worried that they will not be allowed to worship any more, even in their own house,' one pastor said. Shwekey Hoipang, a Chin pastor living in exile, told me that the 2009 crackdown came because the churches were actively helping victims of Cyclone Nargis, and the regime was unhappy that Buddhists were receiving help from churches. 'The regime does not want Buddhists coming in and out of churches,' he said. 'It does not want Christianity to grow in Burma. Ultimately, the regime seeks the destruction of Christianity. This is part of a top-secret plan by the military to stop Christian growth.'[44]

According to Martin Smith, 'school children in Burma are today taught that the Christian churches represented just another branch of the colonial armoury, the three Ms – missionaries, merchants and military'.[45] In Chin State, the authorities state that their three major concerns are 'ABC' – AIDS, Hepatitis B and Christianity. A document believed to have originated in the Ministry of Religious Affairs has been widely circulated, and is headlined: 'Programme to Destroy the Christian Religion in Burma'. Containing seventeen points, the document begins with the statement: 'There shall be no home where the Christian religion is practised. No home will accept any preaching about Jesus.' It then details a variety of somewhat incoherent steps which Buddhists should take to eradicate Christianity, some of which are violent and severe and some are subtle and even laughable.[46]

In 2007 I wrote a report, published by Christian Solidarity Worldwide, called 'Carrying the Cross: The military regime's campaign of restrictions, discrimination and persecution against Christians in Burma', in which I collated evidence of the violations of religious freedom. The regime responded with surprising ferocity. Every day for almost two weeks, full-page denunciations were published in the *New Light of Myanmar*, and broadcast on state television. 'Contents of CSW report are fabricated accusation against Myanmar', screamed the headlines. 'Intention of some big power nations to interfere in internal affairs of Myanmar for political gain through accusation of fabricated story on religions rejected', was another. 'Religion is based on noble kindness and no one should dye it political colour', said a third. The Catholic Bishops Conference and Myanmar Council of Churches were forced to issue a statement distancing themselves from the report, and rallies were organised in Chin State, at which pastors were forced to publicly denounce the report and proclaim that they had full religious freedom.

Two years later, I met a Chin woman in Kuala Lumpur, who had fled Burma just a month before. An ordained pastor, she had served as the Women's Secretary of the Hakha Baptist Association. In March 2007, she was ordered to attend a public meeting, and give a presentation on religious freedom in Burma. 'They told me that they would provide me with the facts they wanted me to express,' she said. 'I was given a piece of paper and told to read it. It was the opposite of the truth. I was told if I did not read it out in full, I would be arrested.' After the event, she managed – at considerable risk – to keep the document, by hiding it in her bra, and she fled. 'I promised myself I would try to declare the truth about religious persecution, by fleeing the country and making the truth known.'

As in the rest of Burma, forced labour is widespread, but as in Kachin State, it is often linked to religious discrimination. The Tatmadaw frequently orders villagers to work for the military on Sundays and Christian festivals, deliberately disrupting church activities. In Sabungte, for example, villagers were ordered to porter for the military from 20 December 2003 until 19 January 2004, meaning they had to miss Christmas and New Year celebrations. In June 2003, soldiers entered a church in Hmun Halh during a Sunday service, and ordered the leaders of worship to go with them to work as porters, thereby disrupting the service.

In 2004 I made my first visit to the Chin people in Mizoram State, on the India–Burma border. I was shown a letter from a Tatmadaw company commander to village leaders in Nga Phai Pi, southern Chin State, issued on 13 December 2003. The letter is a demand for forty porters from Nga Phai Pi and thirty from Sabawngte to report to the nearby Burma Army camp to carry rations for the military. A second letter, dated 19 January 2004, was shown to me. This was sent by the commander of Battalion 268 in Falam, northern Chin State, ordering village leaders to attend a regular monthly meeting to discuss a new special border development project, starting six days later. They are also instructed to bring a chicken to the meeting.

I met one Chin farmer who had been a member of the NLD since 1989. In 1995 he was forced to work for almost a year on constructing the Kalaymyo–Kankaw railway line. Every household in his village was compelled to contribute one person for forced labour. The railway construction project destroyed the paddy fields in the area, and because he was made to work on the construction project he was unable to farm. 'This affected the survival of the village,' he told me. When he enquired about payment for his labour, the soldiers told him 'It is not our job to pay.' They then beat him severely. His arm was broken at the elbow, several of his teeth were smashed and his eye was cut. He was detained for five months, and was not permitted to see his family. After his release, he resumed his

NLD activities, and in 2003 he attempted to meet Aung San Suu Kyi when she visited his village. He was forbidden to meet her, but two of his friends tried to and were arrested. He escaped and fled to India. 'No one dares to enroll as an NLD member now,' he said in 2004. 'People dare not speak the word "democracy".'

Traditionally the Chin do not permit alcohol in their society, although many younger Chins do now drink. The regime has seized on this as a target of attack. During my first visit to the Chin in 2004, I was told that since 1992 the military has deliberately brought into Chin towns large quantities of highly intoxicating liquor known as 'OB', which it sells in the streets, especially on Sundays when people are going to church. Young people as young as twelve years old have been sold the alcohol, at 1,000 kyats (1.10 dollars) a bottle. I was travelling with two British doctors at the time, who assessed that such crude alcohol was probably a mix of methyl and ethyl and would be completely banned in the West. Highly addictive, it leads to social and family breakdown, crime and ultimately death. Toxic liver failure, jaundice and brain damage are some of the physical effects. When people become drunk, the authorities arrest them, and demand a 5,000 kyat (5.50 dollars) bail for their release. As one Chin Christian put it, it causes 'the breakdown of body, mind, spirit and society'.[47]

Rape by Burma Army soldiers is widespread in Chin State, as in the rest of the country, and the Women's League of Chinland have documented this in a report called 'Unsafe State'. In one example, a woman whose son had just been killed by the military was then gang-raped, and strung up on a cross. 'She was hanging outside of the camp the whole night in the freezing winter weather,' said the Women's League of Chinland's coordinator Cheery Zahau. 'Why would they make the cross to hang the women? The cross is the symbol of Christianity in Chin State; it's one of the mockeries against their beliefs.'[48]

All of these violations are the direct result of increased militarisation in Chin State. The Burma Army's presence has grown significantly, even in the space of just a few years. In 2007, for example, there were an estimated thirty-three Tatmadaw camps, whereas now there are at least fifty-five. Human Rights Watch claims that prior to 1988, the Tatmadaw had no battalions stationed in Chin State, and only two battalions, one based in Kalaymyo, Sagaing Division, and the other located in Magwe Division, were in operation in Chin State. Now, over fourteen battalions each with almost 500 troops are stationed in Chin State. In Kalaymyo alone, there are more than nine battalions.[49] Cheery Zahau says that 'as long as [Burmese] troops are there, there will be sexual violence'.[50]

The Chin are facing what many consider 'cultural' genocide as well. Burma Army troops are actively encouraged to marry local Chin women, and are rewarded if they do. In Matupi, the local commander, Colonel San Aung, has apparently offered 100,000 kyats and a pig to soldiers who succeed in marrying a local Chin woman. In Kalaymyo a special army battalion was reportedly established with the specific purpose of incentivising soldiers to marry Chin women, particularly the daughters of Chin pastors. The objective is to 'dilute' their ethnicity and convert them to Buddhism. However, in one area the strategy backfired when the women converted their Burman Buddhist husbands to Christianity. Those who converted were transferred to other places and denied promotion – while those who succeeded in converting their wives were promoted.

The Chin language is forbidden in schools, and the number of Burmese teachers in Chin State has increased significantly. 'The regime is trying to assimilate Chin State,' one Chin women's activist told me. 'Schools are all in Burmese and we are not even allowed to teach Chin language as a subject. Only in some areas can extra language classes for Chin be arranged, through the church. The regime is trying to kill the Chin language.'

History is distorted, according to a Chin university student, and schools do not teach the history of the ethnic nationalities. 'While growing up I was aware that we were a "union" as a country, but I was confused about the so-called "Union of Burma",' he said. 'The reason we didn't understand is that we only learn about the history of Burma in school, and the history we are taught is wrong.' Chin students are never taught that until British colonisation of Burma in the nineteenth century, they had lived as an entirely separate entity, never ruled by the Burmese kings. 'There is nothing about Chin history. We are only taught about the Thirty Comrades and the *Dobama Asiayone*.' As a result, he added, 'the majority and minority populations are separated from each other, and we feel weak and vulnerable because our Chin history is not recognised.' In an examination, this particular student decided to write a paper about the differences between Burman and Chin cultures, and wrote: 'I am not a Burman, I am a Chin.'

He warned that if history continues to be taught in the way it is, ethnic and national identity will be lost. 'I hate Burmanisation,' he said. His history professor called him in and warned him that he would be disqualified from all his subjects if he insisted on submitting this answer. 'He said he would delete my answers and I could rewrite the exam and pass. But I did not want my answers to be deleted, so I failed,' he told me, a look of proud defiance in his eye. 'We cannot learn true history in our country. There is no printed true history available, we cannot print true history, and we cannot learn our own language in school.' He concluded with a plea: 'Please help us to fight for our indigenous rights. I am concerned and worried about our future in Burma. Burma's political crisis is not only a democracy problem, it is also an ethnic and constitutional problem.'[51]

Chin State is widely recognised as the poorest part of Burma. The regime has deliberately withheld investment in health and education, and unlike the Kachin or Shan States, it lacks natural resources. But in addition to its general poverty, approximately every fifty years Chin State is hit by a natural phenomenon which the Chin call the 'Mautam', literally 'dying bamboo'. The flowering of bamboo attracts rats, who multiply in scenes reminiscent of an Old Testament plague, and devour every food source in sight – the bamboo itself initially, then turning their attention to the paddy fields and rice barns. The result: a chronic food shortage.

In 2007 the Mautam hit and, according to the Chin Human Rights Organisation's report 'Critical Point: Food Scarcity and Hunger in Burma's Chin State', over 100,000 people in at least 200 villages were severely affected. This amounts to 20 per cent of the entire population of Chin State. At least fifty-four deaths have been recorded, as a result of extreme malnutrition and famine-related disease, but the real death toll is likely to be much higher. The crisis spread across seven townships in Chin State and part of Sagaing Division, and up to 82 per cent of the farmland in affected areas was destroyed. More than 4,000 people fled to India and Thailand.[52]

During the crisis the regime did nothing to help. Unlike the Indian authorities who responded actively on their side of the border, the junta did not prepare the Chin for the anticipated famine or respond to their needs. Even worse, Chin cross-border relief teams were blocked from delivering much-needed aid.

The Chins themselves established a Chin Famine Emergency Relief Committee, and delivered assistance to the most vulnerable areas, targeting over seventy villages. A few international organisations responded to the emergency, but on a tiny scale. The Humanitarian Aid Relief Trust (HART), whose Chief Executive Baroness Cox had made several visits to the India–Burma border, raised funds for emergency relief, and together with Christian Solidarity Worldwide (CSW) lobbied the British government to help. A journalist from the *Guardian* travelled to the area in the summer of 2008, and a delegation of Chin activists visited London and met Parliamentarians. The *Sunday Telegraph* reported on the famine. Initially, perhaps the most distressing problem they faced was the World Food Programme (WFP)'s denial of the very existence of a famine. It turned out, however, that WFP teams had visited the wrong areas – they had been taken to villages which did not even have any bamboo. When this was revealed, and the crisis began to receive some media coverage, the British government began to consider ways of helping. In September 2008 a BBC World Service radio journalist produced a powerful documentary on the emergency. The WFP acknowledged the crisis, saying that it was 'worse than any other region' that they had visited in Burma.[53] Britain's Department for International Development (DFID) pledged £600,000, later adding a further £200,000.

DFID's aid has certainly made a difference, but it has not been without its problems. DFID insisted on channelling the aid through the WFP in Rangoon, rather than through Chin cross-border relief teams. The reaction of the Chin victims speaks volumes. One man in Matupi told Khin Tun, a young British volunteer working with the Chin along the India–Burma border:

You, the British people, had rescued and saved our spirits as R.A. Laurren (the first missionary from the UK to the people in this region over one hundred years ago) built our community and now you have come to help us for our physical needs . . . We were so heartbroken when we heard that the donations of UK were coming through Rangoon. It is impossible that the donations will reach us through Rangoon. The SPDC have been stealing our belongings. They are thieves; they will surely steal all the assistance from you.

How can your government believe them? We will get nothing, I am sure.[54]

Although DFID aid did reach some affected areas in Chin State, through WFP and the United Nations Development Programme (UNDP), in many areas it was reported to have been delivered through 'food-for-work' schemes. Exhausted, emaciated and starving people were forced to work in exchange for food, and the rations they receive may not have been enough for their families. As one Chin relief worker told me, 'people have to go to work for food, and so they have to leave their own work. It is a kind of forced labour. If they do not work, they won't get food.' In other areas, money was distributed but in the wrong currency. Villagers who had walked for days to receive cash they could use to buy rice then had to walk for several more days to convert the money into a currency they could use. Perhaps most troublingly, I was told on a visit to the border in 2009 that in seventeen villages in Paletwa Township, the worst affected area, aid was distributed in the form of loans, either in rice or cash, which had to be repaid at 200 per cent interest.

According to the Chin Famine Emergency Relief Committee, only 28 out of 87 villages in Thantlang Township had received DFID aid, in Paletwa between 70 and 80 villages out of 401 had received food assistance, and in Matupi Township only 9 villages had been helped. The aid only lasted three months.

Villagers often have to walk long distances to collect the relief, and then struggle through a series of military checkpoints to get the rice supplies home. Even if the aid is not taken by soldiers, they have to pay heavy bribes. From the Kaladan River to Paletwa, for example, there are seventeen Tatmadaw checkpoints. Villagers travelling up the river with supplies for their starving communities have to pay between 500 and 1,000 kyats per boat at each checkpoint.[55]

People have been forced to survive on wild yams and roots, which cause various sicknesses including severe stomach pain, gastric problems and constipation. In addition to hunger and malnutrition, famine-related diseases such as chronic diarrhoea have increased, as has vulnerability to other illnesses. Children in many areas have been unable to attend school, because they are too weak, hungry and ill. The Chin Human Rights

Organisation concludes that 'government neglect and continued abuse; inadequately supported relief efforts; and pervasive hunger and food shortages have the potential for catastrophic humanitarian consequences'. The Chin people 'are on the edge of survival now; but their struggle is far from over'.[56]

In 2010, I met some of the survivors of the Chin food crisis, who recalled their sense of despair that their suffering was largely unknown, and yet they expressed their gratitude for the few people who did know and tried to help. 'We had no place where we could tell our difficulties,' one man said. 'We didn't know anybody to whom we could speak about our suffering and starvation. For many families, the famine meant exodus, because of fear of starvation. Thousands left their villages to go to places where they could get food. They had no food left with them, and they had so many tears.' Mothers were so malnourished that they were unable to breast-feed. 'At night the village was filled with the crying voices of babies,' he said. When help came, however, the situation changed. 'After we got food, we became sure in our hearts that our village would not be destroyed by famine. We had peace, and we knew we could eat as a family. If you hadn't given help, we would have died.'[57]

The lack of health care in Chin State is a particularly urgent concern. In the entire state, according to the Chin Human Rights Organisation, there are only eight permanent clinics, to serve a population of 500,000.[58] There is an acute shortage of doctors, and a severe shortage of medicine.[59] Even if medicine is available, it is unaffordable for most people and is of poor quality.

The majority of the Chin people therefore rely on their own resources: clinics established along the India–Burma border to provide help to those who can reach them, and backpack health workers who travel through villages, at significant risk to themselves. The Women's League of Chinland told me that their health workers face the possibility of arrest every time they go inside the country. But, as one of their leaders said, 'even though it is such a difficult situation, we want to keep going inside again and again. We know it is dangerous, but we want to keep going in.'

I met one female health worker in 2009 who had been caught by the Burmese police, and forced to pay a bribe of 20,000 kyats. Another was caught in Paletwa Township and interrogated for an hour about what she was doing. She was released when two village headmen arrested with her informed the authorities that she was carrying food supplies for them at their request. In another case, Tatmadaw soldiers found medicines which a health worker had left with a village headman, and took some for their own use. 'There are two reasons we do not want to get caught,' a Women's League of Chinland spokeswoman told me. 'Firstly, for ourselves, and secondly, for the sake of the villagers, because they are questioned so much.'

Relief workers travelling inside face other dangers besides the Tatmadaw. One health worker told me that she almost drowned crossing a river. And on 30 October 2008 a Chin human rights activist and relief worker, John Tuihing, died in a boating accident while delivering much-needed food aid to communities in Paletwa Township.

Community health worker training programmes are a vital way of addressing the health crisis in Chin State, as many people are dying of preventable or treatable diseases. The Women's League of Chinland has run a number of training programmes, and the Chin backpack health workers raise awareness about basic primary health care needs. In addition, a Community Health Worker Training Programme has been started in a far corner of the India–Burma border, near a village called Chapi, by an extraordinary young Chin doctor called Dr Sasa.

Sasa was born in a remote village in southern Chin State, into the Mara community. Most of the villagers, including his own parents, were illiterate and he does not know his date or even year of birth. There was no electricity in the village, and many families could not afford candles. The Burma Army had a permanent base with sometimes as many as 200 soldiers nearby, so like most people in military-occupied areas Sasa was forced to porter for the military as a small boy, and his own sister was raped. And the predominantly Christian community was forced to build a Buddhist pagoda in the village.

At a very early age, Sasa's profound intelligence became obvious and the village, motivated by his grandmother, pulled together to give him proper schooling. 'It was very difficult – people wanted to study, but they had no school, no schoolteacher, no textbooks, no pencils, no exercise books,' he recalls. When he was about thirteen, the villagers sent him to Rangoon for education, and the start of his epic life adventure. After walking for three days, accompanied by a pastor, he then travelled by bamboo boat, truck and bus for several more days to reach the city. The entire journey, Sasa believes, took about thirteen days.

After a few years in Rangoon, Sasa returned to his village and worked as a schoolteacher. It was during this time that his most formative experiences occurred, and they were to shape his life's vision. Witnessing the deaths of villagers, sometimes his own students, on an almost weekly basis, Sasa began to question why he was burying people who were dying of treatable diseases. The village had no medical facilities at all and no understanding of primary health care. Sasa began to dream about becoming a doctor, although he says that at the time such an idea was as far-fetched as becoming an astronaut.

Sasa also began to develop an extraordinary wisdom about relationships with the authorities. On one occasion, the local military commander visited his home, and forgot to take his pistol away with him. Sasa instructed everyone to leave the gun untouched, and when the soldier returned to collect it, he was amazed. 'He was about to cry because if he lost his gun he could not go back to his unit – he would be arrested. He was frightened,' recalls Sasa. The brutality of the punishments within the Tatmadaw was shocking, so this soldier had every reason to be afraid. Two soldiers from the same area who tried to run away were caught, shot, and other soldiers were forced to eat the kidneys of the captured men as a warning to others. But Sasa recognised the humanity of some soldiers, and befriended the commander. 'He started to share about his life. I realised that there are some good people in the army who want to do good things but are forced to do bad things.'

To realise his vision of studying medicine, Sasa's village once again united, sold pigs, chickens and cows to raise money, and sent him across the border to India. There, he worked on a construction site to earn money, learned English, and studied in a college in Shillong. When he went for his first interview with the college principal he was rejected for being unable to speak English and being poorly dressed. In a testimony worthy of a stand-up comedian, Sasa recounts that because he was unable to afford a proper shirt and trousers, as stipulated by the college, he turned up in a ladies' shirt several sizes too small, and green ladies' Adidas tracksuit trousers, lent to him by a sympathetic woman. He claims he had not washed for months, and his shoulder-length hair was full of lice and dust. Standing under a ceiling fan in front of the principal, his hair started to blow. 'Dust and all sorts of animals flew into the face of the principal and onto his desk,' recalls Sasa. 'I could not speak English, except for yes and no, so when the principal's face looked positive I'd say "Yes, yes, yes" and if he looked negative I'd say "No, no, no".' The principal told him to go away, learn English and buy some proper clothes, and not to return until he had done so. Sasa did exactly that, was accepted into the college, and graduated as one of its top students.

From Shillong Sasa secured a place at a university in Armenia, and won funding from Prospect Burma. Although he admits he did not know where Armenia was, he chose it because it was cheaper than the United States or Europe. It meant, however, that he had to learn Armenian – his fifth language after his Mara village dialect, Chin, Burmese and English.

Before commencing his final year of medical studies, Sasa had a dream in which he saw starving people from Chin State reaching out their hands and crying for help. Reports of the chronic food shortage developing in his homeland were 'heartbreaking' he recalls, and so he decided to return to the India–Burma border to help. Over the course of two months, during his summer vacation, he treated over 2,000 patients before returning to complete his degree. After seven years of study, Sasa qualified as a doctor in 2009 and returned to the India–Burma border to fulfil his vision: the establishment of a community health workers' training programme. Under a newly formed charity known as 'Health and Hope', Sasa has inspired hundreds of villagers to follow his example. 'My motivation is clear,' he says. 'I believe in my people's future. I want to help my people who are helpless, hopeless and voiceless. Love has no border, no hiding place, it cannot be hidden.'

In November 2009 I had the privilege of attending the opening of the 'Health and Hope' training centre, and a few weeks later I received an extraordinarily moving email from Sasa. Summarising the essence of solidarity, Sasa wrote: 'I thank you for crying with me when I cried for my people, I thank you for feeling with me when I feel for my people, I thank you for studying with me with all you have when I studied medicine for my people who have suffered so much for so long. I thank you for graduating with me when I graduated for my people. I thank you for listening to me when I listen to my people's crying and dying voices . . . I thank you for loving me and my people.'

A year later I returned to meet some of the trainees. Almost all have extraordinary stories of struggles for education and health care. One twenty-three-year-old woman recounted how she had studied in another village as a teenager, because there was no secondary education in her village. Each weekend she would return to her family's home to collect food supplies. 'We would walk the whole of Saturday, twelve or thirteen hours, stay the night, and then walk back on Sunday, sometimes through the night as we did not want to miss our classes,' she told me. 'We would carry heavy loads of rice back, usually between seven and twelve kilograms.' When the time came to take exams, however, she had to walk four days to the nearest school where exams were held. Remarkably, she went on to university in Sittwe, where she worked as a cook for a family. 'For three years, I woke up at 4 a.m., started cooking until 8 a.m., and then I was in college from 8 a.m. until 3 p.m. As soon as classes were finished, I went home and started cooking again, until 6 p.m., and then studied until 11 p.m.' In 2008, she graduated with a degree in botany and then volunteered for the community health worker training programme.[60]

Another trainee had seen two of her siblings die because her mother was unable to produce breast-milk. A brother died of diarrhoea. Some of her other siblings suffered malnutrition, one of her brothers was born disabled, her father is deaf and one of her brothers was taken by the authorities and forced to join the police force. 'He was taken away and we didn't see him for fourteen years,' she says. 'He was a child soldier. Finally we heard he had run away from the police force and had come to India. He got sick . . . and then died.' Recognising the value of education, not only for her but for her community, she worked carrying sandbags from the river, each one weighing twenty-five kilos, for six miles, three times a week for seven weeks to earn money for education. She was then selected for the health workers' training.[61]

Another organisation that provides inspiring leadership for the Chin people is the Chin Human Rights Organisation. Founded in 1994 by student activists Salai Bawi Lian Mang and Victor Biak Lian, it plays a vital role documenting violations in Chin State and engaging in international advocacy.

Both Bawi Lian and Victor fled to the Indian border after the student uprising in 1988, and were originally involved in the armed resistance group, the Chin National Front (CNF). 'I was an angry student after seeing unjust things done by the regime in 1988, and it seemed to me that the only option left was to fight the Burma Army through armed struggle,' says Victor Biak Lian. Both Victor and Bawi Lian received training from the KIA in Kachin State, and endured arduous journeys through the jungle. 'We marched to the China border and it took us eighty-six days,' Victor recalls. 'Then we came to Bangladesh from the China border, another 125 days on foot. We experienced starvation, ambushes by the Tatmadaw and many terrible situations.' Bawi Lian became severely ill with malaria and jaundice, and had to be hospitalised for three months. Unable to return to the front line, he became a volunteer teacher in Manerplaw, the Karen headquarters, and established relationships with other ethnic groups. There he saw the work of other ethnic human rights organisations, and the vision for CHRO was born. 'I spoke to the CNF leaders and said that we need to set up something. The world does not know what we are doing. Nobody can come to us so we need to tell our story to the media,' says Bawi Lian. Human rights specialist Chris Lewa provided some basic training, and a donor gave one hundred dollars. 'We had a two-hour training session in Bangkok, and money which we used to buy a tape-recorder and a camera. That was the beginning of CHRO.'

Victor followed Bawi Lian soon afterwards, swapping the life of a soldier for that of an activist. 'In the jungle, I witnessed many things which made me think differently. I saw children dying due to food shortage, and I lost many friends in combat, some of them dying in my arms. All this made me realise that war is not a solution for the political crisis in Burma. I believe it is essential to tell the world what is happening among our people, by doing human rights documentation and advocacy.'

For the Chin people, wrestling with political oppression, religious and ethnic persecution, severe poverty, lack of education and health care and a famine, life is grim. Many have fled the country, to India, Thailand, the United States, Canada and Europe. At least 25,000 have gone to Malaysia, either as refugees or economic migrants. They go in search of freedom and better opportunities, but in Malaysia they find themselves trapped in another cycle of poverty, oppression, exploitation and victimisation.

I have visited the Chin community in Malaysia several times, and the conditions in which they live are little better than those they fled from.

Many are hidden in cramped apartments in Kuala Lumpur, with poor sanitation, no health care and little food. One two-room apartment housed twenty-seven people from eight families, living in eight-foot by five-foot spaces blocked off with thin curtains or cardboard dividers. Others live in jungle camps on the edges of Malaysia's capital, in conditions no different from the internally displaced peoples of eastern Burma. All of them run the risk of being arrested and deported by the Malaysian authorities – and brutally treated in the process.

The most vicious group among the Malaysian immigration and law enforcement bodies is the vigilante force known as RELA. No more than a gang of thugs used by the Malaysian police to do their dirty work, RELA terrorises the refugees and migrant workers. Regularly launching night-time raids armed with sticks and clubs, RELA is notorious for arresting people without concern for their circumstances. Elderly Chins, pregnant mothers and young children are beaten and taken to detention centres.

Once at the detention centre, they face even more severe treatment. On 9 October 2007, for example, a Chin pastor who had converted to Christianity from Buddhism in Burma was arrested by RELA. The regime in Burma had destroyed one of his churches. 'We cannot worship freely in Chin State,' he told me. 'The SPDC tries to influence people to convert from Christianity to Buddhism. We face Burmanisation.' Denied an interpreter in court, he was sentenced to two months in jail and a caning. Stripped naked, his hands and legs were tied to bars at an angle and he was blindfolded. 'When they removed the blindfold, I could not see clearly. I felt giddy,' he told me. He was caned on his backside, and he showed me the scar which remained, more than a year on. After the caning, antiseptic cream was applied carelessly to the wound. 'They treated me like an animal,' he said. After fifty days he was deported to the Thai border.

Those who are deported to the Thai border then face a desperate struggle to get back to Malaysia and avoid being returned to Burma. Typically, if they can raise enough money, they can pay a trafficker to return them – but leaving themselves very vulnerable to exploitation. Even if they are returned to Malaysia, the whole cycle can start again.

One woman, who was half-Chin and half-Karen, married to a Chin, arrived in Malaysia on 13 April 2005 and was arrested the very next day. She was deported to Thailand, but managed to return to Malaysia, where she was once again arrested. At the time of her second arrest, on 13 October 2006, she was three months pregnant, but the Malaysian immigration authorities sent her to Semenyih detention centre for five months. She was transferred to another detention centre for a further five months. Although she had informed the authorities she was pregnant, she was still forced to work every day cleaning the rooms and toilets, and was denied adequate drinking water. When she complained to the UNHCR (United Nations High Commissioner for Refugees) during one of their fortnightly visits, the prison authorities became angry and increased her workload. Denied proper medical treatment, fresh clothes or rest, she was forced to sweep the floors. When she went into labour, four women police officers took her to the prison hospital, and chained her to the bed. She gave birth on 5 April 2007, and five hours later she was taken back to prison. She was not permitted any visitors and even her husband, who was also in detention, was not allowed to see her or their baby. They were finally released when the baby was four months old.[62] She wept as she sat in a bleak, overcrowded Kuala Lumpur apartment, told her story and pondered her future.

Few foreigners visit the Chin people, either on the India–Burma border or Malaysia. They are among Burma's forgotten people. On my first visit to Mizoram, a Chin refugee told me: 'Many foreigners go to Burma's eastern borders, but until now no one has come to us. We used to pray for foreign NGOs to come to the western borders, and we used to weep when no one came.' The Chairman of the CNF said: 'Your coming here is a godsend.' But even if visits can give the Chin some hope and encouragement, their plight is desperate and it will require more than just encouragement for it to change. One young Chin student, sitting around a dinner table in Aizawl, the extraordinary capital of Mizoram State perched on top of a mountain, looked into my eyes and said: 'We have no hope for a future in Burma.' In a depressing flash of harsh honesty, he said: 'If we want to tell the truth, if we want freedom of speech, then everyone really worries about their life. The younger generation is willing to take risks, they want change, they want to find some hope from someone. Who can change our country? They want to sacrifice their lives. But the situation is hopeless. There is no future.'[63] People such as Victor Biak Lian, Dr Sasa, Cheery Zahau and the Women's

League of Chinland offer their people some hope, and a future, and with the reforms taking place and a ceasefire agreed between the regime and the CNF in January 2012, perhaps the Chin people can have more hope than they had just two years before.

A Stateless People

'Injustice anywhere is a threat to justice everywhere'

Martin Luther King Jr.

THE DESPAIR WAS palpable. Their eyes spoke clearly of their sense of hopelessness, and their testimonies told of their statelessness. One man, a political leader, looked into my eyes and said with genuine fear that he belonged to 'a people at the brink of extermination'.[1]

These were the Rohingyas, a Muslim group of Bengali origin who have inhabited northern Arakan State for generations. Thousands have fled intolerable conditions in their homeland, in the hope of a better life across the border in Bangladesh – only to encounter further misery. Approximately 28,000 have been officially recognised by the UNHCR, and are accommodated in two camps. But tens of thousands more live in dire circumstances in temporary, unregistered camps and settlements, or dispersed among the villages around Teknaf, Ukhiya and the southern Chittagong region. They have almost no access to education or health care, and even in the officially registered camps their shelter is poor. In the rainy season, rain drips through the roof and seeps up through the ground, creating a permanent mudbath. For those living outside the UNHCR camps conditions are even worse.

Not only are the Rohingyas oppressed and abused by the military regime, but they are also subjected to racial discrimination. Tension is particularly acute with some of the Arakan or Rakhine people, and some Burmans and other ethnic people, either as a result of their alliance with the Rakhines or because of their own religious and racial prejudice, also treat the Rohingyas badly. At the core of their plight is the fact that the regime does not recognise them as citizens of Burma.[2]

In Arakan State, there are believed to be approximately 1 million Rohingyas, out of a population of between 2.5 and 3 million. In northern Arakan, their primary location, there are an estimated 725,000, out of 910,000 people. In the major centres of Maungdaw and Buthidaung, they account for 96 and 88 per cent of the population respectively, while in Sittwe, previously called Akyab, the state capital, Rohingyas account for half the population. A further 1 million are living in exile, in Bangladesh, Malaysia, Thailand, Pakistan, Saudi Arabia, the United Arab Emirates, Europe and the United States.[3]

Without citizenship rights, the Rohingyas face restriction in almost every sphere of life. To travel from one village to another, they are required to obtain permission from at least three local authorities – the village-level chairman, the township authority, and the Na Sa Ka border security force. Such permission can be difficult to obtain and often takes up to five days. A bribe of at least 500 kyats must also be paid, and if a Rohingya wants to travel to another township, the bribe is at least 1,000 kyats. Even after having obtained a permit and paid the bribes, Rohingyas face harassment at checkpoints along the way. Engaging in any meaningful economic activity, or gaining access to education or health care, is therefore severely restricted. Rohingyas seeking treatment at the one large hospital, located in Sittwe, are often refused permission to travel.

They also need permission to marry, and approval can take several years and cost between 5,000 and 500,000 kyats. Those who marry without approval are prosecuted and can be jailed for up to five years.

In the words of one Rohingya, 'the education system is grim'. Although there are primary schools in every village, in many schools the vast majority of teachers are non-Muslims, because as non-citizens the Rohingyas are not permitted to be employed as government servants, either as teachers, nurses or in other public services. Rakhine Buddhist teachers employed in Rohingya areas sometimes do not turn up to teach for an entire year, so schools are abandoned. There are only twelve high schools in the three Rohingya-majority townships of Maungdaw, Buthidaung and Rathedaung.

The very few Rohingyas who manage to succeed at school are refused entry to higher education, even if they obtain high marks. Some have been able to follow distance education, but they still have to obtain permission to travel to the only university in Arakan State, in Sittwe, to sit their exams. In 2005 only forty-five Rohingyas were able to sit exams in Sittwe. Since 2005 travel to Sittwe has been systematically denied.

Like Christians, Muslims in Burma have faced persecution at the hands of a fascist military regime which identified itself with extreme Burman nationalism and a perversion of Buddhism for political ends. Rohingya Muslims find it almost impossible to obtain permission to renovate or extend mosques or other religious buildings. According to Rohingya sources, since 1962 very few new mosques have been built. The central mosque in Maungdaw is reportedly still only half-built and without a roof, and between 2005 and 2008 at least twelve mosques and madrasas were demolished. In July and August 2006 the authorities ordered the closure of a large number of mosques and madrasas, on the grounds that they had been built without official permission, or were unable to provide evidence of their funding sources. In north Buthidaung, eight mosques were ordered to close in mid-2006, and a further seventeen mosques and madrasas were ordered to be destroyed at the end of 2006. Eight were demolished. In early 2007, three mosques and madrasas were forced to close in Rathedaung and southern Maungdaw. According to Rohingya expert Chris Lewa in testimony to the US Commission on International Religious Freedom in 2007, at least fourteen people from northern Arakan, including two clerics, are in jail for renovating an Islamic religious building without permission.[4]

Forced labour, extortion and land confiscation are widespread in northern Arakan as in most of Burma. The difference is that in northern Arakan it appears that the Rohingyas are specifically targeted. Three defectors from the Na Sa Ka border force I met in Dhaka in 2008 confirmed that the Rohingyas were singled out. 'Throughout my life in the Na Sa Ka, I was used to this system of arresting Muslims, asking for money, torturing them – every day,' explained one. 'We only arrested Muslims, not Rakhines.'[5] Another confessed: 'When we saw Muslims, we would arrest them . . . After arresting them, we forced them to work for us . . . I did not want to torture and beat Muslim people, but I was ordered to do so. I feel very sorry for what I did. I feel happier now that I have escaped.'[6]

Extortion, said one Rohingya, 'is so serious that if we travel from one village to another, we have to bring money to give to the Na Sa Ka, and we have to send the money for our shopping separately. Economically we are completely crushed.' Sometimes, the authorities find a specific reason for demanding money, accusing Rohingyas of travelling to Bangladesh without permission, or possessing a mobile phone without approval, for example. A few Rohingyas have Bangladeshi mobile phones, but if caught with them, they can be forced to pay between 100,000 and 200,000 kyats. However, often bribes are sought even when the accusations are false. One man had travelled to Bangladesh with permission, but on 27 August 2008 the authorities came to his home and demanded 50,000 kyats from his family while he was gone. And in some instances no reason is even given. People are randomly arrested and a bribe of 1,000 to 2,000 kyats is demanded for their release. The Na Sa Ka come to villages at night, to demand money or livestock. 'This is happening daily,' said one Rohingya.

One of the defectors confirmed this. Based in the Na Sa Ka Area No. 1 at Aung Tha Pray, close to the Bangladesh border, he described how at night, his battalion would go to Rohingya villages to look for those who travel to Bangladesh. 'We kicked open all the doors of people's homes, and arrested all Muslims, demanding money – whether they had been to Bangladesh or not. We did this every day – one village one night, the next night another village,' he recalled. 'Many Muslims are suffering. After arresting Muslims, the Na Sa Ka tortured them. They forced them to give money. The Muslims had to sell their livestock, their cows, goats and chickens, to get the money to give to [us]. If they could not give money, they would be beaten.'

If money or livestock are not demanded, often forced labour is required. 'We used Muslims to dig bunkers,' said the former Na Sa Ka officer. 'Every village had to provide ten or fifteen people. They were not given pay or food. Some families could not eat at all, because they were forced to work all day for the Na Sa Ka.'[7] In July 2008, hundreds of Rohingyas were forced to work on rebuilding the road from Maungdaw to Buthidaung, which had been destroyed by heavy rain. Many Rohingyas have also been forced to buy and plant physic nut saplings or cultivate paddy fields for the Na Sa Ka.

As part of its campaign to subjugate the Rohingyas, the junta has begun to repopulate northern Arakan with Burmans, by constructing a series of what it calls 'model villages', or *natala*. At least fifty of these have been built so far, in eighty-two village tracts in Maungdaw Township, near the Bangladesh border. Usually built with Rohingya forced labour, they are populated by Burman Buddhists. Burmans are offered incentives to resettle, and the plan is that they will then gradually take over ownership of surrounding land and take up leadership positions in area. 'Our land, which we have cultivated, is being confiscated,' one Rohingya told me. 'Muslims are gradually losing lands and becoming landless.' In some cases, land owned by Rohingyas is confiscated, given to Burman settlers, and then the original Rohingya owner is invited to pay rent to the settlers in the form of five-and-a-half bags of the crop per 0.4 acres, each one fifty kilograms, for the privilege of cultivating the land.

While rape is widespread throughout Burma, experts believe it is not as common in Rohingya areas – although it is extremely difficult to obtain evidence, because in the Rohingya Muslim culture attitudes are very conservative and Rohingya women are perhaps more reluctant to speak out. Nevertheless, wherever the Tatmadaw is present, rape cases occur. One refugee woman who fled to Bangladesh in 1991 recalls a terrible night. Her husband had already escaped, her cousin had been killed by the military and a major operation by the Tatmadaw was underway. 'At night, soldiers came to our village, house by house, and pulled out the women to rape them,' she claimed. 'I screamed out when I heard the soldiers, and local people rushed to help. The soldiers did not rape me, but [instead] they demanded a goat. The next day I left everything and crossed the border.' On one occasion a local Tatmadaw captain ordered the village men to provide women for him, she added, and when one man refused to give his daughter, he was severely beaten.

A Na Sa Ka deserter confirmed that rapes occur. 'Sergeants and corporals especially raped Muslim women,' he told me. 'They would gather all the men of one village in one place, and we junior soldiers would have to guard them at gunpoint while the officers abused the women. In one village, I had to watch over the men, while a sergeant and some corporals abused their wives.'[8]

Rohingya activists and resistance groups prompt harsh reprisals from the regime, as with any opposition in Burma. Arbitrary arrest and torture is widespread. In July 2008, a sixty-three-year-old man, Asheraf Meah, from Alethankyaw (Hatchurata) village, twelve miles south of Maungdaw, died after twelve days in police custody. He had been detained without charge, and severely tortured. When he was unable to pay bribes to the police, he was beaten to death.

Typically, extrajudicial killings go unreported. However, on a handful of occasions there have been significant military operations against the Rohingyas, which have resulted in numerous deaths. In 1994, the Tatmadaw launched an offensive in response to the activities of the armed Rohingya Solidarity Organisation (RSO), and it is reported that hundreds of Rohingyas from Maungdaw and Buthidaung were massacred in a military camp. Precise accounts have not been obtained, although an artist's impression exists. Rohingya sources claim that people were lined up in a row in front of mass graves. Soldiers hit each person on the back of the head with a shovel, causing them to fall into the grave. Some died instantly, but many were buried alive.

A senior UN official, who has served in various humanitarian emergencies including Darfur and who, in the words of a foreign diplomat in Rangoon, 'knows human misery when he sees it' has described the plight of the Rohingyas in northern Arakan as as bad as anything he has seen 'in terms of the denial of basic human freedoms'. Médicins Sans Frontières has categorised the Rohingyas as one of the ten world populations in danger of extinction. One Rohingya activist in Bangladesh summed up the situation with these words: 'The regime is trying to take away our identity. We will not be there in the very near future. The disintegration of our society will take place. Our prime concern is that we must not be eliminated. This is our land and we want to live there with full rights and dignity. We need international help.' Another concluded that the regime is 'poised to exterminate' the Rohingya, with the aim of achieving 'Arakan land without Muslims'. His people, he warned, are 'just struggling to survive'.

The Rohingyas' plight is made worse by a continuing debate over their origins. Even their name 'Rohingya' is disputed by many Burmans and Rakhine. Yet these divisions have been stirred by the regime, using its favourite divide-and-rule tactic. A position paper adopted by the NCGUB, the Burmese democracy movement's government in exile, on 24 September 1992 notes that the regime is 'exploiting these differences in order to build up public support for a strong army'.[9]

Although some in the democracy movement refuse to recognise the Rohingyas or at best treat them with undisguised suspicion, others have taken a different approach. The NCGUB affirmed that 'Muslim Rohingyas have lived in Arakan for centuries' and that they should have the same rights as all other citizens of Burma. 'They are citizens of Burma and have in the democratic past participated in Burmese politics. These facts cannot be denied,' the NCGUB notes.[10] And in 2000, one of the Rohingya armed groups, the Arakan Rohingya National Organisation (ARNO), formed an alliance with the National United Party of Arakan (NUPA). In the case of both the NCGUB and NUPA, extremist Rakhines have unleashed bitter attacks on them for even acknowledging the existence of the Rohingyas. NUPA's President Dr Khin Maung, a Rakhine himself, has been given the nickname 'Muhammad Khin Maung' among some Rakhines because of the alliance he has formed with the Rohingyas.

The history of the area is a cause of intense dispute among Rohingyas and Rakhines. Some Rakhines claim that Bengalis only came to northern Arakan State in the nineteenth and twentieth centuries, and that an influx arrived after cyclones devastated Bangladesh in 1978 and 1991.[11] Ironically, those are the years of the largest exodus of Rohingya refugees from Burma into Bangladesh. Some believe the Rohingyas have a secret plot to create a separate Muslim state, pointing to the Mujaheed movement in 1947 that did indeed demand autonomy.[12] The Rohingyas, on the other hand, claim to have inhabited Arakan for centuries. Bangladeshi historian Dr Abdul Karim claims that the Rohingyas came to Arakan in several phases. 'Some came as traders from as far places as Arabia and Persia, others came as conquerors and in the train of the invading army, some came as victims of pirates and still others came in peaceful pursuits . . . In the seventeenth century Arakan reached its pinnacle of glory through the contribution of Muslim poets, Muslim learned men, saints and administrators.'[13] He cites an historical report of a shipwreck in the ninth century, suggesting that 'the Rohingyas have been staying in Arakan for more than a thousand years'.[14]

Some Rohingyas claim that Muslim kings actually ruled Arakan in 1430 for over a hundred years.[15] Martin Smith questions this assertion, noting that this refers to the reign of Arakan King Narameikhla. Smith argues that after King Narameikhla took sanctuary with King Ahmed Shah of Gaur in Bengal during one of the many wars with Burman kings, he and his successors took Muslim titles simply as 'royal honorifics' rather than as a result of conversion. What is not in dispute, according to Smith, is that 'various historians and Muslim scholars have recorded evidence of a Muslim presence or settlement along parts of the Arakan coastline, from as early as the eighth and ninth centuries AD', and that one of Arakan's largest mosques was constructed in the seventeenth century.[16]

Whatever the history, no one can seriously doubt that the Rohingyas have lived in northern Arakan for generations. Exactly how many generations may be debated, but at least we can be certain that they were there before Burma's independence. The former President of Burma, Sao Shwe Thaike, a Shan, is said to have argued that 'Muslims of the Arakan certainly belong to one of the indigenous races of Burma. If they do not belong to the indigenous races, we also cannot be taken as indigenous races.'[17]

Although a large-scale anti-Muslim riot occurred in Arakan in 1942, in which 300 Muslim religious centres were destroyed and thousands of Rohingyas fled their homes, in general Rakhines and Rohingyas lived alongside each other peacefully until Ne Win's rule, and during the democratic period Rohingyas had citizenship rights and played a full part in Burmese society. U Nu, Prime Minister from 1948–1958 and again briefly from 1960–1962, who used the disputed term 'Rohingya', authorised the Burmese Broadcasting Service to broadcast in the Rohingya language, and Rohingyas sat in Parliament.[18] Their fortunes changed when Ne Win seized power.

A former close associate of Ne Win who served as a minister in his government claims Ne Win had 'an unwritten policy' to get rid of Muslims, Christians, Karens and other ethnic peoples, in that order. His hatred for Muslims was especially intense, this source told me.

In 1978, Ne Win launched a brutal campaign known as 'Operation King Dragon' or 'Naga Min'. Although targeted at armed Rohingya insurgents, thousands of ordinary Rohingya civilians were driven out of Burma. In the course of three months, an estimated 200,000 fled into Bangladesh.[19]

Three years later, he began to introduce plans to strip the Rohingyas of their citizenship, as mentioned earlier. A commission of inquiry was established by the regime, headed by a former chief justice of the Supreme Court, which identified eight main ethnic nationalities as traditionally indigenous – the Burmans, Kachin, Karen, Karenni, Chin, Mon, Arakan and Shan – and 135 different ethnic groups altogether. As Errol da Silva reported in the *Bangkok Post*, 'Rohingyas are complaining that the failure to classify them as an entity separate from the general category of Arakanese would render them liable to reduce themselves to either "statelessness" or "alien" status.' The Rohingya Patriotic Front (RFP) spearheaded a campaign against this decision, arguing, according to da Silva, that 'Arakan Muslims would be permanently placed in a position of insecurity because of the absence of a guarantee of Burmese citizenship . . . The revocation of citizenship from such people would make them liable to "deportation to the country of their origin".'[20] Their pleas were ignored, and the following year the 1982 Citizenship Act came into force. Over subsequent years the Rohingyas' status was downgraded to that of 'temporary resident' and they were issued with white 'Temporary Registration Cards'. For the privilege of even temporary residency identification, Rohingyas had to pay 2,500 kyats. As one Rohingya told me, 'the regime claims we are mere residents, not citizens'.[21]

For many years, the plight of the Rohingyas was virtually unknown to the outside world. However, in January 2009, international headlines were dominated by stories of hundreds of Rohingya 'boat people' fleeing persecution and starvation in Burma for Thailand and Malaysia. Although this phenomenon had been going on for several years, assisted by human traffickers, it gained the world's attention when Thai authorities began arresting them when they reached Thai shores, and sending them back to sea. According to the *Nation*, the Thai authorities 'set them adrift on boats without engines or sufficient food and water supplies', and reports suggest that as many as 500 may have drowned.[22] CNN's reporter Dan Rivers conducted an investigation in which he obtained evidence of Rohingyas detained on a Thai beach north of Phuket. They were forced to lie in the scorching sun, and were whipped if they sat up.[23] Even more significantly, the news channel reported that 'extraordinary photos obtained by CNN from someone directly involved in the Thai operation show refugees on their rickety boats being towed out to sea, cut loose and abandoned.'[24]

One young Rohingya who was arrested by the Thai authorities told journalist John Carlin that he was kept on an island for a month, along with 200 others, and then loaded into a barge and towed out to sea. They were provided with food and water, but their engine was removed. 'We drifted for fourteen days. Many of us got sick, many lost consciousness. I had no doubts I would die. There was no hope of land or rescue. We had no energy even to talk any more,' he said. On the sixteenth day, Carlin reports, they saw land, and awoke the next day surrounded by fishing boats. They had reached Indonesia.[25]

Chris Lewa, who runs an NGO called the Arakan Project, estimates that between October 2006 and March 2008, 9,000 Rohingyas left by boat from Bangladesh.[26] The exodus continues to this day. Many never reach Thailand, Malaysia or Indonesia. Travelling in dangerously overcrowded boats with faulty engines through troubled waters, hundreds die at sea, drowning as their boats sink.

In response to growing international concern about the plight of the Rohingyas, the regime intensified its vitriol towards them. Revealing the regime's views, Ye Myint Aung, Burmese Consul General in Hong Kong, wrote a letter to all diplomatic heads of mission in Hong Kong and the editor of the *South China Morning Post* in 2009. Sparing no diplomatic niceties, he observed that:

> In reality, Rohingya are neither 'Myanmar People' nor Myanmar's ethnic group. You will see in the photos that their complexion is 'dark brown'. The complexion of Myanmar people is fair and soft, good looking as well. (My complexion is a typical genuine one of a Myanmar gentleman and you will accept that how handsome your colleague Mr Ye is.) It is quite different from what you have seen and read in the papers. (They are as ugly as ogres.)[27]

In addition to racist language such as this, and religious hostility, there is a third factor in the regime's attitude to the Rohingyas, which the regime has used to considerable effect: the charge of extremism. While generally this is overdone, and deployed simply as a propaganda tool by the regime, there are indications that there may be some legitimate cause for concern. A small minority of Rohingyas have had contacts with extremist groups, particularly in Bangladesh. According to Bertil Lintner, the RSO, which broke away from the RPF in the early 1980s, has become 'the main and most militant faction', and in the 1990s there were allegations that Islamist organisations such as Jamaat-e-Islami in Bangladesh and Pakistan and Hizb-e-Islami in Afghanistan were recruiting Rohingyas. 'Afghan instructors were seen in some of the RSO camps along the Bangladesh–Burma border, while nearly one hundred RSO rebels were reported to be undergoing training in the Afghan province of Khost with Hizb-e-Islami Mujahideen,' Lintner writes.[28] A videotape labelled 'Burma' was found in al-Qaeda's archives in Afghanistan.[29] It is important to emphasise, however, that there have been no recent reports of such activity.

Sitting in an apartment in East London, I spent five hours with a community of Rohingya refugees. They told me their stories, which were similar to so many I had already heard. 'We are stateless people in our own country,' one man said. 'Even animals have the right to move from one place to another, but we don't. And without access to education, we become living dead.'

With tears in his eyes, one young man gently described some of his experiences in Burma. 'Every day of our lives we face harassment and humiliation,' he said. Stories abounded of small but grinding incidents. A seventy-year-old man with tuberculosis denied a seat on a boat because he was a Rohingya. A group of Rohingya students stopped at a police checkpoint on their way to prayers, and ordered to take off their skullcaps. A student with all his papers in order stopped at a checkpoint and turned back – when he asked the police what the problem was, he was told: 'Your religion is the problem.'

As I sat and listened to these stories, it was impossible not to be filled with compassion and anger at the blatant injustice. When I asked them how they felt about radical Islamism and the spread of teachings of hatred in the name of Islam, they smiled. One said: 'Can't you see in our faces what we believe?' I could – their faces were gentle, kind, peaceful, beautiful. Another said: 'Our people don't have time for [Islamism]. Our people think only of the problems they face – our suffering in Burma, and how to put food on the table for their families.'

But then I asked whether there was any danger that the Rohingya could be radicalised – and whether the small number who had links with jihadist groups could become more influential. Nurul Islam, a wise, thoughtful man who had a book about Martin Luther King with him, nodded gravely: 'If the situation does not change, there is a possibility that they could be driven into extremism. If they think they have no friends in this world, no one to stand up for them – and if the Islamists offer them such help – there is a possibility in the future that they could be radicalised.'

This is the crux of it. The rest of the democracy movement need to recognise that unless they embrace the Rohingyas as allies in the struggle against the regime, and include them in discussions about the future of the country, they will be left with a very serious challenge in the future. The Euro-Burma Office knows this, and concludes in its briefing: 'A way must be found to engage them in Burma's nation-building process. Ignoring them or excluding them will not solve the problem. In fact, it will exacerbate and create additional problems.'[30]

Some Rakhine know this too. 'We have to reach out to moderate Rohingyas, and work with them, because if we don't, they will have nowhere else to go but radical Islamism,' one Rakhine leader told me. And the Rakhine are suffering at the hands of the regime too. In schools, teachers use Burmese and the Rakhine language is banned. They have common cause with the Rohingyas, and share a common goal to remove the regime and restore democracy. As one Rakhine leader told me in regard to the Rohingyas, 'when a people have been living this long through history, why should they be deprived of their citizenship rights?'[31]

Currently, the Rohingyas are surviving, but stateless. Refugees on the Bangladesh–Burma border told me repeatedly that it is this statelessness that makes them question their very survival. In Bangladesh, they are told they are Burmese and should go back to Burma. In Burma, they are met with hostility and told they are Bengali and should return to Bangladesh. 'We are trapped between a crocodile and a snake,' said one refugee. 'We are treated as foreigners in Burma. But if we are foreigners, please show us which country we belong to, and we will go there,' said another in a tone of desperation.[32]

Defectors, Deserters and Child Soldiers

'I am still in the land of the dying; I shall be in the land of the living soon'

John Newton

'AUNG SAN SUU Kyi is a very great leader, but our government does not like her very much.' These words caught me by surprise – not because of the words themselves or the sentiment they expressed, but because of who they were spoken by: a serving military officer in Burma. 'She is in a very difficult situation,' he continued. 'But I pray for her.'

Discontent with the current regime, and a desire for change in Burma is not limited to students, monks and political activists. In the junior ranks of the military, morale is believed to be so low that rates of desertion and defection have reached worrying proportions for the regime. A confidential report allegedly from the regime claims that desertion rates have reached 1,600 a month, and that between May and August 2006 alone, a total of 9,467 desertions were reported,[1] while 7,761 desertions were reported between January and April 2000.[2] In early August 2009, seventy soldiers deserted from just one battalion, Light Infantry Battalion (LIB) 324,[3] in Kachin State, and a month later twenty officers stationed near Gangdau Yang and Nam San Yang villages on the Myitkyina–Bhamo highway in Kachin State defected to the KIA.[4] *Narinjara News* reported in 2007 that desertions in Arakan State were increasing 'by the day', with sixty-nine soldiers deserting and twenty-seven retiring in one month alone.[5]

Most of those who desert do so because of the poor working conditions:

low pay, few rations and ill treatment. Some, however, defect, joining the democracy movement or ethnic resistance organisations, literally switching sides. I have met dozens of Burma Army deserters and defectors who have fled to Burma's borders, some of whom were child soldiers. All of them knew the risk they were taking when they fled their units – if they had been caught, they would almost certainly have been executed. Those fighting in the ethnic areas were also fed dire warnings by their senior officers about what the ethnic resistance groups would do to them if they were caught.

Kyaw Zeya was taken from a bus stop in Rangoon when he was eleven years old. A truckload of Tatmadaw soldiers pulled up alongside him as he waited for a bus to go to visit his aunt. They grabbed him, and told him if he did not join the army, he would go to jail. 'I had no choice,' he told me when I met him three years after his abduction.

Taken to Ta Kyin Koe First Battalion Camp in Danyigone district, he was prohibited from contacting his parents. He was one of at least thirty other children of a similar age at this camp, where he was held for eight months before being sent to a training facility for regular soldiers in the Fifth Battalion. There, he went through five months of basic training, which included running five or six miles every morning. He was then transferred to Light Infantry Battalion 341 in Papun District, Karen State, and then sent to the front line. In a unit of thirty soldiers, he said, at least fifteen were children his age.

Subjected to cruel treatment, including regular beatings for failure to carry out basic tasks, Kyaw Zeya said that life in the Burma Army 'was like hell'. He witnessed attacks on Karen villages, civilians being rounded up and forced to work as porters for the military, and claimed that troops were under orders to burn, rape and kill when they entered a Karen village. 'There was no law,' he explained. He was repeatedly warned that if he ever escaped and was captured by the Karens, they would kill him. He believed them, but life became so intolerable that he decided to flee.[6] 'I did believe that the Karen were very bad, and I knew that if I escaped, I might face the Karen,' he admitted. 'But I did not want to live.'[7]

The reality was diametrically opposed to the Tatmadaw propaganda. Almost as soon as he escaped, Kyaw Zeya was captured by the Karen, but instead of killing him, they provided him sanctuary. With the Karen, he told me, he felt 'safe and free and loved'.[8]

Other children tell similar stories. One fourteen-year-old boy was abducted on his way home from watching a film, and forced to fight on the front line against the Karen, where his duties included digging trenches and foxholes. He was fed rice and bananas and paid just six kyat a month – even though at the time military salaries were supposed to range from 3,000 to 100,000 kyats a month.[9] Another boy was taken from a railway station in Mandalay when he was fourteen, arrested because he did not have identity papers, and taken to a police training centre. 'When I arrived at the training centre, all the boys were aged between eleven and fifteen. Nearly three hundred boys had been arrested,' he recalls. 'I lost my childhood. I only had fear and force to drive me.'

Burma has perhaps the highest number of child soldiers in the world proportionate to its population. A 2002 report by Human Rights Watch, called 'My Gun Was as Tall as Me', estimated that the Tatmadaw has at least 70,000 child soldiers, possibly amounting to 20 per cent of the army. A further report by the organisation in 2007, 'Sold to be Soldiers', provides fresh evidence, along with the Watch List on Children and Armed Conflict's report 'No More Denial' in 2009. Other organisations, such as the Karen Human Rights Group, have also provided extensive documentation of the use of child soldiers. A former major in the Burma Army who defected to the KIO told me that he observed many former child soldiers, recruited primarily by battalions trying to meet recruitment targets. Each month, battalions are required to recruit at least five new soldiers, and if they fail they are fined. So soldiers go to railway stations, bus stations, street corners and other public locations and grab whoever they can find. 'Sometimes the children are so young that they still pee in the night,' he said. 'That gives you an idea of the age of the youngest child soldiers.'[10]

In 2006, I walked through the Thai jungle for several hours, to meet two former child soldiers who had escaped from Burma. Defectors, including child soldiers, are not able to obtain refugee status in Thailand and the Thais have an agreement with the junta to hand over any defectors found in Thailand. So, accompanied by the European Parliament's rapporteur for human rights at the time, an Irish politician called Simon Coveney, we trekked through the jungle to a secret location.

The two boys had escaped from their units just nine months earlier. One of them said that he had never been interested in joining the army, but had been captured on his way home from a Buddhist festival. He was detained for four or five days on the pretext that he did not have his identity card, and then given a choice: join the army or remain in jail. From there, he was taken to Shwe Bo military recruiting centre, where he worked for two months doing basic chores, cooking and looking after the livestock. Transferred to Sagaing Division Military Training Camp No. 10, he went through military training for four-and-a-half months, learning to use guns and hand grenades, and was beaten many times. 'I was beaten, especially when I showed no interest in the training,' he said. 'I was beaten with steel rods and bamboo sticks, and once with a bar from the frame of a bicycle.'[11] Of the 250 trainees, most, he claims, were aged around fourteen or fifteen.

After completing his basic training he was sent to Infantry Battalion 112, in Shan State, and from there to Karenni State. Beaten and kicked whenever he stumbled, slowed down or grew tired walking up mountains, he was forced to carry 250 rounds of ammunition, a landmine and a hand grenade. He was ordered to shoot strangers on sight, as they could be 'rebels'.[12]

The testimony of some deserters and defectors is very revealing about the attitudes, conduct and policies of the Tatmadaw. One young man, aged twenty-two, told me that while serving in the military as a forced conscript, he heard his fellow soldiers regularly describing the ethnic nationalities as 'Ngapwe', meaning 'a dirty skin disease'. He escaped specifically because he did not want to carry out the human rights violations that he was ordered to. When fifty soldiers from Light Infantry Battalion 590, where he was stationed, were ordered to go to Rangoon to help in the crackdown on protests in September 2007, he made his decision to run away. He did not want to shoot civilians and monks. 'I want to tell other soldiers who have been forced to join the army to flee if they have the chance,' he said when I met him on the Thailand–Burma border just two months after his escape. 'Don't obey orders any more,' was his message to his fellow soldiers.[13]

Some have heard that message. The Rangoon commander in 2007 was 'permitted to retire' after reportedly refusing to give orders to fire on protestors.[14] Five other generals and 400 soldiers were detained for similarly refusing to follow orders.[15] A major defected, escaping to Thailand, telling the BBC that: '[The demonstrators] were very peaceful. Later when I heard they were shot and killed and the armed forces used tear gas, I was really upset and I thought the army should stand for their own people.' He added: 'I knew the plan to beat and shoot the monks and if I stayed on I would have to follow these orders. Because I'm a Buddhist, I did not want to kill the monks.'[16] A diplomat in the Burmese embassy in London, Ye Min Tun, resigned from his position in protest at the 'horrible' treatment of the monks. He said: 'I have never seen such a scenario in the whole of my life. The government is arresting and beating the peaceful Buddhist monks. This revolution, this incident seemed to be the decisive factor that could persuade the government to go to the negotiation table. But actually the government ignored the reality.'[17]

Typically, however, it is not outrage at the brutality, but rather frustration at pay and conditions, that is the major factor causing desertions. One nineteen-year-old former soldier told me that although he was officially paid 10,500 kyats a month during his training in Thatong, Mon State, and 13,000 kyats when he had completed his training, soldiers often did not receive their full salary. Even when they did, they were not given it in cash, but in vouchers which could only be used in military-run shops. They had to pay for their own uniform, which cost 10,000 kyats – virtually a month's wages. These poor conditions are part of the reason the Tatmadaw loots and extorts money and food from villagers – a practice many believe is deliberately encouraged by the regime.[18] A former Chin major, Thawng Za Lian, who fled Burma to the United States, confirms this. 'The government pushes the army to behave really badly in the front line. They are given five kyats a day for food, which is not enough to buy even an egg. One egg is forty-five kyats. So in the army they just have to try to find food,' he said. 'The government knows that looting and stealing goes on. Why do they allow this to happen? All of this has affected morale very badly. Trying to survive daily life, with not enough to eat, having to lie and steal – it changes the spirit of the soldiers.'[19]

Not all defectors and deserters, of course, had been forcibly conscripted into the military. Some joined voluntarily, in the hope of serving their country, regarding the army as an honourable profession. They left because they were sorely disappointed.

I met one such person at the Karen Revolution Day celebrations in 2009. Aged twenty-four and a Burman, he deserted his unit two years previously, as a lieutenant, after five years in the military. He joined at the age of seventeen, and studied at the Defense Services Academy (DSA). Throughout his three years' basic officer cadet training, he gave little thought to the nature of the regime he was serving. That changed when he was sent to Karen State. 'I saw the imbalance, the discrimination, between the upper and lower ranks in the military. I also saw a lot of incidents of oppression of civilians,' he told me. 'Whenever we went to the front line, we ordered villagers to serve as porters. I did not like these things happening, and I tried to avoid becoming involved . . . When I joined the army, I thought I would serve my country. But I witnessed discrimination, and experienced it myself, and that is why I left.'

The crunch came for him when he fell in love with a Karen girl, while serving in Tarley Mo, opposite Maetan. 'The battalion commander was not happy. He did not allow me to continue a relationship with a Karen girl. That was why I deserted . . . I am a Burman, from Monywa, in Sagaing Division. The army told me that my girlfriend is from a different nationality, and that it is impossible for me to be with her. They were interfering and oppressing me personally.'

Confirming the widespread use of child soldiers in the Tatmadaw and poor conditions, he said that there are many soldiers like him who want to escape. 'Other soldiers have the same feeling as me, but they are denied their individual choices and they are forced to obey the regime.' Escaping, he added, is extremely risky – and once out of Burma, it is impossible to return. 'If I was returned to Burma, I would be jailed for more than twenty years, or possibly executed. I dare not contact my relatives, as they could be charged under Law 17/1, referring to contact with illegal organisations, which carries a three-year prison sentence, or Law 17/2, involvement in the opposition, which carries a seven-year sentence.' But, he concluded, all the people of Burma are suffering. 'I want democracy in Burma, and respect for ethnic rights. The situation in Burma is getting worse and worse and poorer and poorer in every way.'[20]

This call for democracy is more widely felt than may be known. In a rare interview with Radio Free Asia, an active-duty sergeant said that rank-and-file soldiers are extremely unhappy with the regime, particularly in light of the crackdown on the Buddhist monks in 2007 and Aung San Suu Kyi's trial in 2009. 'We all want democracy – both the people and the soldiers,' he told the radio station. 'We sympathise with the monks and feel that the officers who ordered this violence will some day have to pay for their actions.' But he acknowledged that this sentiment is strongest among the junior ranks. 'I would like to stand with the people, but the higher-ranking officers are unlikely to do so.'[21]

A handful of defectors have gone on an active campaign against the regime, speaking out in exile and proactively urging their old colleagues to follow suit. Bo Htet Min, a former major who escaped from Burma in 2005, has established a website to counter the regime's propaganda. Aung Lynn Htut, a former major who served as Deputy Chief of Mission in Washington, DC and defected in 2005, has been overtly critical of the regime, exposing serious human rights violations allegedly ordered by Senior General Than Shwe,[22] and arguing that the regime's elections in 2010 mean that 'the Burmese people will lose all hope of freedom and the generals who now rule the country will retain their power'.[23] In 2008, he called for international pressure on the regime to be intensified, and made a prediction. 'Based on my experience, my view is that General Than Shwe can't bear pressure . . . I have said before that General Than Shwe needs sticks, not carrots,' he told the Democratic Voice of Burma.

When there is effective pressure; from everyone, including the UN and the international community, all at the same time [. . .], his trump card will be to release Daw Aung San Suu Kyi and a few political prisoners for show. As soon as they are released, the international pressure will be reduced. As for Burmese politics, [the Generals] know very well that nothing can be done without Daw Aung San Suu Kyi. So when Daw Aung San Suu Kyi is free, if there is systematic support from people inside and outside, they will inevitably have to hold a dialogue.

Those words have proven prescient. Nevertheless, even with a dialogue beginning and Aung San Suu Kyi participating in the political process, the role of the army is crucial. He emphasised that more should be done to encourage soldiers to abandon the regime. 'In the army, it is not how people think it is, not all soldiers [are against democracy]. There are many people in the army who want the country to prosper, there are many people who want the country to progress. I would say that at least the level below major general – if the situation favours it, if there is trust – would not hesitate to join hands with pro-democracy people. Therefore, we have to think how we are going to entice soldiers and officers below the rank of major general.'[24]

On a few occasions inside Burma, I have met serving military officers, and based on surface impressions of the ones I have encountered, I would be inclined to agree with Aung Lynn Htut. Coming face to face with soldiers is a helpful reminder that it is the system, the regime, that is brutal, and that often people within it, especially at lower ranks, are trapped in a cruel system perhaps against their better judgement.

On one visit to Rangoon, I found myself invited to visit the home of a Burmese family I met by chance. Upon entering their home, I noticed a military uniform hanging on the wall, and so, trying to sound as innocent and naive as possible, I asked: 'Is one of your family serving in the army?' The father, who had welcomed me warmly with a generous smile, nodded. 'Yes, I am. I am Regimental Sergeant Major.' He told me he had served in some of the ethnic states, and in my mind I reflected on what terrible acts he may have had to take part in. As he walked me to the bus stop later, I asked what background the other residents of the area came from. 'All are military,' he said with a smile. 'This is a military camp.' Unwittingly, I had found myself amongst the Tatmadaw, and had they known who I was I am sure the welcome would not have been so friendly. Yet the basic humanity of a man, and his family, working within such an inhumane system illustrates the tragic set of contrasts with which Burma wrestles on a daily basis.

On another visit, I was in a cafe in Maymyo and a Tatmadaw officer walked in, accompanied by two Caucasian women. They sat at the next table, and he struck up a conversation. After building up some rapport, I asked innocently what the two ladies were doing in Maymyo. 'Oh, they are Russian,' he said. Then, volunteering perhaps more information than he should have done, he added: 'They are teaching Russian language at the Defense Services Academy.' I had been told that Russian experts were assisting the Burma Army, and here was confirmation.

Aung Lynn Htut's message is one that the democracy movement and the international community need to listen to. Defectors and deserters have not been given the support and encouragement they need, and yet they are a vital, though much overlooked, part of the struggle. They provide a valuable source of intelligence, not only about human rights violations perpetrated by the Tatmadaw, but also about Burma's wider militarisation, the alleged use of chemical and biological weaponry, the reported development of a nuclear programme, sources of arms and the regime's reliance on the drugs trade. Furthermore, they can play a crucial role in weakening the regime. Some might even argue that the situation in Burma will never change unless there is a major split in the military and mass desertions. More should therefore be done to reassure those who take the brave decision to defect that they will receive the protection they need. If Thein Sein's gradual reform process should stall, the role of defectors will be more important than ever.

The Torture Chambers

'Remember those in prison as if you were their fellow prisoners, and those who are ill-treated as if you yourselves were suffering'

Hebrews 13: 3

WHEN WAIHNIN PWINT Thon was born her father, Mya Aye, was in prison. He had been one of the leaders of the 1988 student uprising, and was held for a month in Maymyo. Although he was briefly released, he was then given an eight-year prison sentence and jailed when Waihnin was five months old. She was four years old in 1993 when she saw him again. 'In between, I only saw photographs,' she recalls. 'It was very difficult. I was always wondering why my father never came home.'

One day, Waihnin's mother told her that they were going to visit her father. 'It was a big building, and I thought wow, this is my father's home. I didn't know it was a prison,' she says. Waihnin and her mother were given just half an hour with him, and the little four-year-old girl was longing to embrace her father. 'I waited for the moment when he could hug me, but he was behind iron bars and so he could not reach me.'

For the first six years of his sentence, Mya Aye was held in the notorious Insein Prison in Rangoon. The family could visit him every week. However, for the final two years he was moved to Taungoo, Bago Division, more than 200 kilometres away. In 1997, he was finally released, and immediately resumed his political activism.

His daughter, Waihnin, left Burma in 2006, to study in the United Kingdom. That same year her father organised a petition calling for the release of political prisoners, signed by 530,000 people.[1] Readers of *Burma Digest* elected him 'Politician of the Year'. In March 2007, he helped organise the 'White Sunday' campaign, where protestors dressed in white and visited the families of political prisoners.[2] A few months later, during the protests that became known as the 'Saffron Revolution', Waihnin spoke to her father on the telephone one evening. 'He seemed very positive,' she recalls.

A few hours after talking to her father, Waihnin received a call from the BBC's Burmese service. 'They told me my father had been arrested. I argued with them, saying "No, that's not possible, I just talked to him,"' she recalls. 'I called my mother, but the phone was disconnected. A day later, she called me. He had been taken in for questioning.' For two months, the family heard nothing, and then they were informed that he had been jailed in Insein Prison, along with other leaders of what had become known as the '88 Generation Students Group, including Min Ko Naing and Ko Ko Gyi. A trial was held in the jail, and he faced twenty-one charges.

On 11 November 2008, he was sentenced to sixty-five years in prison, along with thirteen other activists.[3] These included prominent leaders such as Min Ko Naing, Ko Jimmy and Ko Ko Gyi. It is worth remembering that eleven is said to be Senior General Than Shwe's lucky number by astrologers – hence the choice of date, the eleventh day of the eleventh month, and the length of the sentence, because six and five equal eleven. Mya Aye was moved to a jail in Loikaw, Karenni State, 350 kilometres north-east of Rangoon, making it extremely difficult – and prohibitively expensive – for Waihnin's mother to visit. He was subsequently transferred to Taunggyi, southern Shan State, in 2010. 'Unless the situation in Burma changes, I will never see my father again,' Waihnin told me.

Until the second half of 2011, there seemed little prospect of change in Burma and little chance that the regime would release political prisoners. However, after President Thein Sein indicated his desire to take the country in a different direction, the international community made it clear that the release of political prisoners had to be a priority. Sanctions would not be lifted until all political prisoners were released. In October 2011, therefore, the regime freed approximately 200, including the comedian Zarganar and the labour activist Su Su Nway. On 3 January a further thirty-three were released, but they did not include any of the '88 Generation Students

Group leaders. Waihnin's hopes had been raised and then dashed – she was living on an almost permanent emotional rollercoaster.

Ten days later, however, Thein Sein took his boldest step so far, and freed the most prominent dissidents: Min Ko Naing, Ko Ko Gyi, Ko Jimmy, Ko Htay Kywe, and Waihnin's father, Ko Mya Aye. I was flying to Bangkok that morning, and I heard the news before I boarded my flight. I called Waihnin in celebration. Two weeks later, in Rangoon, I had the privilege of meeting her father and family, as well as many of the '88 Generation leaders. I was struck by how they had not only survived prison and its horrific conditions, but had emerged with their minds clear and their commitment to their struggle intact and strengthened. Just two weeks after their release, they talked to me with an extraordinary and impressive clarity. They gave no thought to their own welfare or rehabilitation – they were focused intently on resuming their activities and contributing to the country's reform.

Yet also, remarkably, they showed no bitterness. When I discussed with Htay Kywe the question of whether the regime should be held to account and brought to justice for its crimes, he acknowledged that truth-seeking was necessary – but for the purposes of reconciliation and preventing the recurrence of such crimes, not for revenge. 'We can forgive,' he said, 'but we cannot forget.' He emphasised his desire to work with reform-minded people in the government. The regime is fortunate to have such generous and gracious opponents.

While their release was certainly a bold move by Thein Sein and a response to international pressure, it is important to make one cautionary note. They were released under Section 401 of the Criminal Code – which meant, technically, a temporary suspension of their sentences, which could be cancelled at any time. That means they still have a criminal record, making them ineligible for any government employment; they are denied passports; and there is no provision at all for their rehabilitation. It may well be that Thein Sein had a battle with hardliners over these releases, and that this was the only mechanism he could use to do it – but it also means that until there is fundamental institutional and legislative change in Burma, dissidents like the '88 Generation leaders will always be vulnerable to re-arrest and re-imprisonment. When I met Ko Ko Gyi, I invited him to speak at a conference outside Burma that I was helping to organise. He replied by telling me that he, and other '88 Generation leaders, were denied passports. He said if the European Union, for example, was to lift the ban on visas for members of the regime, they should at the same time demand that the regime issue passports to former political prisoners to allow them to travel overseas. This has since changed, but only after a lot of advocacy.

I asked Min Ko Naing, the best-known dissident in Burma after Aung San Suu Kyi, how he had survived spending more than twenty years in prison. He reminded me that for fifteen years, he had been kept in total solitary confinement, denied any contact with another human being at all. Even the guards, when they brought food to his cell, turned their backs to him as they handed it through the bars. They had been ordered not to make eye contact with him. His answer to my question was three-fold: 'My Buddhist faith, a sense of humour, and my commitment to the cause.'

Yet as remarkable as the courage of those in prison was, they were not the only victims of the regime's cruelty. Their families suffered, often in silence, and often unknown. Their courage and commitment is worth observing as well.

Despite all the suffering inflicted on her father and the entire family, Waihnin herself became a campaigner for democracy. Using the freedom she has in Britain, she is a prominent activist, speaking at hearings in Parliament and at demonstrations. In 2008, she was part of a delegation of Burmese activists who met the then Prime Minister Gordon Brown. When the regime found out, they increased their harassment of Waihnin's family. But Waihnin shares her father's passion for the struggle and is determined not to waiver. 'I don't blame my father. What he is doing is for all our lives. He is trying to bring change,' she said. 'I shouldn't blame my father, I blame the government. It is the government that has separated us. All I want is to see change in Burma, so I can see my father again.'

The suffering inflicted on the families of political prisoners in Burma is unimaginable. In addition to the emotional trauma caused by separation, families face severe financial hardship. Sometimes this is because the main breadwinner for the family has been imprisoned, but often it is compounded by serious discrimination against family members in the workplace. Employers regard relatives of political prisoners with suspicion and fear, concerned about the consequences for their business if they have people associated with activism in their workforce. Relatives of political prisoners who run their own businesses often find customers are intimidated into boycotting them, or are forced to sign statements disowning the political prisoners and disassociating themselves from their views. In a further, deliberate act of cruelty, many prisoners were jailed in locations hundreds of miles from their families, making it extremely difficult and expensive to make visits.

Despite the release of several hundred political prisoners, hundreds more still remain in jail. The conditions in which political prisoners are held are unimaginable. Burma has forty-four prisons and at least fifty labour camps, according to the Assistance Association for Political Prisoners (AAPP). Until 2011, there were an estimated 2,000 political prisoners, a figure which is now closer to 1,000.

Some political prisoners were sentenced for extraordinarily long terms, and until a new dawn appeared to break in 2011, they faced the prospect of spending the rest of their lives in jail. Bo Min Yu Ko, a member of the All Burma Federation of Student Unions (ABFSU), was sentenced on 3 January 2009 to 104 years. He was denied access to a lawyer, and his family were not permitted to attend the trial.[4] Khun Htun Oo, chairman of the Shan Nationalities League for Democracy (SNLD), a party which won twenty-three seats in the 1990 elections, was sentenced in 2005 to ninety-three years. According to a message from him in 2009, smuggled out of prison, he reminded the world that 'we didn't commit any crime. We reaffirm our aim to empower our people to bring peace, justice and equality to the people.'[5] Both were released in January 2012.

Why are activists jailed? For the very simple reason that they speak their minds, or they enable others to speak theirs – nothing more. Some are very prominent, such as Min Ko Naing, or the comedian Zarganar, jailed for fifty-nine years (later reduced to thirty-five) for criticising the regime's slow response to Cyclone Nargis in 2008. Zarganar, released in October 2011 as part of the regime's efforts to signal reform, had been jailed after organising a relief effort for victims of the cyclone, and was a known democracy activist who had been imprisoned several times before.[6] One of his most famous jokes was this: 'Every country has a success story to tell. Some like to boast about a citizen with no hands who can still write, or another with no legs who can still run. But there is no other country like Burma. Here we have generals able to rule a country for forty years with no brains!'[7] One can understand why the regime did not really like him.

Zarganar has an extraordinary memory for people, facts and jokes, says Htein Lin, an artist who is a close friend of his and who himself spent several years in prison. Zarganar's jokes came to him naturally and were not, it seems, simply restricted to his performances. Most were directed at the regime, and sailed very close to the wind. Htein Lin recalls: 'One day on the phone he said to me, "Htein Lin, do you know instant baby?" I said, "Oh my God, what is instant baby?" He replied: "Oh you're stupid. Don't you understand instant coffee and instant noodle? You just open the packet and pour boiling water. Well, two months ago Senior General Than Shwe's daughter got married, and within just two months she has a baby: instant baby."'[8] On another occasion, when Min Ko Naing and other dissidents had launched a campaign in which everyone wore white, Zarganar told Htein Lin: 'While we have this white campaign, the regime has invented white Internet – you just open the computer and you can see nothing but white!' Even the tapping of his phone is turned into a joke. 'I am very lucky,' Zarganar told Htein Lin. 'If I want to tell anything to the government, I can just pick up the phone and talk to anyone. I have a special way to contact the government.'

Su Su Nway was the first Burmese to sue the regime successfully for using forced labour – and was jailed for her efforts. After two years in jail, she was released, only to be returned to prison a year later for her role in the Saffron Revolution. She was sentenced to twelve and a half years, but was freed in 2011.

Nilar Thein is another prominent prisoner. A campaigner in both the 1988 protests and the Saffron Revolution, she is married to Ko Jimmy. They had a baby in 2007, but when their daughter, Nay Kyi or 'Sunshine', was just five months old Nilar Thein was forced to go into hiding. She took Sunshine with her at first, but the baby's cries risked giving Nilar Thein away, and so Ko Jimmy's elderly mother looked after her. The BBC's Andrew Harding reported in September 2007:

> Their apartment is now guarded by plain-clothed policemen. Two at the door. Two outside. Two across the road. They are waiting to see if Nilar will come back for something rather precious – her five-month-old daughter . . . One night recently, Nilar sneaked back close

enough to hear her baby crying through an open window. 'They are using her as bait,' she said. 'I should be breastfeeding her. But I cannot give in.' She is, a friend told me admiringly, a stubborn woman.[8]

At the time, Nilar Thein said, with defiance mixed with natural human emotion any mother would feel: 'I [was] so choked up with feeling when I had to leave my daughter with my mother-in-law. It [would] not be wrong to say it was the worst day of my life . . . [yet] I don't regret it at all. I don't because just like my daughter I see many faces of children in my country who lack a future. With that I encourage myself to continue this journey.'[9] Almost a year later, Nilar Thein was arrested,[10] and a few months later was sentenced to sixty-five years in jail along with her husband, Ko Jimmy. They were held in different prisons and didn't see each other for over four years. When they were released in January 2012, they had an emotional reunion at Rangoon airport. Two weeks later, I had the privilege of meeting Ko Jimmy. I didn't have the heart to subject him to a detailed political interview; instead, I simply asked him how his wife and child were doing. He smiled, and said they were well.

Other female political prisoners can relate to Nilar Thein's experience. Nita May discovered she was pregnant two months after she had been jailed in 1990. She had been sentenced to three years hard labour, and was held in solitary confinement. Despite being pregnant, she was required to carry out tasks around the jail. 'I was forced to scrub the floors, water the plants, clear the moss from the prison gardens,' she recalls. When she was arrested, at least twenty military intelligence and police officers came to her house, in the middle of the night. 'Arresting one woman with nothing to defend herself – not even a pin! I felt for the first time what the term "helpless" means. You are on your own, nobody can help you.' Even though she worked for the British embassy, not even the ambassador could help her while she was in jail. Despite this, during this time in prison, and her previous detention in 1989, she never betrayed her contacts. 'I didn't name anyone. Nobody was taken in because of me. I sealed my lips, and thought "You can do anything to me, but I won't name any of my associates."'

Another female activist, Mie Mie, a zoology graduate and mother of two children, was arrested on 14 October 2007 after her leading role in the Saffron Revolution. She is alleged to have yelled 'We will never be frightened!' at the judges when she was sentenced to sixty-five years in prison. She had already endured five years in jail for her involvement in the protests in 1996.[11]

Yee Yee Htun was sentenced to fourteen years in prison for her involvement in the 1996 protests. When she was arrested, she was blindfolded, handcuffed and taken to an interrogation centre. Denied a bath for ten days, she was in Insein Prison for eleven months, and then transferred to Tharawaddy Prison. In perhaps one of the worst forms of torment, poisonous snakes regularly came into her cell. 'When snakes came into my cell I shouted for help, but the prison staff did not come. It was a form of torture,' she says. 'I had a fear of snakes and rats, and they both came into my cell often.' She also discovered that the shower room had a peephole. 'Prison guards secretly watched us as we washed.' Along with Nilar Thein, Yee Yee complained to the prison authorities, wrote to the Interior Ministry and informed the International Committee of the Red Cross (ICRC). Three months later, after an ICRC visit, the peephole was covered up.

One of the youngest female political prisoners was Su Mon Aye, sent to Insein Prison in 2000 at the age of just nineteen. As a student she had participated in the 1996 protests, after which the universities were closed for four years. Not able to continue her studies at university, she engaged in political activity, joined the NLD youth wing, and attended discussion groups led by Aung San Suu Kyi to enable young people to continue their education. On the night of her arrest, twenty soldiers, police and township authorities raided her home. 'I was nineteen years old, and very small and skinny. They were more than forty years old – but they look at me as an "enemy",' she recalls. Despite her youth, Su Mon Aye showed remarkable courage and intelligence. 'I asked if they had a warrant to search my room, and the soldier said "Oh, you are very clever!" I told them that if they wanted to enter my room they should show the warrant.' Ignoring her, the soldiers and police pushed past, and gathered everything they could find, including NLD photographs and documents, and an award that Aung San Suu Kyi had presented to her for a poetry competition.

During her interrogation, Su Mon Aye was repeatedly asked to sign a document renouncing her political activities. 'I told them I would not sign because it would be a lie. I could not promise not to be involved,' she says. She also reminded them why she had become involved. 'If the universities had stayed open and we had stayed studying, I would not be here.' Hooded and beaten, she was kept in a cell on death row, and repeatedly told that if she signed a paper promising not to engage in more political activity, she could be released. For four months her parents did not know where she was. Sleeping on a cold concrete floor with no clean clothes and no medical assistance during her period, she sank into depression. But she never gave in.

When physical cruelty failed, the authorities tried 'good cop' tactics. Knowing that Su Mon Aye was struggling with prison conditions, they tried to tempt her with good food. 'The prison food was really horrible, and I told them that not even dogs would eat it. So one day they took me into a beautiful dining room, with a sofa and many dishes on the table. I had never seen such delicious curry before,' she describes. 'When I saw the food, I could not stand it – I really wanted to eat it. But they told me that I had to give them two things first: sign the document renouncing my political involvement, and give information about my colleagues. I would have to betray my people.' In such circumstances, faced with a choice of grim prison conditions or delicious food and the prospect of release, the temptation must have been immense. Remarkably, she stayed firm. 'I told them I wanted to eat this kind of food, but I had no information to give them. I told them I wanted to go back to my cell. I could not betray my people. Back in my cell, I started trying to eat the prison food.' Five months after her arrest universities reopened, and again the authorities tried to tempt her to sign a promise not to participate in politics. 'I smiled, and asked: "Can you promise the university will not close again?" That made them really angry, they told me I was a stupid girl and that they could not promise that. So I told them that I could not promise not to be involved in politics. "If the university closes again, where should I go? I will protest again and be imprisoned again. It's like a cycle."' Upon her release a year later, Su Mon Aye became a reporter in Burma, and then went to work for Radio Free Asia in Bangkok.

The longest-serving political prisoner in Burma until his release in 2008 was U Win Tin. One of the most senior leaders of the NLD, a close associate of Aung San Suu Kyi and a writer, U Win Tin was arrested in 1989. When he was released at the age of seventy-nine he had served nineteen years and three months in solitary confinement. For much of that time he was kept in a cell that had originally been a dog kennel, and was refused bedding. 'The first three or so years were horrid, like hell,' he told Andrew Buncombe of the *Independent*. 'I was tortured, I was interrogated . . . On one occasion they questioned me for five days and five nights non-stop. I was not allowed to sleep or eat.' He witnessed fellow prisoners die. 'Many, many of my friends are dead. I saw them die,' he said. Yet remarkably, like others, he kept his mind focused, writing poems and stories for other prisoners, and even saw his original sentence increase in 1996 when he wrote to the United Nations revealing prison conditions. 'I don't know how I kept my sanity, but I knew I had to work.'[12]

British photographer and activist James Mackay met U Win Tin a year after his release, and photographed him for a global campaign for political prisoners called 'Even Though I'm free, I am not'. Mackay photographed hundreds of former political prisoners, many of them in Burma, each with the name of a current prisoner written on the palm of their hand. His iconic picture of U Win Tin, with Aung San Suu Kyi's name written in black marker pen on his raised palm, made international headlines. But it was U Win Tin's personality that made the opportunity so special for Mackay. 'When U Win Tin arrived at our meeting place, he had this beautiful, broad, beaming smile. Even though he was in quite poor health, he was really vibrant. He realised the power of the picture, and wanted the whole message conveyed to the outside world,' recalls Mackay. The encounter involved careful planning, confidentiality and considerable risk for all involved, particularly U Win Tin, who could easily have been put back in jail for meeting a foreign photographer at that time. 'At any moment he could be hauled away to jail, but that's not going to stop him,' says Mackay. 'He spent nineteen years in prison, his teeth were bashed out, he was in solitary confinement, and yet he sat in front of me saying "I don't mind going back." He refuses to change his opinions. He had this aura of complete invincibility, amazing strength of character, and it rubs off on you, giving you a strength as well.' He is followed everywhere, and in one comic scene during their meeting at the top of a high-rise building, a man appeared at the window. 'We were twenty-four floors up, it was pouring with rain outside, and suddenly this man appears, pretending to clean the windows. It was not even subtle – he was staring straight at us. We looked at each other and decided that was a sign to move.'

Less well-known political prisoners include an Internet blogger, Nay Myo Kyaw, who wrote articles online using the pseudonym Nay Phone Latt. He owned three Internet cafes, and according to *The Times* his blog simply described day-to-day difficulties in Rangoon, and was not explicitly political. He was jailed for twenty years. Saw Wai, who wrote a poem that was a veiled critique of Than Shwe, was given a two year sentence. Even their defence lawyer, Aung Thein, was jailed for four months.[13] In 2009, six months after filming a shocking documentary about the fate of children orphaned in Cyclone Nargis, a cameraman was arrested and charged with a new offence of filming without permission – carrying a minimum jail term of ten years.[14] And when a group of villagers in Natmauk, central Burma, filed a complaint that the Tatmadaw had occupied their land, eight of the villagers were arrested, and although some were released, one man, Zaw Htay, was charged under the Official Secrets Act for approaching a prohibited area and making a record that might be useful to an enemy.[15] On 31 December 2009 an undercover reporter for the exiled Democratic Voice of Burma, Hla Hla Win, was sentenced to twenty years in prison for breaching the Electronic Act. She had already received a seven-year sentence a few months previously, which she was serving when the twenty-year term was added. According to the Burma Media Association, at least fourteen undercover reporters were arrested in Burma in 2009.[16]

With the help of a Burmese interpreter, I spoke by phone to relatives of some of these prisoners in 2010. All of them were jailed in remote prisons far from their families, and most are suffering serious medical conditions. Pyone Cho, otherwise known as Htay Win Aung, whom I subsequently met after his release in 2012, was in an eight foot by twelve foot cell in Kawthaung Prison, in the southernmost part of Burma, near the Thai border. It is one-and-a-half days' journey from Rangoon, but because there is no train or bus, it can only be reached by plane, which is prohibitively expensive. Before his release concerns were growing about his health: he was suffering high blood pressure and gastric problems, but was receiving no medical treatment and was denied exercise. He was reliant on the medicines his wife brought when she visited, but she was only allowed to visit once a month for half an hour. The guards watched them closely during each visit.

When Pyone Cho's wife travelled to Kawthaung, she was only permitted to stay for a maximum of four days at a time. She tried to stay longer with the families of NLD activists, but the authorities were afraid that she would establish contact with democracy groups based on the Thai border, and ordered her to return to Rangoon. The couple had only been married four months before Pyone Cho was jailed.

Min Ko Naing was also in bad health and his relatives expressed their concern about him in our telephone conversation. Held in Kengtung Prison, Shan State, more than 1,000 miles from Rangoon, he also suffered from high blood pressure, as well as gout and a serious eye ailment, and was denied medical treatment or exercise. Food parcels sent by relatives were destroyed in the post, and they were only permitted a twenty-minute visit, once a month. Min Ko Naing previously spent fourteen years in prison. When I met him two weeks after his release in January 2012, he appeared in remarkable form considering what he had been through, but it was clear that he was not in good health.

Htay Kywe was held in Buthidaung Prison, in Arakan State over 700 miles from Rangoon. It cost his relatives almost 800 US dollars each time they travelled to Buthidaung, and when they got there they were only allowed twenty-five minutes with Htay Kywe, with guards standing right beside them. The prison had no electricity, and no doctor. Food parcels sent by the family took five days to reach him, but the postal authorities opened the parcels to check them and didn't put the contents back properly – so the food went bad. He had previously spent twelve years in prison. 'His belief is very strong, his commitment is very strong,' a family member told me at the time. 'But there is a chance he may die in prison.' Thankfully, he too was released in 2012 and when I met him his resilience and renewed commitment inspired me greatly.

Many political prisoners have died in prison. The Assistance Association for Political Prisoners (AAPP), in its report 'Burma's Prisons and Labour Camps: Silent Killing Fields', claimed that at least 139 democracy activists have died in detention, 'as a direct result of severe torture, denial of medical treatment, and inadequate medical care'.[17] In May 2005, for example, Aung Hlaing Win died six days after being arrested. 'According to the autopsy, confirmed by four medical specialists from North Okkalapa Hospital, thirty-year-old Aung Hlaing Win died before he got to the hospital and was sent to the hospital as a corpse,' the AAPP's report 'Eight Seconds of

Silence: The Death of Democracy Activists Behind Bars' claims. Doctors found twenty-four external wounds, three fractured ribs and a fourth rib 'broken in two causing bruising to his heart'. Bruising was also found around his throat and trachea, and his stomach and colon were 'decaying'. He was diagnosed as having died of a heart attack.[18]

The denial of medical treatment for sick prisoners is perhaps one of the harshest policies of the regime. In October 2006, Thet Win Aung died in prison after contracting cerebral malaria at Kham Ti Prison in Sagaing Division. He received no treatment before his death.[19] On 23 December 2009 thirty-eight-year-old Tin Tin Htwe Ma Pae died in Insein Prison, after a ruptured aneurysm.[20] In December 2009 it was reported that the Buddhist monk U Gambira, a leader of the Saffron Revolution and founding member of the All Burma Monks Alliance, was suffering malaria. He was held in Kale Prison, Sagaing Division, over 1,000 miles from Rangoon,[21] serving a sixty-eight-year sentence. After one three-day journey to visit him when he was held in Hkamti Prison, before he was moved to the even more remote location of Kale, his mother said: 'The trip from Mandalay to [Hkamti] prison was like being sent to hell alive. My life, and my family's life, is just like clockwork now. We eat and sleep like robots. There is no life in our bodies. The ordeal we are going through – it's a punishment for our entire family.'[22] U Gambira was released in January 2012, but just a few weeks after he was freed, he faced fresh charges of breaking and entering a monastery that had been sealed by the authorities. He was briefly detained in February 2012, and then released again with further legal action pending. His case shows how fragile Thein Sein's 'reform process' is.

On 2 May 2008 Cyclone Nargis hit Burma – the worst natural disaster in the country's recent history. The storm ripped off the roofs of some of the cells at Insein Prison, leaving prisoners exposed to heavy rains and wind for several hours. They protested, urging the prison guards to move them to another cell, and they threatened to break out if they were not relocated. Armed guards fired shots into the air to calm the prisoners' disturbance, but a bullet hit one prisoner, Thein San, according to witnesses. The guards then beat the prisoners severely, and denied them water for four days and food for eleven days. 'They told us they would give us food if we confessed,' one prisoner told Radio Free Asia. 'But even after some confessed, we didn't get any food. Then, eleven days later, we began to receive a spoonful of rice puree twice a day.' Nine prisoners died as a result of this mistreatment.[23]

These accounts are confirmed by Radio Free Asia, which the UNHCR has also cited. Radio Free Asia reported in March 2009 that: 'Burma's political prisoners – many of them serving lengthy jail terms for their part in the 1988 pro-democracy movement – face harsh conditions in remote prisons where family visits are limited and food supply strictly controlled by the authorities.'[24] Sometimes food parcels brought by relatives are refused, depending on the whim of the prison governor.

Most barbaric, almost medieval, of all are the forms of torture inflicted on prisoners. 'I was sentenced to three years hard labour. I was interrogated and tortured for thirty-six hours,' Bo Kyi, founder of AAPP told Phil Thornton.[25] 'I was given no food or water, and was kept handcuffed and blindfolded. I was put in a small cell. I could see blood and many names, including those of my friends, on the walls. I was not allowed to shower for nine days.' His cell was just three by three metres, with 'blood spattered on the walls' and he was subjected to regular beatings. 'I was blindfolded and repeatedly interrogated. After each answer I gave, I was punched in the stomach so hard it knocked me to the ground. Every time I was forced to stand up and take it, over and over again. I lost all track of time.'[26] On other occasions he was whipped with a rubber cord about an inch in diameter. 'After being hit 150 times, I lost consciousness. When I woke up, I was taken in chains to a solitary confinement cell. I was then forced to assume various *ponsan* positions for one hour at a time, twice a day,' he recalls. *Ponsan* is the term referring to a position sitting absolutely vertical, cross-legged with arms straightened out and both fists on the knees, with the face downward. 'For twelve days I had to perform the same *ponsan* routine, while remaining in chains which encircled my waist and were attached to an iron bar between my legs. I had sores and bruises on my ankles, forehead, elbows and knees. During that time I was also made to "hop like a frog" whilst in chains.'[27]

The regime uses a variety of forms of torture. According to a report by the AAPP, 'The Darkness We See: Torture in Burma's Interrogation Centers and Prisons', 'it is not possible to separate physical torture from psychological torture, as most torture is intended to simultaneously inflict physical and psychological harm'.[28] The degrading humiliation begins from the moment political detainees are arrested, usually in the middle of the night with a knock on the door. As is described in 'The Darkness We See . . .':

> They show no warrant; there is no need for legal matters when the authorities decide to take you away. You are hooded and handcuffed; now you must rely entirely on your captors. You are made to lie down in the back of a van, a gun held at your back . . . You are not told where you are going, and there is no point in asking. Suddenly, the van stops and you hear the cruel voices of your captors ordering you to get out, to jump, to duck, to twist, to turn, all for their amusement. You are taken to a small room where the torture begins.[29]

Typically, according to this report, a prisoner is stripped naked and beaten unconscious. 'You are awakened when your captors drench you with a bucket of water. The beatings begin again. This time a rod is run up and down your shins until you scream out in agony as your flesh peels off. Your captors are laughing and threatening to kill you and your family. You remain hooded and handcuffed, unable to defend yourself or move away.'[30]

A common form of torture is forcing prisoners to sit in excruciating positions for many hours without moving. 'You are forced to hold unnatural positions for extended periods of time until you collapse,' the AAPP reports. These include pretending to ride a motorcycle or fly an aeroplane. 'You are denied food, water, sleep and must beg to use the toilet. You are degraded, bruised and battered. Your entire existence is reduced to the struggle to survive.'[31]

Torture is particularly severe in the interrogation centre, where prisoners are held before being jailed. Moe Aye spent two months in an interrogation centre in 1990, before being sentenced to seven years in Insein Prison for his involvement in the 1988 demonstrations. 'The interrogation centre is worse than prison,' he explains. 'In prison you can see the sky, you can see light, you can see other people, and you can talk to other inmates. In the interrogation centre, they put a blindfold on you. I never knew day or night for two months. If I wanted to go to the toilet, someone would have to show the way. It was very tiring.' He was also subjected to sleep deprivation, held in stocks, and tortured with a hot metal rod on his wrist.

'When they left the room, I took the blindfold off and checked my wrist. My skin was burnt and blistered.'

In September 2009, Myo Yan Naung Thein was released after two years in prison. His description of what happened fits with almost every other account. After being hooded, kicked and beaten, he was forced 'to kneel on all fours like a dog'. One of the interrogators then sat on Myo Yan Naung Thein's back. 'They tortured me very brutally,' he said. 'My hands were tied behind my back, they kicked and punched me. They locked me in a dark, wet room with no windows . . . One of my legs was deteriorating day by day . . . And now I cannot stand up or walk. I can only walk if I have a person on either side to help me.' But, with extraordinary defiance typical of Burmese political prisoners, he expressed a resolve to continue. 'After we were imprisoned, we learned more and more about the injustices carried out by the military government, and that strengthened my beliefs even more. So who will keep fighting if we don't? We have to carry on.'[32]

Being forced to sit as a dog, or worse, being jailed in a dog kennel, is again not uncommon. Zarganar was imprisoned briefly after supporting the Buddhist monks in 2007, and he told Human Rights Watch: 'I was held in the dog cells in solitary confinement for eight days and was not allowed to bathe for three days. I had to relieve myself on a tray. When it became full, I tried to urinate under the door but the dogs tried to bite me.'[33]

Eyewitnesses I have spoken to say that conditions in Burma's labour camps are even worse. Prisoners are forced to work on road construction projects, and rubber and tea plantations, shackled like slaves. In one camp in Chin State, prisoners are yoked like oxen and forced to plough the fields.[34] Known as *yebet sakhan*, it is estimated by some that there are at least 110 such camps, containing between 50,000 and 100,000 prisoners. Some inmates are convicted criminals, although others are jailed for petty crimes – one boy, for example, was sent without trial to a labour camp because he took a horse out for a 'joy ride' and was accused of stealing. According to a man who claims to have visited over thirty of these labour camps,[35] taking medical and food aid to prisoners, they have to keep their heads bowed at all times. If they look up, they are beaten, and if they cry out, they are beaten again. Sleep deprivation is routine. In at least four camps, each prisoner has an empty milk can attached to the end of his bed, and every fifteen minutes throughout the night he is required to strike the can and shout his personal number, to prove he has not escaped.[36] Held in leg-irons, prisoners suffer constant chafing causing lacerations, inflammation and infections. They are forced to work from 6 a.m. until 6 p.m. without a rest, except for one meal a day which may consist of a spoon of boiled rice mixed with wild banana leaf and sweet potato leaf. Prisoners are so hungry that they eat rats,[37] pigswill and some, reportedly, eat their own faeces.[38] 'One man was so malnourished and thin that you could see his intestines moving, looking like worms,' he told me.[39]

Harsh punishments are dealt out to anyone contemplating escape. Some who have attempted to escape have had their hands tied behind their backs and then been dragged along the ground 'like a dead animal', says the pastor. Others have had burning bamboo placed alongside them so that they are slowly 'roasted'.[40] In 2003 at Cang El Zawl Prison in Sagaing Division, soldiers invited prisoners to escape, as a set-up to provide an example to others who might be thinking of attempting it. When they were caught, because they were unable to run fast enough in their leg-irons, they were re-arrested, and placed over a very hot fire. They were then stabbed repeatedly, and put in a tub of salt water. Most of them died.[41]

Even apart from the physical torture, the conditions of prison cells in Burma are almost unbearable. 'You are placed in a cell with five of your colleagues, two criminals and several rats. You are given undercooked and dirty food to eat. You sleep on the cold concrete. Your toilet is a small pot which overflows, creating maggots and a foul, nauseating smell. You are allowed seven plates of water to wash yourself. You have nothing to read, no mental stimulation.'[42]

Khun Saing confirms these conditions. When he was jailed for the second time, in 1990, accused of being a communist, he was tortured in Insein Prison. His trial was held in the prison, and he was brought into the court hooded and handcuffed. When his hood was removed, he found he was surrounded by armed soldiers. 'It was a military court, with judges in army uniforms,' he told me. He was held in an eight- by twelve-foot cell with seven other prisoners, and allowed out for only fifteen minutes a day, for a shower.

Khun Saing was jailed for a third time in 1998. Among the prisoners he shared a cell with, some had HIV/AIDS, tuberculosis and leprosy. Khun Saing contracted tuberculosis as a result, but had to struggle to receive medical treatment. In Shwe Bo Prison near Mandalay, where he was held, there was no doctor, and he had to wait four months before receiving any attention. When he was finally allowed to visit a local hospital, the doctor refused to see him. 'I was in ankle chains and a prison suit,' he recalls. 'I think she thought I was a criminal.' However, after some persuasion, the hospital X-rayed him, but then claimed he was in good health. Using his own medical knowledge, he pointed out a clear 'shadowy ring' on the X-ray, showing a tuberculosis cavity on the middle lobe of his lung. He bribed the prison staff to send the X-ray to Mandalay for examination, as there were no radiologists in Shwe Bo. The result came back – a clear case of tuberculosis. The prison authorities relented, and he was given proper treatment.[43]

Despite the restrictions, political prisoners show an extraordinary degree of ingenuity in finding ways to communicate with each other. According to Khun Saing, they pass messages to each other on tiny pieces of paper, using toothpaste or a small piece of lead from a pencil – 'very easy to hide,' he says. For paper, prisoners improvise, using labels from a piece of bread, leaves, the backs of plates, or cheroots. 'Then we pass the plates by using the criminal prisoners as messengers, and we give them bribes such as a cheroot,' Khun Saing says. Criminal prisoners – as opposed to political detainees – are given jobs by prison authorities, such as cleaning parts of the jail, and so they are able to move around the prison in a way that the political prisoners are not. 'Sometimes we used cheroots to write important information in, and then we ask other prisoners to take this cheroot to this cell, this cheroot to that cell. In this way we can communicate.' Political prisoners who are allowed out of their cell to shower, for fifteen minutes, take the opportunity to exchange news and information with other prisoners too. 'When we get the chance to pass all the cells, we throw [small pieces of paper with information on] to other prisoners. It's a chance of three or four seconds,' says Khun Saing.

In addition to communicating with each other, political prisoners use their time to think, meditate, paint, study and write – again, with ingenuity. Khun Saing composed songs, which were smuggled out by other prisoners who had been released. The AAPP made the songs into an album, called 'Songs from the Cage'. He also taught himself English by reading books provided by the Red Cross. Although he is a Buddhist, he read the entire

Bible in English, twice.[44] Similarly, Bo Kyi had an English dictionary smuggled in, so that he could study. 'I ate the pages as I learned them,' he said. 'I also learned I had no future. It [jail] taught me to live in the present, otherwise I would have gone crazy thinking about the future.'[45]

Tin Aye, who was sentenced to twenty years in jail in 1989, taught himself English in prison. 'I read newspapers, secretly, and when we couldn't get any newspapers, I would ask other people who spoke English to teach me some vocabulary. I learned three words a day,' he told me when I met him on the Thailand–Burma border in 2010. In 1999 he was released after completing ten years as part of a partial amnesty, but it was, he says, a 'sham' release. 'At the gate of Mandalay Prison they told me "We release you now", and showed me the release document. When I reached for the document, they took it from me and showed me another document – "We arrest you". I was immediately jailed again, and served in total sixteen years.' In 2001, he went on hunger strike for five days, demanding an *Oxford English Dictionary*, more time to exercise, better food and medical care. The jail authorities granted him the dictionary and the food improved. Within three weeks of his release in 2005, he enrolled in a computer class. He had never seen a computer before, but within months had qualified as a graphic designer and found work in publishing. When he fled to the Thailand–Burma border, he found work as a translator for UN agencies, the International Rescue Committee (IRC), and other NGOs.

Moe Aye, who also learned English in prison from books that were smuggled in, explains this extraordinary spirit: 'You are put in prison because the regime wants to close your eyes, your ears and kill your brain. So you have to resist. The regime wants to kill our future, so we need to prove that they can put us in prison but they cannot take away our dreams and our future.'

In 1999, the Red Cross was allowed to visit Burma's prisons, and according to Khun Saing, conditions started to improve. 'We were provided with wooden beds, as until then we slept on a concrete floor, and we were given medicine, soap, and enough food,' he recalls. 'After the Red Cross visited, we could spend at least four hours a day outside the cell.' This lasted six years, however, and in 2005 the regime tightened up and the Red Cross was forced to abandon prison visits. 'When the prison visits stopped, the restrictions tightened,' said Khun Saing.

In 2008 and 2009, the number of political prisoners in Burma escalated dramatically, particularly following the Saffron Revolution. The AAPP claims that political prisoners rose 78 per cent in 2008 compared to the previous year,[46] and over 1,000 people were arrested and detained following the Saffron Revolution.[47] By September 2009, the number of political prisoners had reached 2,211, described by the Alternative ASEAN Network on Burma as 'a record high'.[48] On 17 September 2009 the regime released 7,114 prisoners, for good behaviour, but only 128 of these were political prisoners, and some of their terms had already expired. The release was timed a few days before the UN General Assembly was due to consider a resolution on Burma, and was obviously a propaganda trick. As U Win Tin remarked, 'This is the junta trying to make bad things appear good. It's like putting make-up on a dead person's face.'[49] Even in 2011, when the regime was trying to convince the democracy movement and the international community that it was changing, it released a tiny proportion of political prisoners, and very few high-profile activists. It was not until January 2012, as already described, that significant releases occurred and the regime began to show it was serious about change.

Sometimes prisoners are given an opportunity for early release – if they sign an agreement promising to stop their political activities. Khun Saing was offered such conditions twice. 'They give us some questions, maybe seven or eight questions. What is your view on the NLD, what is your view of the army, what is your view of Aung San Suu Kyi, what will you do after you're released? Very simple questions,' he recalls. If you want to be released, says Khun Saing, you can simply tell the authorities what they want to hear. 'I had that kind of test twice in seven years, and I failed both times.' He refused to compromise.

Even when Khun Saing was released, the stigma of being a political prisoner made life for him and his elderly mother a misery. Military intelligence made frequent visits to the tea-shop he ran, and to the medical clinic he managed. 'I was always under surveillance, so life was not free,' he said. A turning point came in March 2006, when another former political prisoner, Thet Naing Oo, was beaten to death by the regime's thugs. Released after serving eight years of a ten-year sentence, Thet Naing Oo was attacked one evening while walking home. Thugs from the pro-regime militia accused him of urinating in public, and set upon him with iron bars, big sticks and machetes. They crushed Thet Naing Oo's head with a stone, and he died in hospital.[50]

Thet Naing Oo's murder shocked Khun Saing's seventy-four-year-old mother, because she worried that Khun Saing could be next. 'After two or three days, she said to me: "I can't sleep very well these days. I always worry about you, and I couldn't make another prison visit if you were arrested again, because I am now seventy-four years old",' Khun Saing recalled. He had spent thirteen years in jail altogether, and his mother had been constantly harassed during that time. What came next, however, was heart-wrenching. As he told his story, for the first time Khun Saing's eyes filled with tears. 'My mother said she would prefer it if I left the country. She said then she would be happy and could live in peace,' he told me. To hear those words from your mother, after so many years of suffering, must have been unimaginably painful, although Khun Saing understood exactly how his mother felt. 'I did not want to leave, but I knew I gave her trouble a lot of the time. I could be arrested again at any time, particularly as my songs had been published and although my name was not on the CDs many people knew the songs had been composed by me. My friends also warned me, and told me that if I did not want to be arrested again, I should leave. I knew that my mother was so worried because one of my friends had been killed. She wanted to make my life safe. It was a mother's love.' In April 2006, he decided to leave Rangoon, and went to the Thailand–Burma border. In order to protect his mother from worry and danger, he did not even tell her he was leaving. He left some money for her as she slept, and with two items of clothing and some money he slipped away to freedom.

It should be clear by now that the regime under General Than Shwe had no regard for human life or dignity whatsoever; only when President Thein Sein took over did it begin to take a softer line. And its disregard for humanity was not limited to its own citizens. In the 1990s and early part of the twenty-first century, it showed little compunction in jailing and ill-treating foreigners who crossed its path. Several Western campaigners staged protests in Burma during these years, and although most were arrested, detained and deported from the country swiftly, British activist Rachel Goldwyn was sentenced to seven years' hard labour for singing pro-democracy songs, although she was freed after two months. Another British activist, James Mawdsley, was given a seventeen-year sentence for handing out pro-democracy leaflets, and was only released after fourteen months due to intense international pressure. He was blindfolded, handcuffed and beaten. In his book *The Heart Must Break: The Fight for Democracy and Truth in Burma*, Mawdsley reflects on the experience. 'How does torture work? It is not all brutality and pain. Half the task of the torturer is to make you feel irrational for holding out. And sure enough, when you are thoroughly exhausted and desperate for food or sleep, it is hard to think clearly,' he writes.[51] However, even though as a foreigner he was treated better than Burmese prisoners, he was physically tortured. On one occasion his interrogators pushed pens between his fingers and then squeezed the knuckles 'until they nearly broke'.[52] Another time guards used catapaults to fire pellets at him,[53] and one day fifteen guards and military intelligence officers burst into his cell, five of them armed with clubs. One guard swung his club at him. 'Before I had a chance to say a word he laid in, swinging the three-foot club with all his power, like a baseball bat, bang! bang! bang!' Mawdsley writes. 'The blows were crashing into my arms and legs . . . It was a savage assault.'[54] There was an even worse beating to come, when he continued to protest in jail about prison conditions by banging on the cell door. 'Within ten seconds the doors were flung open. Again there were about a dozen men . . . Five of them had clubs and there was to be no holding back this time,' he describes. One particularly brutal guard known as 'the Count' was leading the attack. 'I remember seeing the Count's fist, then elbow, smash into my face, and then he grabbed a club off one of his colleagues. As hard as he could he swung it into the back of my head . . . The next thing I saw, though only for a split second, was the Count swinging it again but this time into my face . . . Blood was pouring from my face down my neck and front . . . I had a broken nose, two extremely black eyes, a cheek swollen out abominably, lumps and welts on my head and back.'[55]

It is important to remember, however, that if Mawdsley had been Burmese the treatment meted out to him would have been even worse. Yet in the eyes of the regime, foreign citizenship offers little protection at all, and none whatsoever if you are ethnically Burmese. In September 2009, a Burmese with American citizenship, Nyi Nyi Aung, was arrested when he arrived at Rangoon airport. He had returned to his birthplace in order to visit his mother who has cancer. He had made four previous visits, and experienced no difficulties, but this one came just a few months after he had delivered a petition to the United Nations calling for the release of political prisoners. This marked him out, and the regime exacted its revenge. 'I was arrested by two uniformed officers and one undercover agent, after I passed through immigration. "Nyi Nyi Aung, we know everything about you," one officer said as he handcuffed me,' Nyi Nyi told me when I met him in Washington, DC eight months later. When his fiancee, Wa Wa Kyaw, heard the news of his arrest, her initial reaction was disbelief. Writing in the *Nation*, Wa Wa Kyaw recalls: 'Nyi Nyi is an American citizen, I thought. How could this happen? And then it hit me: I might never see him again.'[56]

Nyi Nyi Aung was taken to an interrogation centre at first, where he was tortured, denied food for over a week, kicked in his face, beaten and deprived of sleep.[57] 'Sometimes they handcuffed me to a chair, sometimes they beat me, punched my face, twisted my arms.' Then he was moved to Insein Prison where, like so many other prisoners, he was held in a dog kennel.[58] 'I could hear the dogs barking at night,' he recalls. He went on hunger strike in protest, and was moved to a cell. 'At midnight one night, the guards woke me up, put a hood over my head, and put me in a cell.'

The torture Nyi Nyi experienced has caused him long-term back problems. 'By mid-December, I was in real pain walking, from the time when they twisted my body in the chair, handcuffing me and twisting my arms. My leg went numb and tingling, and then I could not walk at all.' He asked for medical attention, and eventually a doctor saw him in January. He had an X-ray, and was told that if he did not receive proper treatment, he would end up paralysed. He received injections of painkillers, but no other treatment. When he was released and deported to the United States in March 2010, he required emergency medical attention for his injuries, and when I met him two months after his release he walked with sticks, in excruciating pain.

For the regime, as Bo Kyi concludes, torture is a key instrument. 'The underlying purpose of torture is to effectively destroy the soul of a human,' he writes.

It is designed to break down the identity of a strong man or woman, turning a union leader, a politician, a student leader, a journalist or a leader of an ethnic group into a nonentity with no connection to the world outside of their torture chamber. In Burma, the regime uses torture to create a climate of fear, in order to maintain its iron grip on power. Arbitrary arrest, physical and psychological torture, unfair trials, long-term imprisonment and denial of medical care in prison are all intended to crush the human spirit . . . There is no doubt about it: torture is state policy in Burma.

But, as the testimonies of numerous former political prisoners show, there is another, unintended effect of torture. 'For those of us who share that experience,' says Bo Kyi, 'it creates an unbreakable bond between us . . . We heard each other's screams under torture . . . We will never turn our backs on each other, or our friends and colleagues in prison. As Myo Yan Naung Thein said after his release, "Who will keep fighting if we don't? We have to carry on."'[59] U Win Tin shares that spirit. 'My opinion is that when you have to face a military government, you need a little bit of courage, some sort of confrontation, because if you are always timid and afraid and intimidated, they will step on you. Sometimes you have to force yourself to be courageous and outspoken,' he told the *Irrawaddy*.[60] It is an epic battle of wills.

Bloody Spots and Discarded Flip-Flops: The Saffron Revolution

If you believe in the cause of freedom, then proclaim it, live it and protect it, for humanity's future depends on it.

Henry 'Scoop' Jackson

The only thing necessary for the triumph of evil is for good men to do nothing.

Edmund Burke

ALMOST EXACTLY A year to the day after the Buddhist monks launched a nationwide protest in Burma, I found myself in a rickshaw driving down an unlit backstreet behind the bustling shops of Cox's Bazaar, a remote town in southern Bangladesh close to the border with Burma. By torchlight, my guide took me to a dark, dank apartment covered in mould, where I spent the evening with five Burmese monks. This was their new home, their hiding place, after they had been forced to flee for their lives.

U Pyin Nyar Disa had been responsible for discipline in the All Burma Monks' Representative Committee. On 17 September 2007 he joined the protests, and two days later helped establish the monks' committee at Sule Pagoda in Rangoon. Five days after that, he took part in the famous march down University Avenue, past Aung San Suu Kyi's house. According to one monk who took part and subsequently fled to Thailand, University

Avenue was closed off with barbed wire and a police checkpoint. Initially, and unsurprisingly, the soldiers at the roadblock at the end of University Avenue refused to allow the monks to pass, but after no orders came from Naypyidaw the monks persuaded the soldiers to let them through. They promised that they would not do anything violent, they would only chant, and so the checkpoint was opened and they passed through. To the amazement of the monks, and the entire world, Aung San Suu Kyi herself came to the gate of her house upon hearing their chanting. It was the first time she had been seen in public for several years. 'Some people tried to go to her, but I controlled them,' the monk told me. 'She seemed to be healthy, but also looked sad. She did not say anything. The crowd shouted to her: "Don't worry, we are with you, we have come out for you."'[1] U Pyin Nyar Disa recalled: 'When Daw Aung San Suu Kyi came out of her house, many monks were crying and she was also crying. But she looked strong. Her expression showed she would never give up. The SPDC can arrest Aung San Suu Kyi physically, but they can never arrest her spirit and her mind.'[2]

When the regime announced one month before, on 15 August 2007, that it was removing fuel subsidies, causing immediate and dramatic rises in the price of fuel and basic commodities, it probably had little idea what it had unleashed. Fuel and diesel costs doubled, and natural gas prices increased by 500 per cent.[3] Bus fares rose to exorbitant levels – some Burmese workers earning 1,000 kyat a day would have to spent 800 kyat just to get to work.[4] The people had had enough and, with encouragement from the '88 Generation student leaders such as Min Ko Naing and Ko Ko Gyi, between 400 and 500 people marched in Rangoon four days later, in protest at the fuel price rises.

Although it is commonly believed that the crackdown did not come until later, in fact the regime arrested the key organisers within a few days of the first protests. On 21 August, Min Ko Naing, Ko Ko Gyi, Min Zeya, Ko Jimmy, Ko Pyone Cho, Ant Bwe Kyaw and Ko Mya Aye were all arrested, and by 25 August more than one hundred people had been detained.[5] The junta clearly thought they could nip the movement in the bud by jailing the leaders. They were wrong, and had clearly underestimated the extent of public fury.

The protests continued, and grew in number. Yet although it was still several weeks before the army came out, it is a mistake to assume that the regime allowed the protests to continue unhindered. From almost the very beginning, the junta chose to use its civilian thugs, rather than the military, to try to break up the demonstrations. Its two civilian militia groups, the Union Solidarity Development Association (USDA) and the Swan Arr Shin ('Masters of Force') threatened and physically assaulted those taking part. On 28 August, for example, prominent labour activist Su Su Nway led a group of fifty people shouting 'Lower fuel prices! Lower commodity prices!'[6] Militia attempted to grab her and take her away, and a struggle broke out between them and the protestors who sought to protect her. She managed to escape, but at least twenty others were beaten up and arrested.

Protests began to spread to other parts of Burma. According to the monks I met, as early as 28 August a demonstration was held in Sittwe, Arakan State. Khemin Da was one of the organisers that day, leading monks from Myoma Kyaung monastery to a Buddhist statue. In Sittwe, as in many other towns, the numbers grew. On 9 September, 1,000 monks gathered at the stadium and then marched to a pagoda and then to government offices. By 18 September, more than 10,000 people were involved.[7] Small protests were also held in late August and early September in Meikhtila, Taunggok, Mandalay and in Than Shwe's hometown of Kyaukse.[8]

The turning point came in a town called Pakokku, near Mandalay, on 5 September. Until that day, the monks had not come out in force. Small groups of monks were protesting, but the *Sangha*, the entire community of Buddhist monks, as a whole had not mobilised. That changed on 5 September.

A small group of monks had held up placards denouncing the fuel price rises, and had been cheered on by thousands of local residents. For the first time, the Tatmadaw responded directly, firing a dozen shots over the heads of the monks, and then launching a brutal assault with bamboo sticks. USDA and Swan Arr Shin joined in. It is claimed that one monk was beaten to death, and several monks were tied to a lamp post and publicly beaten.[9] One monk who was present confirmed this to me. '[The monks] chanted "loving kindness", and the soldiers arrested the monks and tied them to lamp posts, where they kicked and beat them with guns,' he recalled.[10] News of this incident spread, adding even more fuel to the public anger. Buddhist monks are revered in Burmese society, and the idea that soldiers should beat them caused outrage and revulsion. The fuse had been lit, and the movement grew.

On 6 September, local officials visited the Maha Visutarama monastery in Pakokku, and almost immediately at least 1,000 local civilians and monks surrounded the monastery and prevented the officials from leaving. They demanded the release of monks who had been detained the previous day, and burned four government cars. After six hours, the officials fled through a back entrance.[11] Three days later, the All Burma Monks Alliance, a new organisation, issued a statement and an ultimatum to the regime. They demanded that the regime issue an apology to the monks for the way they were treated in Pakokku, immediately reduce fuel, rice, cooking oil and other commodity prices, release all political prisoners including Aung San Suu Kyi, and begin an immediate dialogue with the 'democratic forces' to resolve Burma's crisis. A deadline of 17 September was imposed, one day before the anniversary of the crushing of the 1988 democracy movement and the re-establishment of direct military rule.[12] If that deadline was not met, protests would continue and the monks would launch a religious boycott, refusing to accept alms from SPDC officials – in effect, an excommunication.

The regime made no attempt to respond, and the alms bowls were overturned as a consequence. The giving and receiving of alms in Buddhism is a key religious obligation, providing the giver with necessary 'merit' required for life, so the boycott denied regime members and their supporters the ability to advance spiritually, as well as dealing a further blow to the legitimacy claimed by the junta.[13] On 17 September the protests resumed in Rangoon, and the next day 300 monks gathered at the Shwedagon pagoda and marched to the Sule Pagoda.[14] Hundreds of Rangoon residents gathered in the streets to watch, and as the monks passed, people applauded.

'The crowds seemed to get bigger every day,' Jean Roxburgh, a British woman who was in Rangoon at the time recalls.

We decided we would not take our Burmese friends on the streets with us, we would just hang around at the back of the crowds and watch what was happening. We tended to walk along the route of the march, in the opposite direction, to watch what was going on, or sometimes we took a taxi. On one occasion our taxi got stopped by the crowd, it couldn't go any further, and so we got out and walked. The atmosphere was lovely. The people thought we were marching with them, and they really welcomed us. What impressed me was that ordinary people were out, linking hands to form a barrier to protect the monks. It was pouring with rain and they were getting saturated, but they held hands instead of umbrellas. The monks were chanting 'We can do this peacefully.'

On 21 September, the All Burma Monks Alliance went even further, denouncing 'the evil military dictatorship' and promising to 'banish the common enemy evil regime from Burmese soil forever'.[15] Over the course of the following three days, the crowds swelled, and by 24 September between 30,000 and 50,000 monks joined by an equal number of civilians were on the streets in Rangoon, shouting openly political slogans such as 'Free Aung San Suu Kyi' and 'Free all political prisoners'. Similar protests took place in at least twenty-five towns and cities across Burma.[16]

That evening, the minister for religious affairs, Brigadier General Thura Myint Maung, issued a warning broadcast on state television, dismissing the protesting monks as 'only two per cent of the nationwide monk population' and warning that they would 'be faced with the law' if they did not operate 'according to Buddhist rules'.[17] Trucks with loudspeakers then drove through Rangoon, announcing the imposition of Order 2/88, which bans gatherings of more than five people. Anyone taking part in the demonstrations would face punishment under Section 144 of the Burmese Penal Code, which provides for a jail term of up to two years.[18]

Despite this, the protests continued the next day. On 25 September an estimated 1,500 monks marched down University Avenue, as earlier described. U Pyin Nyar Disa marched, along with several thousand others, from Shwedagon pagoda to the Kaba Aye Sangha University temple. 'We had to cross in front of the Ministry of Religious Affairs,' he recalls. 'We knew the authorities might shoot, but we carried on.' That day, the guns stayed silent, but the tension was mounting. 'We delivered speeches at the temple, and then we went to protest, peacefully, outside the radio station. We gave speeches for thirty minutes, urging officials to listen to the people, not to the SPDC.'[19]

The next day, after receiving a notice calling all monks to gather at the Shwedagon pagoda, U Pyin Nyar Disa went out early in the morning, and arrived at 9 a.m. No other monks had come, however, because soldiers had blocked every entrance and junction. Instead, they gathered at a nearby monastery, to decide what to do next. They all knew that Section 144 had been invoked, that they could face jail, and that the military might well adopt a shoot to kill policy. Despite this, they decided to continue, and they marched to the east entrance of the pagoda. 'Many people requested the monks not to go,' said U Pyin Nyar Disa. 'They had seen many tragedies in 1988, they had seen many people die. But the monks explained that we are the sons of Buddha, we work for our country and our people, not for our own interests.'[20]

That day, it became clear that the crackdown would begin. A group of monks who marched to the Maha Wizaya temple, which had been built by Ne Win, were disrupted by the police chief, Major General Khin Yi. People arrived to give food to the monks, but were turned away by soldiers. Two trucks carrying more soldiers, guns and ammunition arrived, and the monks moved back to the Shwedagon, where they found themselves surrounded by police and soldiers. The police chief ordered the monks to disperse, but they refused to move until their four demands were met. 'The police said "These are not your concerns",' recalls U Pyin Nyar Disa. 'They told us to go back to our monasteries, and if we did not move, they would shoot. We moved to the middle of the Shwedagon pagoda. The authorities planned to shoot us there – but then they decided it was not a suitable place. They opened the east gate, and many monks came out.'[21]

At the end of the street, however, soldiers, guns at the ready, were blocking the way. At least 700 monks were hemmed in by soldiers at the front, led by the Rangoon Divisional commander General Myint Shwe. 'All the roads were blocked. We requested the authorities to allow us to go back to our monasteries, and we promised to withdraw the rest of the day's programme. But the authorities refused. We then sat down and prayed. Another 1,000 monks tried to march to the Shwedagon to rescue us, but they were blocked by the army.'

Then the moment many had feared and yet some believed would never happen came. 'The soldiers began to beat us. Four or five monks collapsed. Monks started to jump the seven- or eight-foot walls nearby to escape, and many were crushed. The army began firing tear gas, and disorder broke out,' recalls U Pyin Nyar Disa. 'I was injured on my nose and hand in the crush. The soldiers started beating and kicking people.' Another monk I met in Mae Sot on the Thailand–Burma border just five months after the Saffron Revolution told me he had been a leader of the protest, and had had a loudspeaker in his hand which he used to mobilise the monks. 'I was beaten, but I didn't take any notice because I was looking after other demonstrators who were being beaten,' he said. 'I only accepted medical treatment at 5 p.m. the following day.'[22] A third monk told me he was also beaten with rubber batons, as he tried to protect an older monk. 'I was surprised and shocked,' he said. 'I did not think the soldiers would beat monks. In Burma, religion is like a parent. The military beat their parents.'[23] Yet another monk said: 'I saw many monks with head injuries, and tried to help them. We then tried to march in another direction wearing protective masks against the tear gas. Soldiers shot at the marchers many times. There were many trucks of soldiers. Many people died.'[24]

Two and a half years later, I walked down the street to the east gate of the Shwedagon. My mind was full of the images I had seen on television and the stories I had been told by monks who had escaped. The eerie, calm normality on the surface masked the bloodstains which, though they had long since been washed away from the concrete, remained in people's memories. That evening, listening to a live band in a hotel bar, I requested Bob Dylan's 'Blowin' in the Wind'. The band sang it, but the lyrics referring to freedom, death and suffering were carefully omitted.

In late September 2007 a rumour spread that four monks had been killed, and so more than 2,000 gathered in the street in anger. 'We marched then from Shwedagon to the NLD office in Bahan Township, and from there to Sanchaung Township. We saw three foreigners. Two of them took photographs; one of them was crying. There were many journalists at the NLD office,' said U Pyin Nyar Disa. But at the intersection near the Nine-Steps Buddha Statue at Bagara, the army blocked the way again, and ordered the monks to go home within five minutes or they would shoot. 'The monks refused. The soldiers began to fire into the air, and then ordered the monks to leave one by one,' he described. After about eighty monks had already left, the remaining monks asked that civilians be allowed to leave too, but the soldiers refused. Clearly, the regime was getting ready to punish the civilians once the monks were out of the way. The soldiers warned the monks that they would be shot if they tried to help the civilians.

The monks then dispersed to Sanchaung Township, where many were arrested. 'At that point I escaped,' said U Pyin Nyar Disa. 'I fled into a building, where a resident helped me to get a taxi, and I went directly back to my monastery. When I reached the monastery, I put my monk's robes in a box, and moved to another monastery, but it was impossible to stay there because the army were searching every monastery and many monks had already fled.' Seeking a hiding place, U Pyin Nyar Disa found a bush beside Inya Lake, and spent the night there.

Another monk, twenty-two-year-old U Tiloka, also marched on 26 September, and he witnessed some horrific scenes. 'I saw nearly eighty soldiers shooting at us,' he told me. 'I saw two girls beaten to death with rifle butts. I saw another monk wounded in his left arm, and I am not sure if he died. I saw a young monk beaten with a stick.'[25]

Viro Sana witnessed similar incidents. Soldiers with loudspeakers were declaring that they had orders to shoot. 'They opened fire. I saw four people – a girl and three monks – wounded. I don't know if they were dead or not. I ran away, down a small road, and then took a taxi along with four other monks.'[26]

Across town, Jean Roxburgh, who had witnessed the peaceful build-up of the protests, saw the first signs of the crackdown as well. Sitting at a table near the window in one of the city's major hotels, where she had had lunch, she saw the crowds getting bigger and realised something was about to happen. 'I went through the hotel and out the side entrance, just to be a bit nearer Sule Pagoda. As I came out of that door, that's when I heard the first gunshot, and saw people running for their lives.'

The hotel staff were not allowing any foreigners out at this point, but Roxburgh convinced them that her own hotel was just a few hundred yards away, and they allowed her to leave. 'I went back to my hotel, and the rest of that day I kept my balcony door open and I had the news on the television. It was on all the channels – BBC, CNN and Channel News Asia. The sounds that were coming from the television were exactly the same as the sounds that were coming from the streets,' she said.

The following day, Rangoon descended into bloodshed. U Pyin Nyar

Disa emerged from his lakeside refuge and took a bus into downtown Rangoon, with another monk, to see what had happened. 'I heard many gunshots,' he described. 'When I wanted to get off the bus, many people tried to stop me, for my own protection, but I got off the bus – and I was hit by a rubber bullet in my neck.'

On 37th Street, U Pyin Nyar Disa ran into a building owned by a Muslim family, who helped him to hide. Not far behind him were soldiers, looking for monks. 'Soldiers asked the Muslims, "Where are the monks?", but the Muslims replied, "We are Muslims – how can a monk enter here?"' he recalls, laughing. 'The soldiers left, and I escaped.'

A former schoolteacher from Bago who came to Rangoon to participate in the protests also witnessed the crackdown. He saw people fleeing any way they could, including two people, one of whom was a monk, jumping at least eighteen feet from a bridge. Several monks broke their legs trying to escape, he said. The following day, he went to downtown Rangoon and found a horrific sight. 'There were so many bloody spots on the street,' he said. 'So many discarded flip-flops.'[27]

That day, Roxburgh saw people climbing the fence of her hotel, across the courtyard and out the other side. 'Of course, the soldiers were marching and people were being pursued. That day I saw lorry after lorry after lorry of soldiers, hundreds of them, followed by thugs who would then go and beat people up. I also saw soldiers pointing guns into our hotel – they didn't shoot, but they pointed their guns at us.' At just one barricade alone, on the way to Sule Pagoda, Roxburgh counted forty soldiers.

After the shooting in the streets, the soldiers began raiding apartments and monasteries, searching for anyone who had taken part in the protests. The raids on monasteries actually began on 26 September, when at least fifteen monasteries were raided and 600 monks arrested.[28] On 27 September the Maggin monastery was raided. I spoke to one of the monks who had come from that monastery, and had fled into hiding that night. He told me that at least one hundred soldiers and seventy USDA thugs charged into the monastery. 'Many monks have disappeared, and we do not know where they have gone,' he said. 'Some have been sent to forced labour camps. There used to be 100,000 monks in Rangoon, and now we hardly see any. The SPDC checks all the young monks aged between eighteen and forty, and has arrested many.'[29]

One man from south Okkalapa Township, who fled to the Thailand–Burma border in October, said that a protest was held at Ngwe Kyar Wan monastery on 27 September, after it had been raided the previous night. Many monks had been arrested and beaten, and when they heard the news a group of ten local people came to the monastery the next day and demanded to know what had happened to the monks. According to this eyewitness, tension mounted between the people and the soldiers and the crowd grew to as many as 10,000. At around noon, some people cut down a tree and placed it between the soldiers and the crowd, and the soldiers fired tear gas and started beating people. Two were beaten to death, their bodies dragged into trucks, provoking even more anger from the crowd. Then the shooting started, and five people were killed.[30]

According to U Tiloka, sixteen truckloads of soldiers came to monasteries on the night of 28 September. 'We heard from another monastery that the soldiers were coming, and so we arranged our security – five monks served on lookout duty, so we could know in advance when the soldiers were coming, how many, and where we could hide,' he told me. 'I hid in a water tank, along with two other monks. All the monks fled from our monastery. I heard one monk telling everyone to flee.'[31]

In Burma every locality has a neighbourhood watch scheme, not to fight crime but to keep an eye on the population. In every street, the photographs and names of residents are displayed, and anyone who is not a registered resident must have permission from the police to spend the night as a guest of a resident. According to Roxburgh, soldiers and thugs went door to door and arrested anyone who was not a resident, on suspicion of being a participant in the protests. 'They were released eventually, but they were held for a while, even if they were nothing to do with it,' said Roxburgh. In addition, during the protests the police and military intelligence had been at work, videoing and photographing everyone in sight. Anyone caught on camera clapping as the protestors marched past, giving the monks water, medicine or food, or even simply, as an innocent bystander, turning their head towards the monks as they passed, was tracked down and arrested. Informers passed information to the authorities – incentivised by payment of 3,000 kyats (2 dollars) a day, double the average worker's wage.[32]

A Chin law student at Rangoon University was among the many to be photographed. On 25 September he and a friend donated water to the monks, and the next day he joined the marches, walking hand in hand in a human chain with other demonstrators. The following day he donated food to the monks, and on 28 September again he joined the protests. Then the military dispersed the crowds with tear gas, firing bullets into the air. 'I didn't see if anyone was shot – I was running too fast,' he told me. Not daring to return to his home, he went into hiding, but telephoned friends the next day. They told him that the police and army had gone to his office and his home, looking for him. One policeman saw his photograph displayed in his apartment block, and said: 'I saw him yesterday [in the protest]. Where is he?' Police came again to his office on 12 October, with a photograph of him giving water to the monks. On 16 October, they forced his wife to sign a statement agreeing to assist them in the search for her husband. At that point, he decided to escape, and fled to Malaysia. Breaking down in tears as he told his story just four months later, in February 2008, he said he had had no contact with his wife since he fled.[33]

In the final days of September 2007, Rangoon went quiet. 'The silence was worse than the noise,' recalls Roxburgh. When she went out on the almost-deserted streets and greeted hotel staff, taxi drivers, street children and stallholders, whom she had got to know over previous weeks, 'the impression really was that people were so grateful that we were still there'. In one shop she went into at three o'clock one afternoon, the elderly shopkeeper told her she was the first customer she had had that day. 'Everybody was suffering,' she said. Taxi drivers had no business, and one offered to take Roxburgh somewhere. 'I thought, "Well why not?" So we went to the Shwedagon pagoda. It was havoc. People were absolutely devastated. There were tour guides who tried to grab us because they obviously didn't have any work. There were several groups of workmen mending broken tiles – there had obviously been some damage there. There was an elderly Buddhist monk standing with his hands outstretched, and the look on his face was one of total devastation.' A curfew had been imposed from 11 p.m. until 5 a.m., which initially Roxburgh thought was ridiculous. 'It turned out that they were attacking the monasteries at night, and they wanted to stop the public from trying to protect the monks,' she explained.

During the following days, those who were capable of it fled Rangoon. Two months later, I met three monks and two civilians in hiding in Mae Sot,

Thailand, and in February 2008 I was able to meet three more monks and a civilian in Mae Sot and three Chin activists who had escaped to Malaysia. Their escape stories are extraordinary.

One monk, who had organised a demonstration of at least 50,000 people, including 30,000 monks, in Bago on 24 September, decided to move to Rangoon. On the night of 25 September he travelled with thirty-five other monks to Rangoon, but their path was blocked at Hlegu, a small town between Bago and Rangoon, by troops from Light Infantry Battalion 77. The monks decided simply to take a different route and, walking all night, they arrived the next day in Tamwe Township. There they witnessed one of the Saffron Revolution's worst tragedies.

At the Basic Education High School No. 3 in Tamwe Township, seven truckloads of soldiers arrived. The school was just finishing for the day and children were leaving. As the trucks pulled up, according to the monk who witnessed it, some children were hit by the army vehicles. Eight children and a teacher were killed. The monks tried to rescue the dying children, but when they did the soldiers shot at the monks. Two fourteen-year-old girls were also shot by the soldiers. The monk I met in Thailand five months later told me that when he tried to rescue some of the children, he was knocked unconscious by a soldier. The bodies of the children who were shot, or crushed by the trucks, were thrown into the trucks, and those who died were instantly cremated. According to the monk, the parents were warned not to mourn, weep or even hold a funeral ceremony, but just to keep quiet. The family of the teacher that was killed was given 20,000 kyats compensation, but warned not to speak out. 'If you tell anyone, we will kill you,' the soldiers said.[34]

Despite sustaining serious head injuries, this monk did not dare seek medical treatment – he had heard that monks who went to hospital were arrested. He went into hiding instead, and his friends tended his wounds with lime, using his saffron robes as bandages. On 28 September, he went to the Sule Pagoda, where he witnessed soldiers shooting people, and he hid in a public toilet, still in pain from his injuries, for much of the night. The next day people helped him move to another hiding place, where he stayed until 10 October when he returned to his monastery. He was arrested on 7 November, but escaped to Mon State, and then travelled through Karen State to Thailand. He grew long hair, a moustache and disguised himself as an insane person, dressed in a dirty old saffron robe. His disguise worked, officials thought he was a lunatic and let him pass by.[35]

Ashin Thi La Na Da escaped to Thanbyuzayat in Mon State, by car. He was still dressed in his robes, but at every checkpoint, when asked for his name, identity number and destination, he gave false information. He then got word from his abbot that intelligence agents had come to his monastery at Mekhin, Rangoon, at least four times, and was urged to move to a safer place. 'I went to Apunt Township, Mon State, where I waited to leave for the border,' he recalled. 'One of my former laymen came by private car, and so on 5 November we went to Kawkareik, close to the border, where we spent one night. The next day, because I knew I could easily be noticed at checkpoints, I paid 8,000 kyats to a motorcyclist to take me around the checkpoints. It was early morning and very cold.' At one point he passed a checkpoint manned by the DKBA, the pro-regime Buddhist Karen militia. 'I thought that because they are Buddhists, there should not be a problem. But they checked everything, and found my diary in my bag. I talked my way out of it.' However, despite talking his way out of trouble with the DKBA guards, he encountered a further problem. 'I thought I would be released to leave, but they said no, no monks allowed across the border. They said I had to find another route.' The next day he went through the border town of Myawaddy – and crossed into Thailand with no difficulty.

U Tiloka fled Rangoon when the army came to his monastery again on 29 September. He hid in a hut in a paddy field near his monastery, with six other monks, and then went into hiding in another location for thirteen days. On 13 October, he travelled to Toungup, in Arakan State, and checked into a hotel. But soon, two soldiers came to the hotel and searched him, asking if he was a demonstrator. 'They asked why we left Rangoon,' he recalled. 'We told them we were not demonstrators, we had simply travelled to our home town on a visit.' He then travelled to Sittwe, and by boat to Maungdaw, where he hid for a day in a nearby village. Surprisingly, all this time he had stayed in his monk's robes, but on 27 October he changed clothes and crossed the border to Bangladesh.[36]

U Pyin Nyar Disa went into hiding in Rangoon for four days when the crackdown began, as it was impossible to leave the city. The authorities had his picture. However, on 1 October he managed to make it to Hlaingthaya Township, and from there he escaped to the Irrawaddy Division, and then on to Arakan State hiding among vegetables in a lorry. When he reached Toungup Township, he hid in the countryside for two months, until the authorities heard that he was there and began searching for him. NLD members in Toungup helped him to escape. 'They rescued my life,' he said. 'Some people arranged to send me to Bangladesh in a timber smuggling boat, and on 24 February I arrived in Bangladesh.'[37]

Those who have fled Burma are in no doubt about the sentiment of the people towards the regime. 'People in Burma are really angry,' one monk told me just a month after he had escaped to Thailand. 'The regime has suppressed them very brutally. Inside people's minds they really want to do something to change this regime. Life is getting more difficult.' Although the SPDC succeeded in crushing the protests, it has been weakened. 'The people really hate them now. The regime is still physically strong. It has guns. But it has no legitimacy or moral authority.'[38]

Another monk looked into my eyes and said: 'I came out of Burma because we need help and advice for the suffering people of Burma. I want to tell the world what is happening . . . People in other parts of the world are responsible to protect the people of Burma, in the interests of peace and stability. Please . . . try to increase pressure on the regime to resolve the situation peacefully. Please try to help the people who were injured.'[39]

The events of September 2007 shook Burma. They were the most dramatic protests in almost twenty years – but they were crushed in the same way as all the previous ones. The difference, however, was that with modern technology, the crackdown could not be hidden from the world. Scenes of the peaceful protests, and then the bloody crackdown, were captured on mobile phones, by undercover reporters and on video, and emailed or smuggled out of the country. Footage appeared almost immediately on major international television networks, even though most foreign reporters could not enter the country. Burmese journalists working for exiled Burmese media such as the Democratic Voice of Burma (DVB), the *Irrawaddy* magazine and *Mizzima News* played a vital role in bringing the news and images out of Burma. One Burmese journalist said: 'One man has eyes but no legs and one has legs but no eyes. We need each other. Freedom of the press is our final goal, but in the meantime we have to do what we can.'

The film *Burma VJ* tells the story of Burmese cameramen who risked their lives to capture the evidence. Several were caught and imprisoned, and the central character in *Burma VJ*, a young Burmese journalist with the pseudonym Joshua, had to flee Burma as the monks' protests grew and after he had briefly been arrested. From his base in Thailand, he managed a team of cameramen inside the country. Having previously worked in print media, he is convinced of the power of film. 'Television media is more powerful than print, because in television you can never lie,' he told me when I met him in Bangkok. 'In the press you can write anything you want, and the junta can write what they like in the State media, and people can define what is right and what is wrong, but you cannot prove that what you are writing is the truth. With television, it is different and that is why people paid more attention to the Saffron Revolution when they saw it on television around the world.'

For the domestic audience in Burma, however, print media and radio reach more people. While all domestic media is censored, the print sector has expanded beyond the regime's mouthpiece publications, and there are now more than one hundred licensed journals. Major publications include *7-Day News*, with a circulation of 60,000, the weekly magazine *Newswatch*, with a circulation of 35,000, monthly magazine *Living Color*, reaching 30,000 and smaller circulation journals such as the *Voice*, *Modern Journal*, *Beauty Magazine*, *True News* and *Ecovision*. According to one foreign expert involved in media training, journalists in Burma are unable to write freely, but they show remarkable ingenuity in finding indirect ways to cover controversial stories. For example, when Rangoon University closed many of its departments in the late 1980s, and failed to offer consistent tutoring or modern courses to students, a reporter wrote a story about the courses available in universities in Singapore, Thailand, Vietnam and Cambodia. 'There was no need to say what an abysmal job Rangoon University was doing. It was self-evident.' Other publications often run stories about the political crises in countries such as Zimbabwe or Pakistan, which may contain lessons for Burma. 'We can't criticise the government, but we can educate the people,' says one Burmese journalist. All publications have to be reviewed by the censorship board, and the process can take up to a week. Every independent newspaper receives articles returned from the censors with red slashes through them. Despite this, says a foreign expert, 'most of the independent media never fail to include a story even if they know for sure it will be censored. They just keep pushing.' In the last few months of 2011, restrictions on the media eased considerably, newspapers were able to publish photographs of Aung San Suu Kyi on their front pages and cover her engagements, and speculation mounted that the censorship board might even be abolished. In October 2011 the head of the censorship board went as far as to say that press censorship is incompatible with democracy, and called for greater media freedom.[40]

With television still limited in its reach and print media limited in its freedom, radio is still the most important media. 'Radio cannot be replaced,' says Joshua. 'People can listen to it anywhere, as long as they have a battery, and so it is countrywide, even if there is no electricity.' A Chin activist from the Saffron Revolution confirms this. Internet and satellite television access are still prohibitively expensive for most people in Burma, but even in rural villages people have radios.

During the Saffron Revolution, radio broadcasts into Burma from the exiled BBC, DVB, Voice of America (VOA) and Radio Free Asia (RFA) Burmese services ensured that people inside the country were kept informed. As a result the regime singled them out for attack. The *New Light of Myanmar* published a statement in large bold letters, accusing the exiled media of 'airing [a] skyful of lies'. Described as 'saboteurs' and 'killers in the airwaves', they were warned to 'watch your step'.

British photographer and activist James Mackay visited Burma in December 2007, less than three months after the Saffron Revolution. 'I was the only Westerner on the plane,' he said. The sense of fear among people when they saw him was tangible. 'People didn't want to look at me, for fear. People had a look of "Why are you here? What are you doing?"' Mackay visited many of the monasteries which had been raided, including Ngwe Kyar Yan, Moe Kaung and even Maggin monasteries, each time having to evade the military. Even in December, the raids were continuing. 'I went to Nan Oo monastery, in Upper Pazundaung, which had been raided the night before I went there. I got right outside, then people came up to me and said "No, please go – military".' In Pakokku, Mackay spoke to a young monk who had been tied to a lamp post on 5 September, during those crucial events which sparked the larger movement. 'When they arrested me, they tied me up,' he confirmed. Mackay voiced frustration that foreign media was not more intrepid. 'Why don't other journalists come to these places? Why do they just walk down the main street in Rangoon to Sule Pagoda?'

One man estimates that over one hundred people, and at least fifty monks, were killed in the crackdown. Others would put the figure higher. 'Some of my friends were detained and beaten. Many monks have been tortured,' he told me. 'There are so many human rights abuses. We cannot stay silent any longer. Our country has so many natural resources but the regime only spends money on themselves. We knew the dangers involved in protesting – but we had to act.'[41]

Cyclone Nargis

'We can no longer plead ignorance, we can not evade it; it is now an object placed before us, we can not pass it; we may spurn it, we may kick it out of our way, but we can not turn aside so as to avoid seeing it.'

William Wilberforce

I WAS IN THAILAND when the storm hit. Eight months after the Saffron Revolution, Burma was struck by the worst natural disaster in living memory. On 2 May 2008 Cyclone Nargis ripped through the Irrawaddy Delta, Rangoon and other parts of southern Burma, leaving complete and utter devastation in its wake. Altogether, it is believed that at least 140,000 lives were lost, and at least 2.5 million people were displaced. More than 3.5 million people were directly affected by the storm.

I had been visiting Karen and Karenni refugees on the Thailand–Burma border, and particularly leaders of the KNU for the first time since Padoh Mahn Sha's assassination three months previously. I was due to travel to Kachin State on the China–Burma border, but I got word that the visit was cancelled. When the cyclone struck I was having a few days' break in southern Thailand, and immediately my phone was buzzing and I was inundated with enquiries: was I OK, had I been affected, would I give a comment to the media? I was fine, and I headed back to Bangkok as quickly as I could.

One night, two or three days after the cyclone as the world was starting to become aware of the scale of the catastrophe, I received a telephone call from the BBC. Their ignorance about the geography of Burma illustrates the scale of the challenge for campaigners for Burma – they had heard I was in the region and thought I could report from the ground. I explained that I was not in the areas affected by the cyclone, but I added, hastily in case they hung up, that I was in touch with people who were in the Irrawaddy Delta and that I had, just an hour before, received some photographs of victims of the disaster. 'Send them through,' the researcher said. Immediately, I forwarded them.

A little later, the phone rang again. 'They are too gruesome to show on national television,' the woman told me. The pictures were of dead bodies, lined up beside a river. They were not pretty to look at, but neither were they full of blood and gore. With all the courteous calmness combined with forthrightness I could muster I said: 'Look, firstly people have risked their lives to take these photographs. They would be killed or at the very least jailed for life if the authorities in Burma knew they had taken these pictures. Secondly, they risked everything to smuggle them out of Burma. Thirdly, I have seen far more gruesome pictures in Hollywood movies and British soap operas. These are factual photographs documenting people who have died as a result of the cyclone, and the regime's neglect. We owe it to them to run them.' She said she would see what she could do, and I went to bed, shaking my fist at the world.

When I awoke the next morning there was a voicemail from the BBC producer, telling me that the photographs which I had sent had been the top story on the *Ten O'Clock News* and a major feature on *Newsnight*. 'The head of news at the BBC congratulated us for obtaining such amazing pictures,' the person said. 'We know that the people who really deserve congratulations are the brave Burmese people who took these photographs and got them out. Please will you pass on our congratulations to them.' My anger at the world turned into a profound gratitude. Thank God. Sometimes, what we do is worthwhile.

But important though those photographs were, they did not save lives. The most shocking aspect of Cyclone Nargis was not the natural disaster, for earthquakes, volcanoes, famines and storms are not unusual, but rather the regime's astoundingly apathetic response. As apocalyptic images emerged from Burma, the regime decided to take a three-day public holiday, and closed its embassies around the world. Within one week of the cyclone, at least 100,000 people had died, and 1.5 million people were left homeless.

Around 40 per cent of them were children. The UN described the situation as 'a major catastrophe', and these figures almost doubled after a few weeks.

Despite receiving many warnings of the impending cyclone from the Indian meteorological agency, the authorities did little to forewarn or protect the people.[1] One man told a visiting Roman Catholic Cardinal from Scotland in January 2009 that he heard a radio warning at 3 p.m. on 2 May, four hours before the waters began to rise.[2] Many other people, however, had no warning. 'At 1 a.m., the waters were so high there was no place to cling to, and at 4 a.m. as dawn broke the next morning, I looked for my family but there was nothing left where I had lived!' a witness said. Another person recalled: 'As the waters rose, I expected to die . . . I was thrown into the sea and out onto an island. I tried to go back to my own place – it took four days. I got to my own village, and I tried to find at least one member of my family, but eight of them had died. I lost all and did not even recognise the body of any one of them. I have no hope left.' A third person described how he had sought shelter in the church after his house was destroyed by a falling tree, but then the church collapsed. 'I floated away but managed to climb onto a tree. I stayed in the water for the whole night . . . I later found that both my parents had died along with all of my family. Only my brother and I are left out of eight. There were dead bodies all around.'[3]

When more than twenty-four countries pledged over US$40 million in aid within days of the disaster, the regime initially refused offers of help. It then agreed to accept aid, but refused access to international aid workers. Only the combined pressure of the UN Secretary General Ban Ki-moon, China, India and ASEAN, driven largely by the United Kingdom, the United States, France and Australia behind the scenes, as well as the presence of French, British and American naval ships off Burma's coast, caused the regime to concede access for aid workers. Reports persisted, however, that aid only trickled through to those who needed it, and much was diverted by the regime, to be used for its own purposes.

Stories abound of relief supplies donated by international agencies appearing with labels over the agencies' name and the names of particular Generals displayed instead, a cruel attempt by the regime to use the aid for propaganda purposes. Several relief workers have confirmed this to me. In addition, supplies were stolen for the regime's own use. 'Nutrient biscuits provided by overseas donors were taken by the regime and used for their soldiers. They gave the people poor quality biscuits instead,' said one Burmese aid worker. One Burmese who became involved in the relief effort claims that the wives of several Generals went to the airport to welcome the arrival of UN containers. 'A major general's wife chose one container and said "This is mine." It contained biscuits and other food supplies. She got into a fight with some other Generals' wives over who could have the container.'[4]

A former Tatmadaw soldier has confirmed that aid was taken and sold in the markets. 'I went to some of the markets run by the military and authorities and saw supplies that had been donated being sold there,' he told the Emergency Assistance Team (EAT), a grassroots organisation established to provide relief to the victims of the cyclone. 'These materials were supposed to go to the victims. I knew what materials were being donated so I could recognise them in the market.' These included noodles, coffee mix and soap. 'The money from selling these things would go to the shop owner, but they are all part of the military. The shopkeepers are all families of the military.'[5] Yet another eyewitness claimed:

> supplying through the [Burmese] government doesn't work. At the [Rangoon] airport, you can see supplies landing there but they are stored at a government warehouse. You can see army trucks carrying it out and in some areas you can see them reaching the army camp. The army camp gets [the supplies], not the villagers. Some was labelled with USAID. In some areas, there are seven villages and only one received supplies with the USAID logo, not others. Local commanders don't dare distribute and need to wait for permission from the top.[6]

In some places local people who had cleared fallen tree trunks and debris from the streets, because the authorities had failed to do so, were then ordered to put it all back again so that soldiers could be filmed for state television in the act of clearing. Compounding this cynical act, the soldiers simply posed for the cameras, pretending to clear the trees – but in reality, once the cameras had finished filming, they left the debris where it was and ordered local people to clear it a second time. Children who had been orphaned were reportedly taken around and people required to make donations, supposedly for the care of the children. 'Then they take the money themselves and do nothing for the children,' a Burmese relief worker told me.[7] Camps were set up for those who had been displaced, with pristine tents and relief supplies provided, and senior Generals and UN officials were filmed visiting, inspecting the rows of tents and handing out aid. As soon as they left, the tents were taken down, people were ordered to hand back the relief supplies, and they were sent away, without food, medicine or shelter. The rows of blue tents were simply props in the regime's propaganda war.

Those directly affected by the disaster were not fooled by the regime's propaganda, but according to a representative of one international aid organisation, people in the north of the Delta, who had not been so severely hit, initially believed the regime. Only when they began to hear reports, by word of mouth or via exiled Burmese radio broadcasts, that aid organisations were denied access did they begin to realise the truth. 'One man in the Delta exploded when he heard that an aid organisation had not got permission,' an international aid worker told me. 'He said: "We have listened to the [state] radio and television, and the government says it is doing all this. But now you are telling us you have not got permission. We have been lied to."'

Instead of helping the people, the regime used the crisis to pursue two other objectives. First, the referendum on a new constitution, which will be examined in the next chapter, went ahead, to the world's astonishment, on 10 May – just one week after thousands had died and hundreds of thousands of people had lost their homes and loved ones, and were barely surviving. Second, numerous attacks were launched against civilians in Karen State, taking advantage of the world's focus on the Irrawaddy Delta. According to the Free Burma Rangers, hundreds of people were displaced and villages burned down as the Tatmadaw 'stepped up its efforts to terrorise villagers into hiding'. Hundreds fled as the military 'mortars villages, captures and kills villagers, and continues to expand its network of military camps into the farms and villages of the local people'.[8]

For the first time ever, people began to talk seriously about invoking the UN's 'Responsibility to Protect' mechanism and forming a military coalition to intervene in Burma for humanitarian purposes. Air drops of aid were considered, and some argued that the naval ships off Burma's coast should deliver aid into the country, with or without the regime's approval, by force if necessary. The NLD issued an appeal urging the international community to help 'by any means',[9] and Charm Tong, from the Shan Women's Action Network, issued a rebuke to the international community for its tough talk but lack of action. At a press conference in Bangkok she said: 'The survivors must be wondering if the world has forgotten them. This is not the time to go along with the regime's restrictions. Now is the time when humanity must be more important than diplomacy.'[10] A coalition of Burmese democracy groups wrote to President Bush, saying: 'Intervention will be seen as divine intervention by the Burmese people, not only to help the cyclone victims but also to finally free the entire nation from the military yoke. Please do not compare Burma with Iraq, because Buddhist monks, students, Burmese patriots will happily assist you with whatever you need to go inside Burma and help the cyclone victims and entire nation. Many concerned Burmese citizens are willing to join the intervention. Please do not waste precious time.'[11]

For a brief period even world leaders talked tough. As the French naval ship Le Mistral, the British ship HMS Westminster and the Americans' USS Essex, as well as several other naval vessels, sat off the coast of Burma laden with aid supplies, US Defense Secretary Robert Gates said the regime was guilty of 'criminal neglect',[12] and British Prime Minister Gordon Brown described the regime's behaviour as 'inhuman'. He said: 'We have an intolerable situation created by a natural disaster. It is being made into a man-made catastrophe by the negligence, the neglect and the inhuman treatment of the Burmese people by a regime that is failing to act and to allow the international community to do what it wants to do.'[13] Britain's then Leader of the Opposition, now Prime Minister, David Cameron said the Generals should be brought before the International Criminal Court if the situation did not change,[14] and US First Lady Laura Bush held a press conference and delivered a strongly worded critique of the regime's failures.[15] French Foreign Minister Bernard Kouchner advocated a UN Security Council resolution that would authorise the delivery of aid regardless of the regime's wishes, invoking the Responsibility to Protect. Many took the view that if the regime's deliberate and calculated failure to protect and assist its own population in the face of a devastating catastrophe did not invoke the UN mandate, what would?

Yet the moment passed. The bodies continued to decompose, the aid trickled through, the will of the international community crumbled and the ships sailed away. UN Secretary General Ban Ki-moon visited Burma and met Than Shwe on 23 May – three weeks after the cyclone – and then told a press conference in the Sedona Hotel in Rangoon: 'I am happy to report that we have made progress on all these issues. This morning I had a good meeting with Senior General Than Shwe. He agreed to allow international aid workers into the affected areas, regardless of nationality. He has taken quite a flexible position.'[16] It was reminiscent of Neville Chamberlain's return from Munich, in which he proudly declared 'peace in our time'. As one Burmese relief worker complained, 'the UN described our government's response to Cyclone Nargis as slow. The UN should be on the people's side. The response was not slow, it was silent. I don't understand why the UN didn't say this.'[17] Another criticised the slowness of the UN's efforts. 'I would also request international organisations to put more pressure on our government if there is another catastrophe. We need political pressure exerted at UN headquarters in a much shorter timeframe.' Ban Ki-moon, the relief worker added, 'was effective once he arrived here but it took one and a half months for him to arrive. This is too late.'[18]

Than Shwe's 'flexible' position was short-lived. As soon as Ban Ki-moon left the country, Prime Minister Thein Sein announced that the regime would merely 'consider' allowing access to international aid workers, but only 'if they wish to engage in rehabilitation and reconstruction work'.[19] The regime declared the relief phase 'over' before it had even begun. Talk of reconstruction and rehabilitation was scandalous, when victims of the cyclone urgently needed food, medicine and shelter and were dying of starvation and treatable diseases.

The regime's conduct was shockingly callous. But it got worse. In its Orwellian eccentricity, it announced that the cyclone had killed precisely 665,271 ducks, 56,163 cows and 1,614,502 chickens. Loss of human life, in contrast, appeared irrelevant to the Generals. One official told foreign aid workers: 'What you, Westerners, don't seem to understand is that the people in the delta are used to having no water to drink and nothing to eat.' With echoes of Marie Antoinette, the state newspaper, the *New Light of Myanmar*, declared that farmers could 'go out with lamps at night and catch plump frogs' and did not need 'chocolate' from foreign countries.[20] In June, the regime hit out at the foreign media, describing them as 'the enemy who is more destructive than Nargis'.[21]

Meanwhile, bodies continued to float in the floodwaters and hang uncollected in trees. Snake-bite became a common cause of death as people and snakes competed for shelter. There were reports, in the first few weeks after the cyclone, that the military forbade the burial of corpses, leaving them to decompose and spread more disease. And people continued to die. According to one relief worker, 'a huge number of people actually died after surviving Cyclone Nargis. They had injuries and infections from holding on to coconut trees for eight hours straight. Nargis emergency relief came two days late, people had fevers and no food or water for that whole time. They were in an area far from town so it was difficult to get transport to seek assistance. Within one week so many people had died again.'[22]

There is a widely held view that the reason the regime did little to help the victims of the cyclone, and actively blocked efforts initially, is that a large proportion of the population in the Irrawaddy Delta are Karens. The junta saw the storm as doing their dirty work for them, eliminating a proportion of an ethnic group which they had been trying to eliminate militarily for years. Some also point to the fact that Senior General Than Shwe had been the regional commander in the Irrawaddy Delta in the early 1980s, and had confronted the Karen insurgency during that time. In 1991 Than Shwe had presided over a military offensive ironically called 'Operation Storm', in which several hundred Karen were killed. In some villages, all the young men were taken away, tortured and executed. Perhaps he saw this natural disaster as completing what he had started. According to Karen sources, a Tatmadaw officer was overheard, a few weeks after the cyclone, saying: 'There are a lot of bullets for the Karen people in eastern Burma, but Cyclone Nargis has already cleansed Karens in the Delta.' A Burmese relief worker from an international agency confirms this. 'The SPDC cannot win over the Karen rebels, so this is another strategy to destroy the people. Like rape, it was used as a weapon, to destroy an ethnic group. The regime has lots of resentment towards the Karen,' she said.

The Emergency Assistance Team (EAT) and Johns Hopkins Bloomberg

School of Public Health confirm in their report 'After the Storm: Voices from the Delta' that 'discrimination existed in the distribution of aid to cyclone victims, particularly in the Irrawaddy Delta, which had significant non-Burman and non-Buddhist populations'. One relief worker told EAT that 'at first the government only supported the Burmese [Burmans]. Not Karen people . . . When the government came to help the people, they came by boat, they took the Burmese [Burman] people in the boat. But . . . the Karen people, they kicked them down, they didn't let them on the boat.' Another relief worker claimed that religion was a factor as well. 'When the government comes to help people in the affected area, they leave behind the Christian groups because they know they may be helped by Christian organisations.'[23]

Any hint of criticism drew a sharp reaction from the junta. A Burmese aid worker employed by an international aid agency to lead their efforts in the country went on Canadian television and said that in a disaster of this scale, even the United States or the United Kingdom would not be able to cope alone, so Burma would certainly require international assistance. He was called in that night for questioning.

Slowly, the situation began to change, as a result of international pressure. Aid agencies were permitted to operate, and according to one aid worker from a major international organisation, 'by September, the aid situation had improved significantly. A lot of good work had been done.' However, while some in the international community believed this was a genuine opening, and spoke optimistically of lifting sanctions and pouring aid and investment in, others are more realistic. 'I am very sceptical that there is more space,' a representative of an international aid agency told me. 'The Generals will always find a reason to close it off again. They may be biding their time, but it is not as open as people think it is.'

The real problem, this aid worker argues, is at the very top of the regime. 'At a local level, local authorities eased restrictions early on, but then closed off. The central government was very closed, until about five or six weeks after the cyclone when they began to open up more. This was due to the influence of ASEAN and others.' Even then, however, there were still restrictions on access to some areas. 'Access did not open up immediately after Ban Ki-moon's visit. We still had to go through various processes to get permission. The regime appeared to say you could go in "only if we deem that it brings added value". There were strings attached.' Local authorities sometimes refused permission even when the central government had agreed it. 'The government sometimes said yes, in order to ease pressure on themselves, but then sent a message to the local commander telling them to refuse access. The central government could then say "It's not our fault, it's the local authorities."' An added problem was that the central government was so suspicious of international agencies, it took care to reshuffle ministerial responsibilities regularly. 'If government officials show any relationship to an international NGO, they are moved or removed. They constantly move senior officials and ministries' responsibilities around. The Ministry of Forestry and Tourism was responsible for dealing with the disaster response in Bogolay for a time.'

While international agencies battled for access and struggled to overcome the red tape, an informal and diverse network of Burmese civil society addressing the crisis was growing. Businessmen, Buddhist monks, Christian churches and prominent activists and celebrities all responded to the disaster. They too faced significant risks and challenges, but performed a vital role.

Two young foreign volunteers contributed to this effort. Khin Tun, a half-Burmese student from the United Kingdom, was able to slip in to some restricted areas and help deliver medical and food aid. 'We were continually hampered by local authorities who were highly suspicious of our motives, and by restrictions from Rangoon and Naypyidaw,' Khin Tun recalls. The need, however, was enormous. 'We saw a great need for food, clean water, shelter, medical supplies, mosquito nets and other basic needs such as footwear. People were sustaining further injuries with debris cutting their feet.'

Trauma counselling was also a major unmet need. 'Survivors were still in great shock from the horrific experiences they had encountered, such as seeing local community leaders and a pregnant mother hanging dead on trees.' Another aid worker agrees. Speaking almost a year on from the cyclone, she told me that in some areas people are still afraid when they hear the rain. 'They still see what happened [in their minds], but they can't talk about it.' In some areas, all women and children were killed, and only the men have survived. 'Waves of nine or ten feet tall destroyed all the houses, and the women and children died. The men survived because they were physically stronger.' Another aid worker told me: 'Our team returned from Bogolay traumatised. They saw bodies, human and animal, floating all over the place, and no one was allowed to do anything.'

Eventually, the local authorities tracked Khin Tun and his friends down and forced them to leave. 'But before we left we were able to visit the Nargis victims one last time, but under the condition of not taking photographs and not going to the refugee centres,' he recalls. 'We ended up having to distribute supplies and games to the children through a closed metal gate. Words cannot describe the feeling we experienced of being able to touch them, but feeling so powerless. Were we really a threat to national security, distributing medicine and footballs to children?'

Tens of thousands of children had been orphaned or separated from their parents in the cyclone, and had to survive on their own. Older children found themselves caring for younger siblings, and many had to find work to support themselves. Sixteen-year-old Khine, whose story is told in a remarkable documentary film *Orphans of the Storm*, worked a ten-hour shift pushing a heavy roller on a military-owned salt field. Ten-year-old Ye Pyint was left to look after his six-year-old sister and three-year-old brother. 'We never found my mother,' he said. 'Someone told me they saw my father's body with some rubbish on a beach.'[24] The DVB camera crew risked thirty years in jail to make the film and defy the regime's media blackout.

Extortion and theft were rampant. On 31 May, a Burmese Christian lawyer went with a friend into the Irrawaddy Delta, to do what she could to help. They loaded up a pickup with thirteen 50-kilogram rice bags, as well as noodles, salt, clothing and twenty packs of water – each pack containing twelve 1-kilogram bottles. 'When we reached a checkpoint at the bridge at the junction of the road to Twante and the road to Daydaye and Laputta, we were stopped by two police officers,' she recalls. 'They asked me what the supplies were for, whether they were donations for relief, and I said yes. They asked if I had permission. I told them the supplies were for labourers on my fish farm. They told me the supplies were too many, and that I could only take half the amount. I paid 20,000 kyats (approximately 20 dollars) "tea-money" and they let me through.'

After delivering the relief, they drove back to Rangoon. 'At 5 p.m., on our way back, we found a long line of cars, at least fifty, standing still at the checkpoint. We were stuck in the line until 11 p.m. A captain came to us and I asked him what the problem was. He told me he had instructions from his senior officers to take our driving licences and tax certificates.' After giving him the documents, she was told to follow him, and was taken to the Insein Government Technology Institute. 'We saw at least one hundred cars in the compound. I was told to write down my name, address, driving licence number and other details, and then at around midnight, I was allowed to go home by taxi. The next day I was told to go back to the compound, and pay 30,000 kyats (30 dollars) for the release of my car.'[25]

Initiatives varied – some were simply taken by individuals, such as the Burmese lawyer already quoted, others were more formalised. Groups such as the Myanmar/Burma Emergency Aid Network (MBEAN) were formed by civil society organisations and individuals to try to coordinate efforts. The MBEAN provided both emergency relief as well as longer-term assistance, such as stationery to schools, the construction of latrines, repair work and agricultural equipment.[26] Some work went unnoticed, under the radar, or the authorities turned a blind eye. Others, however, got into serious trouble for their efforts. One foreign aid worker observed: 'In the immediate aftermath, many small groups of friends got together as volunteers and went back and forth from Yangon to the Delta providing small amounts of relief because they felt the government was not doing enough. Some told me that they never expect the government to act appropriately, whatever the circumstances. When I made informal suggestions about fundraising methods we use routinely here, such as progressive dinners, raffles etc., I was told that any of these would lead to arrest and probably a long gaol sentence.'[27]

As Human Rights Watch concluded, while 'some observers suggested that the resurgence of civil society in the wake of the cyclone showed an opening of humanitarian space', for Burmese who attempted independent relief efforts or spoke openly of their frustrations with the regime, 'the threat of arrest or intimidation was all too real.'[28] In June 2008 alone, according to Human Rights Watch, at least twenty-two people were arrested for providing assistance to victims of the cyclone. They included a doctor, U Nay Win, who founded The Group that Buries the Dead, an initiative to collect the corpses of cyclone victims for burial. He and his daughter were arrested and jailed for unlawful association. Journalists Eine Khaing Oo, a twenty-four-year-old reporter for *Ecovision Journal*, and Kyaw Kyaw Thein, a former editor of *Weekly Journal*, were arrested and jailed for bringing cyclone victims to Rangoon and interpreting for them at meetings with the UN Development Programme and the International Committee of the Red Cross.[29] The most prominent person arrested for his involvement in the post-Nargis relief effort was, of course, the comedian Zarganar.

Despite having been in and out of jail several times since 1988, Zarganar continued to be a powerful voice of dissent against the regime. After the cyclone struck the Delta, he mobilised a network of several hundred people to drive supplies down to the affected areas, and to raise money for urgently needed relief. On 2 June, Zarganar spoke out in an interview with the BBC. 'The victims are very angry with the military junta,' he said, but added that they were not the only ones. 'The second group is the donors . . . They want to donate directly to the victims but the military junta and some police are stopping them from donating directly.' Some government officials, he added, are unhappy too. 'They are human beings. Some of their relatives disappeared in the Delta region but they couldn't go there, so they feel anger towards the military junta.'[30] He told the *Irrawaddy* magazine: 'I want to save my own people. That's why we go with any donations we can get. But the government doesn't like our work. It is not interested in helping people. It just wants to tell the world and the rest of the country that everything is under control and that it has already saved its people.'[31] Two days later, he was arrested and in November 2008 he was sentenced to fifty-nine years in prison. Three months later, the sentence was reduced to thirty-five years, although he was released in an amnesty in 2011.

Foreign journalists who attempted to cover Cyclone Nargis were turned back or, if caught, deported. CNN's Dan Rivers and his camera crew were chased through the Delta by the military for a week in the days immediately after the cyclone. According to Human Rights Watch, the CNN team were 'hiding in the back of cars, walking through the jungle to sneak into villages to interview survivors, bluffing their way through checkpoints and sending out broadcasts of the scale of the disaster.'[32] Eventually, the authorities caught up with him and he was deported. *Time* magazine reporter Andrew Marshall was similarly kicked out. He wrote later: 'The junta's pitiless response to the cyclone is alienating the very people it depends on for its own survival. One young Special Branch officer at the airport seemed embarrassed to be expelling a foreign journalist whose only crime was trying to publicise the plight of Burmese disaster victims. "Please forgive me," he kept telling me. "Please forgive me." I now realise he wasn't embarrassed at all. He was ashamed.'[33]

If there was any faintly positive outcome of the truly awful events of 2008, it was that the regime's refusal to help inadvertently empowered Burmese civil society groups. According to a report titled 'Listening to Voices from Inside: Myanmar Civil Society's Response to Cyclone Nargis', 'on the one hand, Cyclone Nargis brought so much destruction. At the same time, it brought people together and provided the opportunity for people in civil society to take action and mount a response to the disaster.'[34] A foreign observer who left the country three months after the cyclone concluded that 'small acts of heroism will continue', and that given the regime's attitude, 'without the superhuman efforts of local NGOs, church groups and monasteries, there would have been much more suffering and death. It was these groups who found temporary shelter, provided food, clothing and medicine for survivors.'[35]

As a result of their efforts, people of different ethnic and religious backgrounds became more unified, one Burmese aid worker concluded. 'Civil society has been strengthened. Because of the cyclone, our local people are more unified. It is a good thing – we could develop empathy, and mobilise resources in-country.'

The words of one woman involved in the relief effort, writing to a relative abroad, sum up the spirit of all those Burmese who reached their people when the regime would not and the international community could not. 'In situations like these, the important thing is to remain focused on the situation at hand and the person with whom we come into contact, and leave things (or at the very least try to) better than we found them initially. I keep in mind the starfish story[36] and affirm what we are doing by reminding myself constantly that it does make a difference (however slight) to that one person we serve.' Acknowledging the criticism made by professional aid workers that the local efforts were not as well coordinated as they might have been, she concluded: 'There are many personal, professional and "official" limitations and even negligences. We could have done things differently, in a more "systematic" manner, or even been more effective and efficient but, despite all this, I know that we can rely and lean on each other's kindness and generosity and resilience – my people have depths of inner strength and are deeply spiritual, capable of amazing *rétablissement*, and I trust in this.'

Out of Uniform but Still in Power

'Despots themselves do not deny the excellence of liberty; only they want
to keep it all to themselves. They do not think that anyone else is entirely
worthy of it.'

Alexis de Tocqueville, *L'Ancien Régime et la Révolution*

ONE OF THE strange facts about Burma is that history keeps repeating itself. Just as Ne Win drew up a new constitution, established a political party, put the constitution to a referendum, albeit one that was completely rigged, and turned a military junta into a nominally civilian government, although with many of the same ministers, history came full circle in Burma in 2010. If imitation is the highest form of flattery, Than Shwe clearly has unbounded admiration for Ne Win.

Than Shwe's plans began in 2003, following the attack on Aung San Suu Kyi and her supporters at Depayin. Although there is little doubt that Than Shwe had ordered the attack, he had to do something to quell growing international anger. The Thai Foreign Minister Surakiart Sathirathai proposed a road map to democracy at a conference of foreign ministers in the Asia–Europe Meeting (ASEM). In his mind, such a road map would include the release of Aung San Suu Kyi, an investigation into the Depayin massacre, peace talks with the ethnic groups, a new constitution drawn up through an inclusive process, a transitional period leading to elections, and ultimately democratic elections monitored by international observers.[1] The third-ranking General in the regime at the time, Khin Nyunt, responded by announcing a seven-stage road map to 'disciplined democracy' – but the only thing in common between his plan and the Thai proposal were the words 'road map'. No mention was made by the SPDC of their road map involving Aung San Suu Kyi, let alone her release, and there was no question of an inquiry into Depayin.

The constitutional element of the new road map was not, however, new. Three years after the 1990 elections, a National Convention was initiated to draw up a new constitution. At the beginning the NLD took part, but they withdrew in protest at the fact that the process was completely rigged. 'We are not trying to destroy the National Convention,' Aung San Suu Kyi said at the time. 'We are trying to make it one that will be acceptable to the people of Burma and to the international community.' She complained that 'decisions are laid down before an issue has been discussed'.[2] The regime packed the National Convention with hand-picked delegates and imposed tight restrictions on the agenda, making it impossible for the NLD to achieve anything. Of the 702 delegates, only ninety-nine were Members of Parliament elected in 1990, out of which eighty-one were from the NLD. The remaining 603 delegates were all appointed by the SLORC, and included cronies and suspected drug warlords.[3] Some ethnic representatives participated, and were initially optimistic that they could create a constitution that would lead to a federal structure with ethnic autonomy. It quickly became apparent that such hopes were false, and that the regime never intended an inclusive, genuine constitution-drafting process.[4]

After the NLD's walkout, the National Convention stalled for eight years. When it resumed in 2004, nothing had changed. Confined in a military location with no contact with the outside world, delegates were forbidden to discuss the draft constitution outside the conference hall. Anyone criticising the National Convention could be jailed for up to twenty years. The regime's '104 principles' for the constitution, providing a basic structure for the final document, offered little hope for democracy. Among the 104 principles were provisions for the Tatmadaw to govern its own affairs without oversight from the civilian government eventually elected, and for the Tatmadaw to seize power again in the event of a 'state of emergency'. The principles also included a requirement that the President of Burma 'shall be a person who has been residing continuously in the country for at least twenty years' with 'political, administrative, military and economic experience' and whose spouse, children and spouses of children are not citizens of another country. The President should also have at least fifteen years of military service. These requirements automatically disqualified Aung San Suu Kyi. It was a sign of things to come.

I have spoken to some delegates from the National Convention, who confirm that the entire process was simply a rubber stamp for the regime's agenda. 'No discussions were allowed,' one Kachin former delegate told me. 'Every day we attended we only listened to the speeches. After that, we took a rest.' Each morning, from 9 a.m. until 11 a.m., delegates listened to regime officials delivering their speeches, and were then free in the afternoons. 'Most delegates brought a book to read during the speeches. For some, such as the Kokang, they couldn't understand Burmese so they sat reading Chinese books.' When asked whether they learned or achieved anything during the National Convention, one looked at me with a wistful smile and said: 'We learned to play golf.'

In July 2007, the KIO submitted a 'Proposal for Constitutional Provisions and Clauses', otherwise known as the '19-point proposal', in which they advocated 'a specific constitutional mandate' to be included providing for 'a federal system of union'. They also sought guarantees for religious freedom. Their submission was not even discussed in the proceedings, and received no response from the regime. A proposal submitted by thirteen ethnic ceasefire groups three years previously was similarly ignored.[5]

A major in the Tatmadaw, in charge of hospitality and recreation facilities during the National Convention, observed that during the second session of the newly resumed process ethnic delegates were separated from each other and housed in different accommodation. The regime, he said, did not want representatives of different ethnic groups to conspire with each other. After receiving requests from ethnic delegates urging him to reinstate the previous accommodation arrangements, he spoke up for them. In response, his superiors warned him not to even discuss such matters. 'I was demoted, and ordered to serve in a [location] far away from Rangoon. They confiscated my car and phone, and forced me out of my government apartment where my family was living. So I fled to Thailand.'

When the National Convention finally concluded, after thirteen suspensions over fourteen years, its outcome was not a constitution – it was a hand-picked fifty-four-member drafting commission to produce a text based on the 'fundamental principles' finalised by the National Convention.[6] However, the draft constitution was finally ready a few months later, and in February 2008 the regime announced plans to hold a referendum in May that year.

The regime had learned its lesson from the voting in 1990, and was determined that in the referendum, and no doubt any future ballots, its desired result would be achieved. So government-controlled media offered, according to Human Rights Watch, 'only crude propaganda in favour of a "Yes" vote' and spread rumours that those who opposed the referendum might go to prison. The proposed constitution itself was only available to limited audiences – it was not published much in advance of the referendum, and when it was available, it went on sale for 1,000 kyat, a price that was unaffordable for many Burmese. It was available in only Burmese and English, making it impossible for many of the non-Burman ethnic nationalities to read it, and was not distributed in rural areas where the majority of the population live. A report by the Institute for Political Analysis and Documentation (IPAD) called 'No Real Choice: An Assessment of Burma's 2008 Referendum', claims that most people 'were never provided with an opportunity to read the draft constitution. Indeed, most have never seen it. Copies of the draft constitution were released on 9 April, just one month before the referendum.'[7] As Human Rights Watch concluded, 'The generals are sending a clear message that their hand-crafted constitution will continue the military rule that has persisted for more than four decades.'[8] Critics of the constitution were not permitted to distribute their own literature, and those who campaigned for a no vote did so at significant risk of imprisonment.

In the days leading up to the referendum, the regime used a mixture of fear and incentivisation to encourage people to vote for the new constitution. Civil servants were told if they did not vote for the constitution they would lose their jobs, communities were warned that water and electricity would be cut off if at least 80 per cent did not vote for the constitution, students were warned that only those who voted in favour would be able to graduate and people were threatened with jail if they voted no.[9] Thugs from the pro-junta militia, the USDA, went around villages intimidating voters, usually accompanied by military intelligence officers and local officials. One former USDA member involved in this told Human Rights Watch that people suspected of intending to vote no were targeted at night, often threatened, abused and beaten up. 'The people who say "no" we write down their name and address. If they still say "no" we go back late at night and beat them. We . . . take them to the jail. We accuse them of being a thief, a drunk. We explain we can give them trouble, give them many problems. Most are scared. [One person] we talked to about the referendum . . . he said he was not interested, he was against it. We came back later to his house and took him to the *ya ya ka* office and pushed and beat him and told him he faced many problems.'[10]

Despite these severe restrictions, an extraordinarily courageous campaign against the constitution did develop. On 27 March 2008 more than thirty NLD activists in T-shirts with 'NO' emblazoned across them marched in Rangoon.[11] A network of underground activists across the country organised a 'vote no' campaign.

As has been described in the previous chapter, Cyclone Nargis struck Burma on 2 May 2008, just a week before the date of the referendum. With several million people homeless and grieving, and hundreds of thousands dead, one would have expected the regime to delay the ballot. UN Secretary General Ban Ki-moon called for a full postponement, but on the contrary, the junta saw the opportunity to ram it through, calculating that people would be less able to organise to vote against it. Only as a result of international pressure did the regime decide to postpone the vote in the most affected areas, and so it was the worst of all worlds: most of the country voted on 10 May, while the Irrawaddy Delta voted two weeks later, on 24 May, leaving the counting of votes wide open to abuse. To compound the farce still further, the junta announced the results of the referendum on 15 May – before the second ballot. According to the regime, turnout was 99 per cent of the electorate, and the constitution was approved by 92.4 per cent.

If the accounts of what happened on polling day are true, it is no surprise that the regime achieved that result. Stories of massive abuse abound.[12] In some villages local authorities handed out ballot papers already marked with a tick in the 'yes' box, while in other places voters were simply informed that their votes had already been cast for them and that they did not need to go to the polling station. In other areas, voters were watched closely as they cast their ballot, and were advised how to vote if they showed signs of casting a 'no' vote. Relatives were told to vote on behalf of family members in some places, while in other areas multiple voting occurred, and according to one report, in one village 'a polling station officer stretched out the hand of an eighty-year-old man and forced him to vote yes. Local authorities promised villagers that if they voted yes then the village would receive development assistance for the building of necessary infrastructure.'[13]

Millions of people were disenfranchised. Religious leaders, including the country's more than 500,000 Buddhist monks and nuns as well as Christian pastors and Islamic clerics were denied a vote, as were refugees who had left Burma and internally displaced peoples in the ethnic states. At the same time, according to IPAD, 'thousands of minors and non-citizens were wrongfully allowed to vote'.[14]

IPAD concludes that 'the National Referendum Commission (NRC) not only violated every minimum standard for a free and fair referendum, its officials blatantly cheated. Three fraudulent practices appear to be particularly widespread: ballot stuffing, the falsification and corruption of advance ballot voting, and the systematic cancellation of no-votes.'[15] The claim that 98.58 per cent of the population in Kachin State, for example, turned out to vote, and in eight out of ten townships in Kachin State 100 per cent of the electorate turned out, is simply not credible. Kachin State is one of the most remote and sparsely populated parts of Burma, in which transportation and roads are severely limited. 'These statistics defy rational belief,' IPAD concludes.[16]

A Rakhine eyewitness from Arakan State confirms these reports. In northern Arakan State, he told me, authorities summoned only one person from each family to cast votes on behalf of their entire family, and often they were presented with a ballot paper already completed in favour of the constitution, and simply instructed to place it in the ballot box. They were threatened with seven years in jail if they refused. In Kyee Dwe village, Sittwe Township, the local Peace and Development Council chairman tried to replace 'no' votes with 'yes' votes, stuffing the ballot boxes. 'Another villager and I opposed this,' a Rakhine student told me. 'We dared to advise the chairman to submit the results according to how people had actually voted. He said he had been ordered to ensure a high "yes" vote, and had been warned that if there were many "no" votes he would be fired. He was afraid. After I opposed his action, he informed the police and they came looking for me.'[17] The student had to go into hiding, and eventually flee to Bangladesh.

The constitution that has come into force through this sham referendum has been described by the General Secretary of the KNU, Zipporah Sein, as 'a death sentence for ethnic diversity in Burma'.[18] It is simply a way for the regime to secure its rule, she argues, and offers no prospect of democracy and no protection of ethnic identity, language or cultural rights. One quarter of the seats in both houses of the new national Parliament are reserved for the military, and a similar proportion is reserved in state and regional assemblies. In addition, serving military officers are permitted to stand for election in the non-reserved seats.[19] Most significantly, any attempt to amend the constitution would require more than three-quarters of both Houses of Parliament and a majority in a nationwide referendum. With a quarter of the seats in Parliament reserved for the military, the armed forces will hold an effective veto over any changes.[20] The constitution also gives the military immunity from prosecution for any crimes committed.

As the International Center for Transitional Justice concludes, 'instead of being a true catalyst for lasting change, it [the constitution] further entrenches the military within the government and the associated culture of impunity'.[21] The result is 'a carefully planned strategy in which a functioning democracy is impossible' under this constitution, and amending its 'fundamentally undemocratic provisions is virtually impossible'.[22]

Having finalised a new constitution that effectively enshrines military rule, the regime then set about planning elections that would, it hoped, create a veneer of respectability and legitimacy for its continued rule. As part of its preparations for a transition to a 'civilian' government, the junta began to demand that ethnic ceasefire groups merge with the Tatmadaw. The proposal, as touched on earlier, was that they should form a border guard force, under the command of the Tatmadaw – in effect, a total surrender enabling the Tatmadaw to assume total control of all areas of the country. Each border guard force battalion, the regime proposed, would consist of 326 soldiers including 18 local officers. Thirty Tatmadaw officers would be posted to each battalion.[23] Some ethnic ceasefire groups, particularly those already aligned to the regime such as most of the DKBA, accepted the deal; others, such as the KIO and the KNU/KNLA Peace Council, a breakaway from the KNU, have refused.

The key question for the democracy movement in the run-up to elections in 2010 was what they should do: take part, in the full knowledge that it would be rigged and they would lose, or boycott, and risk being made illegal and closed down. Similar choices faced the ethnic nationalities. U Win Tin emphasised that the democracy movement is 'ready to engage' in a genuine dialogue, but would not endorse a sham process.[24] That message was developed in the NLD's Shwegondaing Declaration in April 2009, in which it stated that if all political prisoners were released, the new constitution amended and the elections held on a free and fair basis, monitored by international observers, the NLD would take part. It quickly became clear, however, for anyone in any doubt, that the regime was not interested. The democracy movement followed up with a 'Proposal for National Reconciliation: Towards Democracy and Development in Burma', in which it reiterated its call for dialogue. In Insein Prison on 20 May 2009, Aung San Suu Kyi said 'it is still not too late to achieve national reconciliation'. The movement's proposal, signed by all the major organisations within the democracy movement including the NCGUB, the NCUB, the Ethnic Nationalities Council, the Women's League for Burma and the Forum for Democracy in Burma, declared that it was 'extending an outstretched hand, inviting a dialogue with the Tatmadaw leaders which would contribute to the creation of the necessary conditions for the holding of free and fair elections'.[25] Still, the regime's hand remained tightly clenched. As a Kachin activist told me, 'there is no freedom of expression. The regime always violates fundamental human rights. The elections cannot be free and fair.' Another described the road map as 'fake democracy'.[26]

Even though the new constitution alone gave the military a guaranteed place at the centre of government, the regime was determined not to allow any loopholes through which freedom could inadvertently emerge. After an American Mormon, John Yettaw, swam uninvited across Inya Lake to Aung San Suu Kyi's home, the regime saw it as an opportunity to keep her locked up and out of the way until after the elections. Charged with violating Article 22 of the 1975 State Protection Law, by allowing Yettaw to stay for two nights in her home without permission, Aung San Suu Kyi was put on trial and sentenced to three years imprisonment with hard labour. General Than Shwe then reduced the penalty to eighteen months' house arrest, in an effort to appear compassionate. 'In considering a military dictatorship such as the government of Burma, it is easy to see only its crudity and absurdity . . . But if Burma's generals are cruel, stubborn and pompous, they are also cunning and strategic,' wrote Richard Lloyd Parry in *The Times*. The Generals had a plan, he said, and Aung San Suu Kyi's sentencing 'is part of its unfolding'.[27]

As if that were not enough, election laws issued in March 2010 required any political party that wished to contest the elections to expel political prisoners among their members. The NLD, therefore, would have been required to expel a significant proportion of their members, including possibly Aung San Suu Kyi, who spent more than fifteen years under house arrest. The NLD was left with little choice but to boycott the elections, and as a result, its status as a legally registered party was removed.

In addition, the regime then announced that candidates had to pay 500 dollars to run, a fee that is more than the average annual salary and totally unaffordable for most parties other than those backed by the regime. All election literature had to be approved by the regime, and candidates were forbidden to make statements that might 'tarnish the image of the state'. Restrictions on movement and gatherings made election canvassing or rallies impossible. The electoral commission was entirely hand-picked by the junta, several political parties and candidates were barred from standing, foreign journalists were banned and in 3,400 villages in ethnic areas polls were cancelled, leaving at least 1.5 million people disenfranchised. No international observers were invited, apart from a North Korean delegation. A few days before the election, Britain's ambassador Andrew Heyn summed up the situation. 'As we approach the elections and I get out talking to ordinary people about their voting intentions, I am often met by two apparently illogical statements. The first is that there is a strong sense that the regime's proxy party, the USDP, will win the elections; the second is that none of my contacts has met anyone who will willingly vote for the USDP . . . People here believe that the vote will somehow be fixed.'[28]

Two weeks after the elections, I travelled to the India–Burma border, and the evidence that the polls had been 'fixed' was overwhelming. I heard stories of intimidation and harassment, and the manipulation of advance postal votes. In some areas, particularly Tedim and Kalaymyo, USDP officials reportedly cast ballots on behalf of voters. The USDP is what used to be known as the USDA – the thugs had formed a political party. Villagers were forced to make financial contributions to the USDP campaign in parts of Chin State, and in the aftermath of the elections, in the few areas where the USDP had lost to the pro-democracy Chin National Party (CNP), the regime ordered an investigation into how civil servants had voted. Any government official found to have voted the wrong way faced a severe punishment. The conclusion of the Chin people I spoke to was that 'the elections amount to nothing more than a change of clothes for the military' and 'a sham'.[29]

Similar stories of electoral fraud, irregularities, harassment and abuse were reported from all parts of the country. The Chairman of the National Democratic Force (NDF), Than Nyein, said that while his party had never expected the polls to be free and fair, the abuses were 'far more than we anticipated'.[30] The Executive Secretary of the Democratic Party, Cho Cho Kyaw Nyein, said the electoral fraud was 'the ugliest and most extreme level of vote-stealing'. The end result was as predicted: an overwhelming victory for the regime. The USDP won 883 of the 1,154 seats contested. In the Lower House, the People's Assembly, the USDP won almost 80 per cent of the seats, and in the Upper House, the National Assembly, they gained 76 per cent of the seats. In some of the division and state legislatures, ethnic and pro-democracy parties fared better, but the USDP remained in control. Adding the seats won by the USDP to the 25 per cent of seats reserved for the military, the regime has a total grip on the new legislatures at national and regional levels.

To add to the cards stacked in the regime's favour, real power does not lie with the legislature anyway. An eleven-member National Defence and Security Council, chaired by the President, and dominated by the military, is established under the constitution. Compared with this governing body, the Parliament has little power. The military remain largely unaccountable to legislators, and the President and Vice-President, elected by a hand-picked electoral college of MPs, must be military officers. Former general Thein Sein, who served as Than Shwe's Prime Minister under the previous system, is the new President, and of the thirty-member cabinet, only four are civilians and none are women. The head of the military appoints the Ministers of Home Affairs, Border Affairs and Defence. U Win Tin's words written more than a year earlier proved prescient: 'The showcase election planned by the military regime makes a mockery of the freedom sought by our people and would make military dictatorship permanent.'[31]

Nevertheless, within a few months of their election some MPs did begin to test what little space they had, by tabling questions and debates that would previously have been unthinkable. They started gingerly, with questions about land rights and child rights, but quickly became more confident, raising questions about the ethnic conflict and political prisoners. Five ethnic political parties formed an alliance, the Nationalities Brotherhood Forum, bringing together Shan, Mon, Rakhine, Chin and Karen parties in a grouping in Parliament. In February 2012, Parliament debated the country's budget for the first time. As United Nations adviser Aung Tun Thet told the media, 'it's a very refreshing step forward. It's a demonstration of the checks and balances between the legislative and the executive.' Under previous regimes, which spent almost half their budget on the military and less than 2 per cent on health, there was, said Aung Tun Thet, 'no assessment, no discussion, no dialogue. Now for the first time in many, many years, we have a chance to discuss the budget and its priorities.'[32]

It remains to be seen whether these steps will lead to more substantial reform. With its victory secured and its continued rule guaranteed, the regime could afford a face-lift, and went vigorously into public relations mode. Six days after the election, Aung San Suu Kyi was released from her latest period of house arrest. Under Burmese law her detention had expired, and the regime clearly wanted to improve its international image and divert attention from the elections. The crowds who had gathered outside her home showed that, more than two decades after the Shwedagon speech at which she had first captured the imaginations and affections of Burma's people, she is as relevant to the country and its future now as she has ever been.

Immediately, she re-energised her supporters. 'Please do not give up hope. There is no reason to lose heart,' she told the crowds in front of the NLD's offices the day after her release. 'Even if you are not political, politics will come to you. None of us can do it alone. We must work together.'[33] With that theme of unity echoing in the ears of those who heard her, she then displayed an extraordinary absence of bitterness towards her former captors. 'I have no negative feelings towards the government,' she said. Her message to Than Shwe? 'Let's meet each other directly.'[34]

For nine months, the regime ignored that offer and there appeared to be no hope of change any time soon. Although President Thein Sein spoke of reforms in his inaugural speech in March 2011, few people believed him at the time and there were few signs of substance to back up his pledges. Yet just as history repeats itself in Burma, so Burmese politics is capable of producing surprises. On 19 August 2011 Aung San Suu Kyi received a sudden, and apparently unexpected, invitation to Naypyidaw, where she met President Thein Sein for the first time. Even more surprising than the meeting itself was her positive assessment of the new President. After years of stalemate, in which the regime either refused to talk or offered nothing substantial to talk about, Aung San Suu Kyi repeatedly claimed that Thein Sein was a man she could trust, and that he was 'an honest man'.[35] In January 2012, I asked Aung San Suu Kyi why she believed Thein Sein, and she told me that her meeting with him was completely unlike any previous meeting with anyone from the regime in the past two decades. All her previous conversations with Generals had contained no substance whatsoever. They were, in her words, 'nothing'. In contrast, Thein Sein immediately got down to detail, telling her that he wanted her to be part of the process, and asking what the government needed to do to make it possible for her to participate. They discussed substantive issues such as the 2008 constitution, election laws and other concerns. His willingness to engage at that level made her feel, as Margaret Thatcher famously said of Mikhail Gorbachev, that he was a man she could do business with.

In subsequent months Thein Sein talked increasingly of reform, and her engagement with the process deepened, to such an extent that the President's adviser was openly talking about the possibility of her being offered a position in government.[36] A significant number of political prisoners, including the high-profile '88 Generation leaders and the comedian Zarganar, were released, censorship was eased, bans on websites were lifted, and most significantly, the NLD was permitted to register as a political party and contest parliamentary by-elections. On 1 April 2012, the NLD won 43 of the 45 parliamentary seats contested, and Aung San Suu

Kyi won her constituency of Kawhmu in a landslide. She told the BBC that she believed Burma would see real democracy in her lifetime. [37]

Within less than a year the mood changed from near-despair to cautious optimism. A Burmese journalist who is a known critic of the regime told me in January 2012 that for the first time since 1962, Burmese people were praying for the President to live, not to die. People were becoming increasingly persuaded that Thein Sein was, at least personally, sincere. But there is a recognition that as things stand, much is riding on the shoulders of two human beings: Thein Sein and Aung San Suu Kyi. It is no secret that Thein Sein, in his late sixties, is not in good health. 'We're all praying for his pacemaker to keep working,' said the Burmese journalist.

Yet sceptics are right to remind the world that there is still a long way to go, and that until all political prisoners are released, there is significant legislative, institutional and constitutional reform, the rule of law is established, and – crucially – the military stops attacks on ethnic civilians and declares a nationwide peace process, one cannot be confident of real freedom in Burma. When I returned from Rangoon in January 2012, I said I believed in 'cautious optimism' – with equal emphasis on both words. There are reasons to be hopeful, but still plenty of grounds for caution. Some, including Aung San Suu Kyi's own colleague U Win Tin, warn that Thein Sein's reforms are a ploy to neutralise her and gain international legitimacy. Ludu Sein Win was even more scathing, believing she is walking into a 'trap' that will lead to her spending months in Naypyidaw, isolated and separated from the NLD and the people, and that it would spell the end for her party. 'A leopard never changes its spots,' he told me. Without doubt, the regime's motives remain those of self-interest. It is unlikely that the Generals have had an epiphany and woken up as true believers in democracy – instead, they want to see sanctions lifted, China's influence counter-balanced by that of the United States, their pariah status removed and legitimacy secured.

As to where Than Shwe is in all this, there are three possibilities. The first, but least likely, is that he has confounded everyone's expectations and genuinely retired, which is what the regime would like us to believe. Indeed, Burma's Information Minister Kyaw Hsan told the *Wall Street Journal* that Than Shwe is 'in his house, doing a lot of reading, and enjoying a peaceful time'.[38] The speaker of the Lower House of Parliament, Shwe

Mann, said that 'the senior general is really retired', and went on to state that 'The senior general is absolutely not concerned with the party, nor the government, nor our parliament, nor legislative organisations.' While it is true that he is no longer involved in day-to-day policy matters, it seems very unlikely that he would have disengaged completely. Most people tell me that his role is rather like that of Ne Win; government ministers pay courtesy calls on Than Shwe from time to time and seek his views on the key issues of the day, but that his influence will gradually wane. It is possible, though, that the whole reform exercise is a clever game of divide and rule masterminded, or at least approved, by the great psychological warrior himself, to undermine the democracy movement and play games with the international community. A third possibility, which has a certain logic, is that Than Shwe saw what happened to Egypt's Mubarak, Libya's Colonel Gaddafi, and other dictators, and concluded that a controlled, gradual transition process in which his security and that of his family is protected, is preferable to a violent popular uprising in which his own fate could be in jeopardy. After all, Father San Germano's description of the Burmese people in the early twentieth century is still an appropriate description of Than Shwe and the regime today: 'There is no contempt, oppression or injustice they will not exercise towards their fellow men when they can assure themselves of the protection of government.'[39]

The Future?

'Those who love stay awake when duty calls, wake up from sleep when someone needs help; those who love keep burning, no matter what, like a lighted torch. Those who love take on anything, complete goals, bring plans to fruition. Those who do not love faint and lie down on the job.'

Thomas à Kempis, *The Imitation of Christ*

BURMA TRULY IS at a crossroads. For the first time since Ne Win's coup in 1962, there may finally be a possibility that Burma could establish a meaningful democracy – something few would have dared predict until very recently.

Yet there is still a long way to go. Although Thein Sein and his regime have promised that the reforms they are implementing are 'irreversible', Aung San Suu Kyi rightly warns that the test will be how much support for change exists within the military as a whole. 'I wouldn't say it is unstoppable. I think there are obstacles, and there are some dangers,' she says.[1] U Win Tin is more outspoken, warning that hopes have been raised and if they are not met, another popular uprising is likely. 'The simmering discontent is there,' he told *The Times*. 'President Obama said that there is light in Burma and we can see the light. But, here in Burma, we are still inside the tunnel.'[2]

Nevertheless, Thein Sein's reforms are evidence that years of international pressure have begun to make an impact. Bringing Burma's human rights record to the agenda of the United Nations Security Council, threatening the establishment of a United Nations Commission of Inquiry into war crimes and crimes against humanity, which could have led to a prosecution of the Generals in the International Criminal Court, combined with targeted economic sanctions have been the campaign themes of activists around the world. No single measure can be accorded credit for impacting the regime, but the combination of pressure and, more recently, high-level engagement appears to have communicated a clear message: keep suppressing, raping, enslaving and killing your people, and you will remain a pariah state; but if you change your ways, pressure can be lifted and you can be welcomed as an accepted member of the international community. That message was most clearly articulated during the historic visit of US Secretary of State Hillary Clinton in December 2011, followed a few weeks later by that of British Foreign Secretary William Hague, both the first visits of their kind since 1955. On 13 April, 2012, David Cameron became the first British prime minister to visit the country in living memory, and the first Western leader to meet Aung San Suu Kyi and Thein Sein in Burma. The unprecedented, and previously unimaginable, photo-calls, and substantive meetings, they all had with Thein Sein and Aung San Suu Kyi symbolise the crossroads which Burma has reached. Their visits have been followed by countless others.

The courage of the Burmese people is primarily responsible for bringing them to this point. However, the support of international human rights organisations and aid agencies, large and small, politicians of all political perspectives, and ordinary, unknown individuals from a wide range of countries who have stood in solidarity with the people of Burma should not be underestimated. When foreigners have taken the time to learn about the people of Burma, and their suffering, particularly by visiting the country and its borders and hearing stories first-hand, they can rarely walk away from the cause.

Politicians whom I have taken to Burma's borders have been converted into some of the country's strongest champions. Andrew Mitchell, Britain's former Secretary of State for International Development, was one. 'It was horrendous. The stories that were told, mostly by widows, were heart-breaking. It is the only time in my life that I have ever been seized by an almost uncontrollable spasm of fury,' he said after a visit to a camp for internally displaced peoples just inside Karen State, Burma in 2007. 'These people, with horrendous stories, were living in dire conditions. They had a stream that they used for washing, drinking, defecating. But there was a wonderful sense of community and solidarity. The Burma Army was terrifyingly close, separated from us by a short distance with just a few landmines and Karen soldiers.' Similarly John Bercow, now Speaker of Britain's House of Commons, visited the Thailand–Burma border with me in 2004. 'I was struck by the sheer savagery of some of the human rights abuses about which we heard testimony. I met parents who had seen their children shot dead in front of them, and children whose parents had been shot dead in front of them.' His commitment was fuelled by memories of the people he had met.

> I recall meeting a man who had been subjected to water torture. I asked him what he thought of the Tatmadaw soldier who had done this to him, and he replied in a very matter-of-fact way: 'I love him. He is my brother.' Someone who combines determination with such dignity and grace deserves our continuing support and advocacy. I felt that if that is how he behaved, it is my job to use what limited influence I have got, and certainly the voice I have and the pen I possess and the opportunity of a public platform that I enjoy, to ratchet up the level of attention to what is going on in Burma.

The challenge also motivated him. 'There was the sense that there is this utterly incorrigible, shameless, sadistic dictatorship putting two fingers up at the world and that I regarded as a challenge. I believe passionately in the UN Responsibility to Protect mechanism, and I believe we have a duty to protect the people in Burma and on the borders who are innocent victims of one of the most hideous regimes on the face of the planet.' In 2007, Bercow and I travelled to the India–Burma border to meet Chin refugees, the first time an elected politician from the West, and possibly anywhere in the world, had been to that border.

Glenys Kinnock, a former British Foreign Office Minister, former Member of the European Parliament and wife of the former leader of the Labour Party, now in the House of Lords, is another champion of Burma. In 1996, she went to Rangoon to meet Aung San Suu Kyi, and left just two hours before a mob attack on the democracy leader. 'It was a very unpleasant atmosphere and a very tense trip,' Kinnock said afterwards. 'I have never seen such deprivation and such malnourished children.'[3]

Politicians from other countries have visited the borders as well, including Irish MP Simon Coveney, who travelled with me in 2005, US Congressman Joseph Pitts, Australian parliamentarians and members of the ASEAN Inter-Parliamentary Myanmar Caucus, established to bring together MPs with a concern for Burma from across the South East Asia region.

But you don't have to be a politician or a full-time activist to make a difference. People such as my great friend Martin Panter, an Australian doctor who has travelled twice a year for the past two decades to the Thailand–Burma border, and occasionally the India–Burma border, to conduct medical training, and who introduced me to Burma, deserve recognition.

The role of the individual is illustrated perhaps most inspiringly by Deklan Stokle and his family. At the age of just eight years old, Deklan's parents took him to the Thailand–Burma border for the first time, and what he learned there changed his life. He and his family have returned to the border to visit refugees most years since then, and when he was sixteen he travelled inside Burma. He returned home to Newcastle, in the north of England, having visited orphans in Pathein, promising himself to tell others about Burma. He has spoken in churches, youth groups and schools, and in 2010 when Pope Benedict XVI visited the United Kingdom, Deklan was given an opportunity to speak at the vigil in Hyde Park. In front of 80,000 people he told the crowd:

Six years ago, at the age of twelve, I looked into the eyes of an orphan from Burma. For the first time in my life I saw the poor and oppressed as human beings. I saw a child who was no different to me. I saw a child who deserved everything I had. I could see that and I was only twelve.

I have lived with the refugee children of Burma and I have shared their meagre rations of food. In return they ask I share their story with the world. I have a hope that one day all the children of Burma, Buddhist, Christian, Muslim, Hindu and those of no religion will live together in freedom and peace . . .

I am asking you to fight the Burmese Junta, not with guns and bullets, but with prayers and actions. I am asking you to fight against this injustice and to be the voice for the voiceless. These people are human beings and deserve the same dignity and reedom that we enjoy. For me being a Catholic means standing up for those suffering an injustice – whether on my doorstep or 6000 miles away.

Such international efforts appear to have led Thein Sein to recognise that the status quo is unsustainable. Even with the political, diplomatic, economic and military support of China, India, the Association of Southeast Asian Nations (ASEAN), Russia and North Korea, the humanitarian and economic catastrophe awaiting Burma if it does not change is too great to keep things as they are. He, and others in the regime, do not want to become a client state of China, which is what they will fast become if they do not take steps to improve relations with the United States and Europe, to act as a counterweight. Could Thein Sein prove to be Burma's equivalent of South Africa's F.W. de Klerk, the Soviet Union's Mikhail Gorbachev or Indonesia's B.J. Habibie? Quite possibly, precisely because in all three cases their motivation was similar. None of these reform-minded leaders were originally real democrats – they embarked on reforms with the intention of preserving the system and protecting themselves, recognising that leaving things as they were would lead to chaos and upheaval. In all three cases, however, once the door to reform was opened a crack, the momentum grew until complete change became unstoppable. Events moved far faster than Gorbachev, de Klerk or Habibie anticipated. If Thein Sein proves to be in the same mould, the scenario in Burma could be similar.

History shows that dictators do not last for ever. Herculean struggles that at times appear hopeless have resulted in astonishing transformations. The collapse of the Soviet Union and the spread of democracy throughout Eastern Europe; the end of apartheid in South Africa; the fall of Suharto and the establishment of democracy in Indonesia; the independence of East Timor after a quarter of a century of Indonesian military occupation; the demise of the Marcos regime in the Philippines; the transformation from authoritarianism to democracy in South Korea, Taiwan and much of Latin America; the toppling of Slobodan Milošević in Serbia; the victory for democracy against Asia's longest serving dictator, Maumoon Abdul Gayoom, in the Maldives; and even the overthrow of Saddam Hussein in Iraq and the Taliban in Afghanistan, albeit by controversial international armed intervention – all these and other examples demonstrate that the human spirit yearns for freedom, that such a desire is universal, and that in the end, freedom will win.

In 2011, a movement swept through North Africa, bringing down the twenty-three-year rule of Zine al-Abidine Ben Ali in Tunisia, the thirty-year rule of Hosni Mubarak in Egypt and the forty-two-year rule of Colonel Muammar Gaddafi in Libya. Driven by the traditional methods of mass popular protest, combined with the use of modern technology to communicate developments, this could provide a model for future freedom movements, although what then followed in these countries clearly is not.

In the demonstrations in Burma in 2007, mobile telephones and Internet technology proved vital to communicating news to the outside world from a country whose regime banned foreign journalists from entering. Facebook, Twitter, Google, BlackBerry messenger, email and other technologies will take on ever-increasing importance. An editorial in *The Times* describes Twitter, along with Facebook, as 'a potent tool for democratic engagement' and concludes that the movements in Tunisia and Egypt were not only precipitated, as in Burma, by rising prices and anger at corruption. 'They are also the product of a heady atmosphere seeded by new freedoms of expression and information,' the newspaper concludes. 'This kind of freedom of information and freedom of communication has many positive sides. It undermines regimes that have sought to bolster their power by keeping their people ignorant. It makes strangers less strange to each other. It also exposes bad arguments to daylight and scrutiny . . . Social networks were built to make friends: they are turning into places to take on your enemies.'[4]

I have had the privilege of witnessing and, in a small way participating in, transitions from oppressive rule to democracy in two countries. In 2002, I was living in East Timor, having for several years supported the campaign for its liberation. At midnight on 20 May 2002, after centuries of Portuguese colonial rule, twenty-five years of brutal Indonesian military occupation, and three years of UN-led transitional administration, the Democratic Republic of Timor-Leste was born. Moments after the new flag had been raised and the national anthem sung, I turned to the man next to me, who had been the first Timorese to be forced into exile soon after the Indonesian invasion in 1975. He was a Catholic priest, Father Francisco Maria Fernandes, and he was an old friend of mine. I asked him if he had ever believed in all his years of exile that he would live to see this day. He smiled, nodded, and said: 'Yes I did. Throughout our struggle, people all around the world used to say to me, "Why do you carry on? You are fighting a losing battle. Indonesia will never give you freedom. The world will never help you. Why don't you just give up." But we had one thing those people did not know about. We trusted God. This was a victory of faith.' As he uttered those final words, fireworks lit up the night sky, providing a tangible symbol of light penetrating the darkness. That principle of faith – whether religious or philosophical – applies to all movements for freedom: faith in philosophical and moral, religious and spiritual beliefs, not giving up, not allowing circumstances or doubt to deter, not losing hope.

In 2006, I visited the Maldives, a country more often associated with tropical paradise vacations, beautiful beaches and bright blue seawater glistening in the sunlight than with dictatorship. In reality, the Maldives was ruled with an iron fist by Maumoon Abdul Gayoom, who suppressed critics and jailed opponents. Gayoom, who had ruled the archipelago since 1978, had, however, appointed some ministers in his government who were reformers, and in the face of growing pressure from his people and the international community, he allowed a reform process to begin. Precisely what his intentions were only he knows, but my strong suspicion is that he intended it as a public relations exercise, to buy off his opponents and keep his critics at bay. It snowballed into a more meaningful transition. When I visited, I met the lead reformer, the Foreign Minister Dr Ahmed Shaheed. He arranged for me to visit a journalist, Jennifer Latheef, and the Leader of the Opposition Maldivian Democratic Party (MDP), Mohamed Nasheed, both under house arrest. Nasheed had spent several years in solitary confinement in prison, and had been repeatedly tortured. After my visit, I produced a report, in which I concluded that if it was serious about reform, the regime needed to release Nasheed and Latheef as a matter of urgency. Within months, they were freed and two years later the Maldives' first free multi-party elections were held. The man I had met under house arrest in 2006 became the first freely elected President of the Maldives.

In all these struggles, the courage of the people of these countries themselves, combined with solidarity and support from people outside, took them from tyranny to liberty. The same can be achieved in Burma. The people of Burma have shown extraordinary courage, commitment, sacrifice and hard work in their struggle for freedom, and in Aung San Suu Kyi they have a leader every bit as inspiring and unifying as Václav Havel, Nelson Mandela, Desmond Tutu, Xanana Gusmão or Mohamed Nasheed. There is no doubt in my mind that, one day, Burma will be free.

When and how? The first of these two questions is impossible to answer. History says it can happen, and the courage of the people inspires confidence that it can happen, but the timing cannot be predicted. Change happened in Eastern Europe, Indonesia, East Timor and Egypt rapidly, and when we least expected it, and the same could be true in Burma. Even the current period of reform was unexpected, and the pace surprising. The question of how is also difficult to predict precisely. If Thein Sein's reforms take root, if a genuine peace can be negotiated in the ethnic states, if religious intolerance can be curbed, and a gradual transition to democracy can be developed, then it could happen in an orderly way. The next major test will be the elections in 2015. They will inherently be unfair, not least because the constitution has not been amended and it prohibits Aung San Suu Kyi from becoming President. But they may be much freer than previous elections, and the NLD may well win a majority in Parliament and some influence in government. If, however, there proves to be no real substance to Thein Sein's promises of reform, or an internal coup by hardliners in the regime stalls them, and hopes are dashed, then a more chaotic upheaval is likely, but one which would probably require a convergence of three factors: popular uprising, division within the military and intensified, targeted international pressure. There are many within the ranks of the military whose morale is low, who hate the country's pariah status, who are not inspired by the Generals, and who harbour a secret admiration for Aung San Suu Kyi. Were they to be reassured that if they defected they could be given safety, and that if change comes they would not be punished, then at the right moment they could turn. The factor that holds them back is the same factor that makes most ordinary civilians in Burma think twice before speaking out: fear. Yet if they heed the words of Aung San Suu Kyi, in her book *Freedom from Fear*, the potential for

Burma is unlimited: 'Don't think about whether these things [justice and freedom] will happen. Just continue to do what you believe is right. Later on the fruits of what you do will become apparent on their own. One's responsibility is to do the right thing.'[5] Many Burmese people, whose stories are told in this book, are already following this path. The question for the international community, individuals, organisations and governments, is will we be with them?

When democracy truly comes to Burma, new challenges will arise which will be as difficult to overcome as the current ones. There will be no panacea. Post-apartheid South Africa, independent East Timor, a democratic Maldives, not to mention the former Soviet Union and Eastern Europe show that a transition to freedom and democracy is not easy. A free Burma will need continued international support and solidarity. Resolving conflicts within ethnic groups, between the ethnic nationalities and the majority population, between different Burman factions and between the population and the military will require time and expertise. Questions of how to balance the apparently conflicting principles of justice and reconciliation will dominate, as they did in South Africa and East Timor. Developing skills and infrastructure will need international resources. There may be further conflict, tension and turmoil even when Burma has won its freedom, if the experiences of the Maldives and East Timor are anything to go by. In the Maldives, a coup d'état in 2012 by forces close to the previous dictator, in collusion with Islamists, in which Mohamed Nasheed was forced to resign at gunpoint, set back democratisation.

Fresh elections were held in 2013, but were declared void when Mr Nasheed emerged as the winner, and a re-run was held until the polls yielded the result the old dictatorship desired. Abdulla Yameen, the brother of the former dictator Mr Gayoom, was elected President. He appointed Mr Gayoom's daughter as Foreign Minister. The Gayoom family were back in power. Eighteen months later Mr Nasheed was arrested, put on trial, and jailed for thirteen years. He has later moved to house arrest – back where he was when I first met him nine years earlier – and then back to prison. President Yameen appeared determined to do everything possible to ensure that his rival never returns to politics.

In East Timor in 2008, tension between the government and rebels within the army threatened the country's new-found fragile independence, led to violence and the displacement of thousands, and assassination attempts on José Ramos-Horta and Xanana Gusmão. Building an open society after decades of repression is not easy, as these examples show.

What are the lessons for Burma? Firstly, that transitions are fragile, and that vested interests can be powerful. Secondly, one of Mr Nasheed's failures, with hindsight, was his considerable generosity of spirit towards his former oppressors. He staunchly resisted any suggestion of bringing the old regime to justice for their crimes. Thirdly, when he did try to reform the one key institution whose reform was essential if democracy was to be assured – the judiciary – he came into collision with those vested interests that were close to the old regime, and that led to his downfall. If he had taken a more robust stand on judicial reform earlier in the process, perhaps his fate would have turned out differently. But then again, perhaps not. Nevertheless, questions of judicial reform and the rule of law, and the balance to strike between justice, accountability, ending impunity and reconciliation, are questions that face Burma as they do the Maldives.

Developing the building blocks of democracy – the rule of law, respect for basic freedoms and human rights, the conduct of multi-party and multi-ethnic politics – will pose further challenges as well as opportunities. Yet if the peoples of Burma can agree on a plan for genuine federal democracy, and embrace the principle of unity in diversity, then these hurdles can be overcome and Burma can be the thriving, beautiful, successful land it deserves to be. The rising awareness of the centrality of the ethnic question among some prominent Burman dissidents encourages me to believe that the challenges are not insurmountable. The '88 Generation leaders have started to show a level of understanding and concern about the ethnic situation that had not previously been seen, as has Ludu Sein Win. 'I fully support the ethnic people,' he told me in January 2012. 'They are fighting for their freedom. As a Burman, I hate the Burman mentality of seeing ourselves as the "elder brother", and the ethnic people as "younger brother". Who gave the Burmans "elder brother" status? All the peoples of Burma should have equality, secured by federalism.'

In February 2012, Aung San Suu Kyi visited Kachin State and delivered a speech in which she promised to work for the establishment of a genuine federal union. This pledge should go some way towards reassuring the ethnic people, some of whom have questioned her commitment to addressing their plight. Most ethnic people, however, recognise that Aung San Suu Kyi is their best hope for a resolution. 'We understand that she is struggling for the people of Burma, and we appreciate what she is doing,' one Kachin told me just a month before she visited the state. 'We request her to think about the Kachin people, who have suffered a long time. We are left far behind the other people of Burma. We hope she will consider protecting the Kachin people. We trust her, and that is why we ask for her help to protect our people and our rights.' A Kachin pastor emphasised her responsibility as the daughter of Aung San, whose legacy included the Panglong Agreement. 'We Kachin people have really high regard for her father's legacy. We hope it will be fulfilled one day.'

The choice Burma faces is illustrated perhaps most colourfully by the story of one of the NLD's by-election candidates, Zayar Thaw, founder of the Generation Wave movement of activists established in 2007. Zayar Thaw was a hip-hop singer, but in April 2012 he contested, and surprisingly won, one of the parliamentary seats in the regime's stronghold of Naypyidaw. The juxtaposition of contrasts – hip-hop singer in his thirties takes on ex-Generals in their sixties – represents the choice Burma must make between its future and its past. So too does Zayar Thaw's vision. When I met him in January 2012, he talked about the need to unite the country, to end the brutal persecution of ethnic minorities, to guarantee equal rights for all, to develop understanding between the Burmans and the ethnic groups, and to help people understand the real meaning of federalism and its benefits for the country. He also talked about his own experience of three years in prison, and his desire for reconciliation with his adversaries. 'We don't want to live with hate, we want to look forward. If our hearts are filled with hate, we cannot do anything else,' he said. 'The system made us – whether we are activists against the system, or officials within the system. In our struggle, we, the activists, are trying to push the system, and the people within it are trying to protect the system. But if together we change the system, then the problem is solved.' This desire to look to the future was reiterated to me by Aung San Suu Kyi. 'There are some people who think it is still 1988,' she said. 'It isn't. It is right to be sceptical or cautious, but to not want to try – that I don't understand.'

In their struggle for freedom, as they approach the crossroads of potential change, the people of Burma deserve the continued support of the international community. The vision is clear, as Aung San Suu Kyi has articulated it: 'We want a Burma where there's freedom to debate, and to exchange ideas, and to analyse the situation as we see it. Burma is now at an important juncture in its modern history. We have come to a path where we may be able to progress towards our long-cherished goal of democracy and freedom,' she told Chatham House in 2011.[6] As Burma approaches this crossroads, the time has come to redouble our efforts, individually and collectively. A banner hanging in a bamboo hut in a Karen village of internally displaced people, orphaned, widowed, wounded and dying of treatable and preventable diseases, presents a challenge for us all. On the banner was the question: 'Are you for democracy or dictatorship?' We all need to consider our response, and what that means in terms of action.

Epilogue

'**B**URMA stands on a knife-edge of hope and fear,' wrote the Catholic Archbishop of Rangoon who became Burma's first cardinal, Charles Maung Bo, in the *Washington Post* in June 2014. Warning against 'premature euphoria', Cardinal Bo said: 'Concern fills our hearts as we see darkness compete with hope. We pray this is not a false dawn. For five decades Burma endured crucifixion on a cross of injustice bearing five nails: dictatorship, war, displacement, poverty and oppression. Today, a new crucifixion threatens the country, with five new nails: land-grabbing, corruption, economic injustice, ethnic conflict and displacement and religious hatred and violence . . . Burma's future hangs in the balance.'[1]

Those words vividly describe the challenges Burma continues to face today. Even though some political liberalisation has occurred, political prisoners have been released, space for civil society and media expanded and a torturous process of ceasefire talks with the ethnic nationalities continues, other challenges such as land confiscation, crony capitalism and religious nationalism have emerged, and the ethnic conflict remains unresolved. The military is continuing an offensive in Shan and Kachin states, for example, resulting in the displacement of over 100,000 people. A new offensive was launched against the ethnic Chinese Kokang people in northern Shan State in 2015. Rape is still being perpetrated by the Burma Army, as illustrated by the brutal rape and murder of two Kachin school teachers in January 2015. The production and spread of narcotics, particularly in Kachin and Shan states, is having devastating social consequences, just as illegal logging and mining is having a serious environmental impact. Crony capitalism, with oligarchies and monopolies close to the government or the military, stifles opportunities for potential entrepreneurs, while the trade in jade and other gems primarily benefits the military and the ethnic armed groups, with little economic gain for the population-at-large.

Since 2013 there have also been signs of regression on the political front, with the arrest and imprisonment of demonstrators and journalists, filling the prison cells that had been emptied of previous political prisoners in 2012. At the beginning of 2014, for example, there were reportedly thirteen political prisoners; at the time of writing, there are over 150, with almost 1,500 farmers and activists also on or awaiting trial. Crucially, there have been no new political reforms despite a flurry of activity and hype between 2011 and 2012, and on the fundamental issue of the constitution, attempts at amendment have failed.

Aung San Suu Kyi approached the elections in November 2015 able to contest her parliamentary seat, but ineligible to be a candidate for the presidency, due to the unreformed provisions in the constitution designed to bar her. President Thein Sein's major rival for the presidency, the Speaker of the Lower House of Parliament, Shwe Mann, was purged as leader of the ruling party in August 2015. At the time of writing, the regime's carefully constructed veneer of reform was wearing incredibly thin, revealing a government led by people who had changed their clothes and their image and introduced some surface-level changes but whose *modus operandi* remained the same: hold on to power, crush any opposition and keep international pressure at bay by doing the bare minimum to create a semblance of progress without any fundamental change.

Burma appears to be less at a crossroads and more at a roundabout. Many, on the other hand, would say that whatever the regime's intentions, the genie is out of the bottle. Steps by the government, albeit faltering and inconsistent, towards transparency and consultation with civil society and non-governmental actors could drive democratisation forward. With a freer media, better communications, a vibrant civil society sector and therefore greater availability of information, a better-informed and better-organised public, combined with the eyes of the world continuing to watch, a formidable force could be created which the government and businesses would more reluctant to ignore than they did before. Time will tell.

Of the new challenges, the most dangerous is the emergence of militant Buddhist nationalism, and the relative silence on the part of the democracy movement in response. In June 2012, violence broke out in four townships in Arakan (Rakhine) State, resulting in the displacement of over 140,000 mainly Rohingya people. Sparked by the alleged rape of a twenty-eight-year-old Arakanese woman by three Muslim men on 28 May, the violence began when a large group of Arakanese villagers in Toungop stopped a bus and beat and killed ten Muslim passengers. The spiral of violence intensified, with victims among both the Arakanese and the Rohingyas, while the state security forces looked on passively, doing nothing to halt the carnage. Indeed, before long the security forces actively participated in attacks on Muslim neighbourhoods.

An uneasy, fragile calm followed for three months, although the tensions remained high. In October 2012, the conflict erupted again, affecting nine townships in the state and involving what Human Rights Watch described as 'a coordinated campaign to forcibly relocate or remove the state's Muslims'.[2]

The violence in October, claims Human Rights Watch, was well-planned. 'For months, local Arakanese political party officials and senior Buddhist monks publicly vilified the Rohingya population and described them as a threat to Arakan State,' the organisation notes in a 2013 report titled 'All You Can Do is Pray: Crimes Against Humanity and Ethnic Cleansing of Rohingya Muslims in Burma's Arakan State'. 'On October 23, thousands of Arakanese men armed with machetes, swords, homemade guns, Molotov cocktails, and other weapons descended upon and attacked Muslim villages in nine townships throughout the state. State security forces either failed to intervene or participated directly in the violence. In some cases attacks occurred simultaneously in townships separated by considerable distance. In the deadliest incident, on October 23 at least 70 Rohingya were killed in a massacre in Yan Thei village in Mrauk-U Township. Despite advance warning of the attack, only a small number of riot police, local police, and army soldiers were on duty to provide security. Instead of preventing the attack by the Arakanese mob or escorting the villagers to safety, they assisted the killings by disarming the Rohingya of their sticks and other rudimentary weapons they carried to defend themselves.'

Satellite images that Human Rights Watch obtained show 27 specific 'zones of destruction' in just five of the 13 townships affected by violence. In Sittwe, the capital of Arakan State, there were at least 2,558 'destroyed structures'. At least 4,862 structures were destroyed in Arakan State as a whole in June and October 2012.[3] Human Rights Watch concludes that what took place in Arakan State amounts to ethnic cleansing and crimes against humanity. Other international experts, including Tomás Ojea Quintana, former UN Special Rapporteur on Human Rights in Burma, warn of possible genocide. 'There are elements of genocide,' Professor Quintana said in 2014. 'The possibility of a genocide needs to be discussed.'

President Thein Sein himself revealed the regime's mindset in July 2012 when he called on the international community to resettle the entire Rohingya population in a third country – tantamount to ethnic cleansing, albeit in slightly more sophisticated packaging.[4] In February 2014, Fortify Rights released a report, 'Policies of Persecution', revealing the restrictions in place against Rohingyas.[5] Restrictions on marriage, on religious practice and on movement have been in place for many years, and amount to a deliberate campaign of persecution. Furthermore, according to Fortify Rights, there is evidence of senior government officials planning to tighten the noose around the Rohingyas. In 2011 the Minister of Defence, Hla Min, made a speech calling for tougher restrictions and in 2012 General Ko Ko, the Home Affairs Minister, did the same.[6]

A humanitarian crisis followed the violence, not only with over 140,000 people held in desperate conditions in camps for displaced people, but also for the thousands of Rohingyas who have fled the misery they face in Burma for an equally horrific plight on boats at sea, at the mercy of traffickers, dangerous weather, inhumane travelling conditions and brutal rejection by the countries they flee to in the region.

Several prominent international figures have visited the camps in Arakan State since 2012, and all report some of the worst conditions they have witnessed. The UN Assistant General-Secretary for Humanitarian Affairs, Kyung-wha Kang, said after visiting camps in June 2014 that: 'I witnessed a level of human suffering in the IDP camps that I have personally never seen before . . . appalling conditions . . . wholly inadequate access to basic services including health, education, water and sanitation.'[7] Those words echo the words of the Under-Secretary-

General for Humanitarian Affairs, Baroness Amos, who said after visiting the camps in December 2012: 'I have seen many camps during my time but the conditions in these camps rank among the worst. Unfortunately we as the United Nations are not able to get in and do the range of work we would like to do with those people, so the conditions are terrible . . . It's a dire situation and we have to do something about it.'[8] The UN Special Rapporteur on Human Rights in Burma, Yanghee Lee, said in early 2015 following her visit that she 'witnessed how dire the situation has remained . . . The conditions in Muslim IDP [internally displaced persons] camps are abysmal and I received heart-breaking testimonies from Rohingya people telling me they had only two options: stay and die or leave by boat.'[9]

The situation is not only dire inside the camps. For Muslims in northern Rakhine, the humanitarian crisis is also desperate. At least 70 per cent of Rohingya currently have no access to safe water or sanitation services. In Maungdaw Township, there is just one doctor per 160,000 people. The World Health Organisation recommends one doctor per 5,000 people. Only 2 per cent of Rohingya women give birth in a hospital.[10]

The desperate plight of the Rohingyas, one of the most persecuted minorities in the world today, has finally gained some much-needed and long overdue international media and political attention. However, it is important to remember two vital points.

Firstly, while undoubtedly the Rohingyas are the primary victims, Rakhine Buddhists have also suffered in the conflict, and their sense of grievance should not be ignored. The international community is perceived within Burma as being unduly biased towards the Rohingyas. Given the extent of the persecution and dehumanisation that the Rohingyas face, the fact that they are receiving attention is both right and unsurprising. However, the international community should be mindful of the Arakanese perceptions, in what is in any case one of the poorest and most deprived parts of Burma. Arakanese hostility to foreign aid agencies can have dangerous consequences. In March 2014, for example, UN agencies and NGOs in Arakan State were attacked by violent Buddhist mobs, forcing them to withdraw from the area temporarily.[11] This only served to compound the humanitarian crisis.

Secondly, it is essential to realise that the Rohingyas are not the only victims of anti-Muslim hatred, discrimination and violence in Burma.

In March 2013, Meikhtila – a city in central Burma, far from Arakan State and with no connection to the Rohingyas – was struck by an orgy of violence against the local Muslim community. According to Physicians for Human Rights, over 100 people were killed in the course of three days, over 1,500 homes burned down and more than a dozen mosques destroyed.[12]

Throughout much of the rest of 2013, a wave of anti-Muslim violence swept Burma. From Oakkan near Rangoon[13] to Lashio in northern Shan State and Thandwe in Arakan State, a pattern emerged. Typically the spark would be a rumour – sometimes false, sometimes exaggerated, sometimes true – of the rape of a Buddhist woman or the desecration of a Buddhist monument. That was all that was needed to incite violence, and while in some places the security forces did act to bring the situation under control, in many incidents they stood by and let it happen. And in most instances, the instigators were outsiders, not locals, although local people participated after the incitement. In July 2014, anti-Muslim violence hit Mandalay, Burma's second largest city. An investigation by the Justice Trust detailed the role of outsiders in stoking the Mandalay riots.[14]

I was in Burma when the tragedy in Meikhtila occurred in March 2013. I took a British Parliamentarian, Lord Alton of Liverpool, with me, and we visited Ayela, a village on the outskirts of the capital, on 25 March. Three days earlier, Muslims in Ayela had been attacked, and we saw the burned-out madrassah and the desecrated, burned mosque. We met with the few remaining Muslims, and one man described what had occurred:

At 10 p.m. on 22 March, people gathered in the village, having heard that a mob was on the way. I sent news to the authorities. Then a big crowd – maybe as many as 1,000, but I am not sure – came. When the mob came, the people ran away. Only 15 police came, but they also ran away, instead of doing their duty. The mob came from outside, maybe from Meikhtila or motivated by Meikhtila. Now, only a small number of Muslims remain. Out of 260 Muslims, only 15 have stayed. The mob burned down the madrassa, attacked another building, our dining hall, and destroyed the inside of the mosque. They went into houses, stole possessions – clothes, money, food. They were shouting, 'Kill Muslims, kill Muslims, kill "Kala."' No one was injured or killed, but that was only because they all managed to run away. It was very frightening. We have never had problems before. Buddhists and Muslims never had any conflict in this area. We have lived here for 200 years with no problems, but now there is absolutely no communication with Buddhist neighbours. We don't dare greet each other on the street. If the security forces are here and do their duty, then we will dare to live here. If they cannot protect us, we won't dare to live here. Four or five people were subsequently arrested for the violence, and we were asked to write a list of what was destroyed, which we submitted to the authorities. But we don't think people will pay compensation. We just hope everything will be peaceful.[15]

What is behind this outburst of anti-Muslim violence? And is it confined to just anti-Muslim sentiment? And who will speak out or work to counter it?

There are several threads to the answer to the question of who, and what, is behind all this. Firstly, there is a history of anti-Muslim prejudice in Burma. Anti-Muslim riots broke out periodically in the 1920s, 1940s, 1960s, and more recently in Mandalay in 1997 and in Taungoo in 2001. Scratch the surface of Burmese society only a little, talk to just a few Burmese people including some dissidents, and you will find shocking anti-Muslim prejudice. Economic grievances against Muslims who are successful traders and businesspeople, concern about the growth of the Muslim population, a perception that in recent years Muslims have dressed more conservatively and separated themselves from Burmese society, and a fear of radical Islamism based on what is happening in Syria, Iraq and Nigeria, and on Burma's doorstep in Bangladesh, Pakistan, Malaysia and Indonesia, all fuel the prejudice.

The public face of radical Buddhist nationalism in Burma is a monk known as U Wirathu, whose face adorned the cover of *Time* magazine in July 2013 with the headline: 'The Face of Buddhist Terror'.[16] His preaching is appalling. His vile personal attack on the UN Special Rapporteur on Human Rights in Burma, Yanghee Lee, is just one example.[17] He and other like-minded Buddhist monks formed a movement known as '969', a name derived from Buddhist scriptures, and they are largely responsible for the distribution of anti-Muslim hatred through leaflets, books and sermons. 969 transformed into the Ma Ba Tha – the Committee for the Protection of Race and Religion – and has proven to be an influential political force,[18] lobbying successfully for the introduction of new laws to restrict religious conversion and inter-religious marriage, which completed their legislative process in both houses of Parliament in August 2015.[19]

Ma Ba Tha has been responsible for the recent resurrection of Burma's blasphemy laws. In March 2015, two Burmese Buddhists, Tun Thurein and Htut Ko Ko Lwin, along with New Zealander Philip Blackwood, were jailed for two and a half years for 'insulting religion', because the bar they ran in Rangoon had used an image of Buddha in its promotional material.[20] And in June 2015, a Buddhist democracy activist, Htin Lin Oo, who criticised Ma Ba Tha and other Buddhist nationalists for preaching in contradiction to Buddha, was jailed for the same crime of insulting Buddhism.[21]

While Ma Ba Tha is not an entirely uniform or cohesive entity, and nor is the government, it has become clear that its links with the government, and particularly the ruling party, the Union Solidarity and Development Party (USDP), are close. Ma Ba Tha leaders have urged people to vote for the USDP, and are travelling the country, including to remote areas, preaching hatred. They appear to have complete freedom to operate, at a time when the UN special rapporteur says space for freedom of expression is shrinking.[22] While there is ingrained prejudice against Muslims in Burmese society, and that should not be denied, there is little doubt that the forces of Buddhist nationalism could not have become so prevalent without powerful political backing. The violence since 2012, the legislation, the hate speech, the intolerance were pre-meditated and orchestrated for political purposes. The government has been complicit through its failure to stop violence and hatred, its refusal to act against monks who preach and incite hatred, and its active implementation of legislation drafted by Ma Ba Tha. This is a government that has shown it is perfectly capable of cracking down on groups in society that it does not like, in the name of 'stability', and that it is perfectly willing to reject legislation that does not suit its agenda. President Thein Sein himself has defended U Wirathu,[23] and his own popularity among ordinary people increased significantly after he proposed deporting Rohingyas. Therefore one is left with only one conclusion: the government supports Ma Ba Tha and is using religious nationalism for its political ends.

And yet – I have met many Buddhist monks who truly live up to the precepts of Buddhism, and who work to counter such voices of hatred. In several places, particularly Lashio and Meikhtila, some monks gave sanctuary to thousands of Muslims who might otherwise have been killed. I took four Buddhist monks to Indonesia in February 2015, and watched as a Buddhist monk from Burma hugged a Muslim leader from the nation; as that same monk observed Friday prayers in an Ahmadiyya Muslim mosque in Bandung, West Java; and as another monk stood hand in hand with Christians and Muslims at a demonstration outside the Presidential Palace in Jakarta. In Mandalay, as I showed the photograph of the Buddhist monk hugging the Islamic cleric in Indonesia, a young Burmese monk approached me at the end of my lecture and said: 'I want to do the same,' and flung his arms around me. He accompanied me to the top of Mandalay Hill where, as the sun set, we discussed deep questions of the soul, spirituality, religion, peace, beauty, love and life. There is an urgent need to strengthen and support those Buddhist monks who are speaking out against the voices of hatred.[24]

One Buddhist civil society activist told me, 'It is not a religious clash, it is a creation. There is something behind it. Muslims, Christians and Buddhists have been living here a long time together. How and why did this happen? It is created by elements who do not want change, or who are trying to bolster votes for a particular party, or want to create the circumstances whereby the military can retake direct power due to unrest.'

Another activist said, 'Most communities want peace. Some political actors created this issue. They want to unsettle the situation ahead of 2015. If the situation is too unsettled, there will be no election.'

So what is being done? It is encouraging that there are a growing number of actors within civil society, of different religious backgrounds, who are working to counter religious hatred. Women's organisations have played a courageous leading role in campaigning against the race and religion laws, receiving death threats in the process. Others are working to try to build inter-faith understanding. As Htuu Lou Rae, founder of Coexist, an organisation working for inter-religious harmony, said, 'The tensions between Muslims and Buddhists arise because of misunderstanding about one's own religion and about other religions. We need to raise awareness, to see the relationship between Muslims and Buddhists improve. We are not alone. There are many like-minded people. We encourage people to take part.'

Another activist, Thet Swe Win of Myanmar Youth Empowerment Programme, said that after the violence in Meikhtila 'we felt unsafe and uneasy', and for that reason he and other young activists contacted young Muslims and requested a meeting: 'Our common ground is peace.' He acknowledged that 'hatred between Muslims and Buddhists started a long time ago,' and that even though the violence may have stopped temporarily, 'it is still burning inside.' His group and others have launched a sticker campaign promoting religious harmony and peace. 'Hate speech is still circulating, and we are trying to counter it. We can never get true peace without dialogue and transparency, and just posting stickers cannot bring harmony, but we want to post stickers to our inner hearts and minds. It will take time. We just want peace. We must open our fists, and show we have nothing, show that we are willing for peace, and then we can start the conversation.'

There is a danger that if the anti-Muslim hatred is not tackled, it could spread into a wider intolerance of all non-Buddhist minorities. There have been reports of propaganda DVDs circulating which describe Christianity as a 'guest religion' and which contain false accusations of Christian involvement in forcible conversion. Rumours, which proved to be unsubstantiated, of possible violence against churches in Rangoon were also allegedly spread. I myself saw posters from '969', the militant Buddhist group that preceded Ma Ba Tha, in Putao in northern Kachin state – a remote and overwhelmingly Christian area. I also met relatives of Kachin political prisoners in Myitkyina, who described how Kachins in prison were tortured by being forced to sit on sharp stones with their arms outstretched as if on a cross, in deliberate mockery of their faith. Male prisoners were also forced to engage in sexual acts with each other.[25] The military's use of religion as a political tool against Christian minorities in Burma, particularly among the Chin and Kachin, is longstanding and reported earlier in this book, so there is no reason why Ma Ba Tha and the Buddhist nationalists might not extend their campaign of hatred.

When asked whether religious intolerance could spread to target other non-Buddhist minorities such as Christians and Hindus, one civil society activist said that 'everything is possible in Burma. If these people really want to establish their Burman Buddhist nationalism, they may attack other minorities.' The rise of anti-Chinese sentiment, particularly following the conflict with the Kokang in northern Shan State and in reaction to the economic and political influence of China and Chinese businesses in Burma, is concerning.

There is also a danger that outside radical Islamist or jihadi groups will turn their attention to Burma, and foment retaliatory violence and extremism among the Muslim community. The Indonesian Islamist cleric Abu Bakar Bashir, in prison on charges of terrorism, has called for 'jihad' against Burma, and an attempt to attack the Burmese Embassy in Jakarta was recently discovered and prevented by the Indonesian authorities. Growing radical Islamism in Bangladesh and attacks by Muslims against Buddhists on the Bangladesh side of the border with Burma indicate the potential for a disturbing cycle of religiously-motivated violence, which could have devastating consequences for the region. On 28 March 2013, despite his subsequent defence of U Wirathu, President Thein Sein made a televised address to the nation in which he blamed 'political opportunists and religious extremists' for sowing hatred between faiths and warned that he would 'not hesitate to use force as a last resort' to quell religious violence.[26] Two days later, he appointed a committee responsible for tackling the violence, consisting of five ministers and five deputy ministers. Perhaps the government was, with hindsight, shocked by what it had unleashed and realised it might have created a monster it could not control. On 3 April, the Foreign Minister announced that 142 people had been arrested for their alleged involvement in violence. Despite those promises of action, however, there is still widespread concern about the attitudes of the security forces. A disproportionate number of Muslims have been arrested and jailed, while relatively few Buddhists have been held to account. A junior police officer in Meikhtila reportedly said, 'We received an order to do nothing but extinguish fires. Obedience is more important than anything else in our service.'

The then UN Special Rapporteur on Human Rights in Burma, Tomás Ojea Quintana, has said he has received reports of 'state involvement in some acts of violence' and that the Government of Burma had 'not done enough' to address the rising religious intolerance or tackle the 'organised mobs' inciting hatred and violence against Muslims. The UN Secretary-General's Special Adviser on Burma, Vijay Nambiar, said that the attacks were 'clearly targeted' and carried out with 'brutal efficiency'. Unless and until the culture of impunity and the attitude of complicity on the part of the security forces are addressed, religious intolerance and violence will continue, with potentially devastating consequences.

Most Burmese pro-democracy activists have stayed silent in response to this challenge. Some have even made remarks that have fuelled this religious nationalism. One of the few clear, consistent voices among national leaders in Burma today, for religious freedom and inter-religious harmony, has been Cardinal Bo, who has the advantage of being an ethnic Burman speaking for ethnic minorities; a religious leader who is neither a Buddhist nor a Muslim; and a cleric protected by a worldwide infrastructure. When he was appointed Burma's first ever cardinal in early 2015 he pledged to be a 'voice for the voiceless'.[27] In countless sermons before and since he has been as good as his word. In his Christmas homily in 2014, his message was clear. 'Do not be afraid,' he said. 'Do not be afraid to seek your rights to dignity. Do not be afraid of resisting injustice. Do not be afraid to dream, to imagine a new Burma where justice and righteousness flow like a river. . . .'

Since the first edition of this book, Burma has become even more of a riddle and a paradox. On some levels little has changed, in some respects there has been a deterioration, and yet some things have clearly changed for the better and certain things are now possible. Aung San Suu Kyi has travelled the globe. World leaders, including President Barack Obama, have visited Burma. I myself have been able to travel inside Burma regularly, to go to parts of the country – such as Hakha and Falam in Chin State – which were previously closed to foreigners, to conduct training workshops and public lectures that would previously have been inconceivable. People have much greater access to mobile telephones, the Internet, social media, print media and cars, and greater freedom of expression. Censorship of the media, at least at a formal level, has been abolished. These are, on the face of it, positive developments and should be welcomed.

Yet Burma remains at a crossroads, waiting for the traffic lights to change. Or, as already suggested, perhaps it would be more accurate to say it finds itself at a roundabout. Some aspects are moving, but the fundamentals have not changed. The changes are surface-level, but the institutional and constitutional change that is so urgently needed still appears far-off. Even those reforms that may be underway will take time. Ask a Kachin or a Rohingya and they would say their lives have got worse.

While it is right to welcome positive steps made by brutal regimes, and to encourage reform when there appear to be hints of it, and to engage with dictators if they show signs of change, the international community has, so far, been taken for a ride. Britain, the EU and the US were far too quick to lift sanctions. It was right to relax some sanctions in recognition of change, for to let tentative reforms go unrecognised, unwelcomed and unrewarded would be foolish; but at the same time, there was no need to take all our leverage off the table in one go, and to give the regime everything they wanted before they had done what was needed. The Generals have been canny and calculating, and the international community should have been cleverer in its response.

Burma's history has a habit of repeating itself. Just as Cyclone Nargis preceded the referendum in 2008, in 2015 Burma was struck by horrific floods just three months before the elections, resulting in devastation, death and displacement for thousands. The regime did behave differently, however – unlike in 2008, it quickly appealed for international aid and President Thein Sein visited some of the affected areas. The regime might not have changed their hearts, but they have become more subtle and sophisticated at diplomacy and public relations.

The military remains the dominant force in Burmese politics. The Commander-in-Chief, Min Aung Hlaing, told the BBC the military would respect the results of the elections in November 2015.[28] But that is what Saw Maung promised in 1990, and look what happened. The one thing I have learned after almost two decades of working on Burma is never, ever to predict the outcome.

Notes

Author's Note

1 Hugh C. MacDougall, 'Burma Press Summary No. 27', May 1989, citing
   SLORC Information Minister coverage in *Working People's Daily* newspaper

Introduction

1 Bertil Lintner, 'The Staying Power of the Burmese Military Regime', paper
   presented at a public forum on Burma at Aichi Gakuin University, Nagoya,
   Japan, 11–17 March, 2009
2 Chin Human Rights Group, 'Critical Point: Food Scarcity and Hunger in
   Burma's Chin State', 2008
3 Christina Fink, *Living Silence in Burma: Surviving Under Military Rule*, second
   edition, Zed Books and Silkworm Books, 2009, 3

Chapter 1: From Rice Bowl to Basket Case

1 Fink, 18
2 Kin Oung, *Who Killed Aung San?*, White Lotus, 1996, 17
3 Ibid., 74
4 Aung San Suu Kyi, 'Aung San', *Asiaweek*, 12 June 1998
5 Burma Centre for Ethnic Studies, Peace and Reconciliation, Analysis Paper
   No. 2, 'The Challenges of Ethnic Politics and Negotiated Settlement: From
   Ceasefire to Political Dialogue', February 2012
6 Ashley South, *Ethnic Politics in Burma: States of Conflict,* Routledge, 2008
7 Ibid., 24
8 Thant Myint-U, *The River of Lost Footsteps: A Personal History of Burma*, Faber
   and Faber, 2008, 209
9 Ibid., 209

10 South, 21

11 Field Marshal Viscount Slim, *Defeat Into Victory: Battling Japan in Burma and India, 1942–1945*, Cooper Square Press, 2000, 519

12 Ibid., 485

13 Martin Smith, *Burma: Insurgency and the Politics of Ethnicity*, Zed Books, 1999, 65

14 Paul Gore-Booth, *With Great Truth and Respect: The Memoirs of Paul Gore-Booth*, Constable, 1974, 212

15 Ibid., 30

16 Kin Oung, 40

17 Ibid., 67

18 Smith, 305

19 As quoted in Kin Oung, 31

20 Ibid., 69

21 Ibid., 71

22 Fink, 22

23 Gore-Booth, 223

24 Fink, 23

25 Ibid., 23

26 Gore-Booth, 223

27 Thant Myint-U, 290

28 International Crisis Group, 'Myanmar: A New Peace Initiative', Asia Report No. 214, 30 November 2011

29 Inge Sargent, *Twilight over Burma: My Life as a Shan Princess*, University of Hawaii Press, 1994, xxiii

30 Gore-Booth, 220

31 Ibid., 224

32 Ibid., 224

33 Ibid., 26

34 Thant Myint-U, 292

35 Ibid., 293

36 Smith, 1

37 Fink, 32

38 Thant Myint-U, 311

39 Ibid., 312

40 Ibid., 312

41 Fink, 40

Chapter 2: Cry Freedom

1 Ibid., 47

2 Bertil Lintner, *Outrage: Burma's Struggle for Democracy*, Review Publishing Company, 1989, 16

3 Smith, 2

4 *Asiaweek*, 'Burma: A Raging Discontent', 8 July 1988

5 Fink, 49

6 'Bogyoke' means 'General', and is typically used in reference to both Aung San and Ne Win.

7 *Asiaweek*, 'Burma: A Raging Discontent', 8 July 1988

8 Ibid.

9 Ibid.

10 Lintner, 117–19

11 Ibid., 119

12 *Asiaweek*, 'Burma: Revolt in the Streets', 19 August 1988

13 Ibid., 135

14 Ibid., 144

15 Ibid., 154

16 Ibid., 156

17 Aung San Suu Kyi, *Freedom from Fear*, Penguin Books, 1991, Introduction by Michael Aris, xvii

18 Aung San Suu Kyi, 'Belief in Burma's Future', *Independent*, 12 September 1988

19 Aung San Suu Kyi, *Freedom from Fear*, xix

20 Lintner, 157

21 Aung San Suu Kyi, *Freedom from Fear*, 193

22 Ibid., 195

23 Lintner, 159

24 Fink, 55

25 Ibid., 55

26 Lintner, 166

27 Ibid., 167

28 Ibid., 171

29 Ibid., 181

30 Ibid., 184

31 *Asiaweek*, 'Interview with Aung San Suu Kyi: "I am the Target"', 21 July 1989

32 Lintner, 'The Rise and Fall of the Communist Party of Burma', Cornell South-East Asia Program, 1990, 1

33 Ibid., 49

34 Fink, 63

35 Lintner, 'The Rise and Fall of the Communist Party of Burma', 50

36 *Asiaweek*, 'Interview with Aung Gyi: "I Trust the Army"', 21 July 1989

37 *Asiaweek*, 'Interview with Min Ko Naing: "Fighting a 'Bad King'"', 28 December 1988

38 Aung San Suu Kyi, 'Belief in Burma's Future', *Independent*, 12 September 1988

39 *Asiaweek*, Interview with Saw Maung: 'I Saved Burma', 27 January 1989

40 Ibid.

41 *Asiaweek*, 'Burma: Debating the Polls Promise', 21 October 1988

42 Aung San Suu Kyi, *The Voice of Hope: Conversations with Alan Clements*, Rider, 2008, 52

43 Dominic Faulder,'The Burmese Way to Steal an Election', *The Asian Wall Street Journal*, 7 May 1990

44 Lintner, *Aung San Suu Kyi and Burma's Unfinished Renaissance*, Peacock Press, 1990, 28

45 Maung Aung Myoe, *A Historical Overview of Political Transition in Myanmar since 1988*, Asia Research Institute, National University of Singapore, August 2007

46 Ibid.

47 Ibid.

48 Anthony Spaeth, 'Student Power', *Time*, 16 December 1996

49 *Irrawaddy*, ' "Fighting peacock" on the streets again', January 1997 – http://www.irrawaddy.org/article.php?art_id=183

50 Dr Michael Aris, 'A Tribute for James Leander Nichols', 23 July 1996

51 *Independent*, Obituaries, Leo Nichols, 26 June 1996

52 *Asiaweek*, 'On the Streets', 20 December 1996

53 Statement released by Dr Michael Aris, Oxford, 30 November 1992

54 *Asiaweek*, 'A Careful Hero: Suu Kyi Confronts Some Tough Choices', 4 August 1995

55 Preliminary Report of the Ad Hoc Commission on Depayin Massacre (Burma), 4 July 2003

56 See www.burmapartnership.org

Chapter 3: A Campaign of Brutality in the East

1 Christian Solidarity Worldwide, 'Burma: Visit to the Thailand–Burma Border', February 2010

2 Smith, 44

3 Christian Solidarity Worldwide, 'Burma: Visit to the Thailand–Burma Border', February 2010

4 Smith, 72

5 South, 30

6 Ibid., 57

7 Ibid., 58

8 Christian Solidarity Worldwide, 'Burma: Visit to the Karen and Mon Peoples on the Thailand–Burma Border', 27 February–8 March 2007

9 Christian Solidarity Worldwide, 'Burma: Visit to the Thai–Burmese Border', November 2006

10 Christian Solidarity Worldwide, 'Seven Year-Old Karen Girl Raped and Killed by Burma Army Soldier', 5 January 2009

11 Karen Human Rights Group <http://www.khrg.org/khrg2006/khrg06b4.html>

12 Free Burma Rangers reports, 2006

13 Free Burma Rangers, 'Over 2,100 displaced as Burma Army mortars villages and burns homes in new attacks', 8 March 2008

14 Christian Solidarity Worldwide, 'Burma: Visit to the Thai-Burmese Border', 19–26 April 2004

15 Ibid.

16 Bernice Koehler Johnson, *The Shan: Refugees without a Camp*, Trinity Matrix, 2009, 31

17 Shan Human Rights Foundation, 'Dispossessed: A report on forced relocation and extrajudicial killings in Shan State', April 1998

18 Shan Women's Action Network, 'License to Rape', 2001

19 Women's League of Burma, 'System of Impunity', 2004

20 Chris Beyrer and Richard Sollom, 'Burma's Rising Toll: The Junta Widens a War on Ethnic Groups', *Washington Post*, 3 September 2009

21 Shan Human Rights Foundation, '10,000 Shans Uprooted, 500 houses burned in Burmese regime's latest scorched earth campaign', 13 August 2009

22 Shan Women's Action Network, 'Forbidden Glimpses of Shan State: A Brief Alternative Guide', 2009

23 Ibid.

24 Christian Solidarity Worldwide, 'Burma: Visit to the Thai-Burma Border', November 2002

25 Democratic Voice of Burma, 'Burma conflict due to "misunderstanding": Thein Sein', 2 March 2012 – http://www.dvb.no/news/burma-conflict-due-to-misunderstanding-thein-sein/20528

26 Smith, *Burma: Insurgency and the Politics of Ethnicity*, 32

27 Christian Solidarity Worldwide, 'Visit to the Karen and Mon Peoples on the Thailand–Burma Border', February 2007

28 Zoya Phan, *Little Daughter: A Memoir of Survival in Burma and the West*, Simon and Schuster, 2009, 226

29 Ibid., 232

30 Ibid., 236

31 Ibid., 252

32 Ibid., 263

33 Ibid., 287

34 Andrew Marshall, 'Dr Cynthia Maung – Healer of Souls', *Time*, 28 April 2003

35 Benedict Rogers, *A Land Without Evil: Stopping the Genocide of Burma's Karen People*, Monarch Books, 2004, 184

36 Free Burma Rangers, 'Torture, Capture, Uprooted Villages and Child Soldiers: Life in Northwestern Karen State', 16 May 2009

37 Free Burma Rangers, April–May 2005 report

38 Free Burma Rangers, 'Eliya Samson: First Ranger', 26 September 2008

39 Humanitarian Aid Relief Trust (HART), Visit to HART Partners in and from Eastern Burma, 25–31 October 2009

40 Thein Sein, 'Inaugural address to the Pyidaungsu Hluttaw', Naypyidaw, 30 March 2011

41 Thailand Burma Border Consortium, 'Protracted Displacement and Chronic Poverty in Eastern Burma', 2010, 3

42 Amnesty International, 'Crimes against humanity in eastern Myanmar', 5 June 2008

Chapter 4: A Silent Cry in the North

1 Project Maje, 'The North War, Part II: Kachin Conflict Continues', December 2011 – www.projectmaje.org

2 South, 18

3 Ibid., 18

4 UN Development Programme, 'UN Myanmar Vulnerability Mapping and Monitoring System', June 2005, as quoted in South, 151

5 'In His Own Words: Colonel Chit Myaing', *Burma Debate*, July/August 1997

6 Ibid., 152

7 Ibid., 152

8 Ibid., 152

9 Christian Solidarity Worldwide, 'Burma: Visit to the Thailand–Burma Border and Malaysia', February 2008

10 South, 154

11 Transnational Institute, 'Neither War Nor Peace: The Future of the Ceasefire Agreements in Burma', July 2009, 14

12 Ibid., 14

13 South, 155

14 Transnational Institute, 17

15 Ibid., 14

16 Christian Solidarity Worldwide, 'Burma: Visit to Kachin State', May 2009

17 Christian Solidarity Worldwide, 'Kachin School Girl Gang-Raped, Mutilated and Killed by Burma Army Soldiers', 15 August 2008

18 South, 153

19 Transnational Institute, 23

20 South, 159

21 Ibid., 159

22 Christian Solidarity Worldwide, 'Burma: Visit to the Thailand–Burma Border and Malaysia', February 2008

23 South, 159

24 Christian Solidarity Worldwide, 'Burma: Visit to the Thailand–Burma Border and Malaysia', February 2008

25 Christian Solidarity Worldwide, 'Burma: Visit to Kachin State', May 2009

26 Christian Solidarity Worldwide, 'Burma: Visit to Kachin State', 25 August–1 September 2006

27 Christian Solidarity Worldwide, 'Burma: Visit to Kachin State', May 2009

28 Benedict Rogers, 'Carrying the Cross: the military regime's campaign of

restriction, discrimination and persecution against Christians in Burma', Christian Solidarity Worldwide, 2007, 40

29 Christian Solidarity Worldwide, 'Burma: Visit to Kachin State', 25 August–1 September 2006

30 Christian Solidarity Worldwide, 'Burma: Visit to Kachin State', May 2009

31 BBC, 'Burma dam: work halted on divisive Myitsone project', 30 September 2011

32 Ibid.

33 Kachin News Group, 'Over 1,000 HIV positive patients in 2008: KIO', 3 December 2008

34 Kachin News Group, 'Battle Between Burmese Army and Kokang Intensifies', 29 August 2009

35 Michael Sainsbury, 'Burma Death Toll Reaches 500', *Australian*, 2 September 2009

36 *International Herald Tribune*, 'A Rebel Stronghold in Myanmar on Alert', 5 November 2009

37 Kachin News Group, 'KIA on high alert after clashes in Kokang territory', 28 August 2009

38 Ben Blanchard, 'China raps Myanmar after recent border unrest', Reuters, 25 September 2009

39 KIO Central Committee, Ref: #272/M-1/CC/2009, 7 October 2009

40 Peter Janssen, 'Post-election offensive feared against Myanmar rebel groups', Deutsche Press Agentur, 28 October 2010

41 *Economist*, 'Myanmar's Border with China', 25 November 2010

42 Christian Science Monitor, 'Cut out of Burma election, Kachin minority could turn guns on junta', 29 October 2010

43 Christian Solidarity Worldwide, 'Burma: Visit to Burma and Kachin ethnic group on the China–Burma Border', February 2012

44 Aung San Suu Kyi, 'Open letter to President Thein Sein, KIO, KNU, NMSP and SSA', International Crisis Group translation, 28 July 2011

45 Christian Solidarity Worldwide, 'Burma: Visit to Burma and Kachin ethnic group on the China–Burma Border', February 2012

Chapter 5: A Cross to Bear in the West

1 Benedict Rogers, 'Carrying the Cross: the military regime's campaign of restriction, discrimination and persecution against Christians in Burma', Christian Solidarity Worldwide, 2007, 3

2 Christian Solidarity Worldwide, 'Burma: Visit to the India–Burma Border', 14–21 September 2007

3 Lian H. Sakhong, 'In Search of Chin Identity: A Study in Religion, Politics and Ethnic Identity in Burma', Nordic Institute of Asian Studies, 2003, 17

4 Ibid., 2

5　The Chinram is the name the Chin gave to their land, according to Lian H. Sakhong

6　Ibid., 85

7　Ibid., 21

8　Ibid., 21

9　Ibid., 86

10　Ibid., 87

11　Ibid., 87

12　Ibid., 88

13　Ibid., 95

14　Ibid., 96

15　Ibid., 101

16　Ibid., 98

17　Ibid., 102

18　Ibid., 101

19　Ibid., 107

20　Ibid., 108

21　Ibid., 110

22　Ibid., 11

23　Ibid., 116

24　Ibid., 119

25　Ibid., 119

26　Ibid., 126

27　Ibid., 131

28　Ibid., 131

29　Ibid., 132

30　Ibid., 131

31　Ibid., 136–37

32　Ibid., 244

33　Salai Bawi Lian Maung, 'The Persecution of Chin Christians in Burma', Chin Human Rights Organisation, presentation to the Sixth Hong Kong Christian Human Rights Conference, November 2005

34　Chin Human Rights Organisation, 'Religious Persecution: A Campaign of Ethnocide Against Chin Christians in Burma', 52

35　Ibid., 53

36　Ibid., 55

37　Chin Human Rights Organisation, 'Junta Coerces Chin Christians to Pull Down Cross', 29 June 2002

38　*Irrawaddy*, 'Junta closes popular Rangoon church', 9 September 2005

39　Benedict Rogers, 'Carrying the Cross: the military regime's campaign of restriction, discrimination and persecution against Christians in Burma', Christian Solidarity Worldwide, 2007, 37

40　Ibid., 36

41　Christian Solidarity Worldwide: 'Burma: CSW, HART and Norwegian Mission to the East Visit to the India–Burma Border', 3–9 March 2006

42 Chin Human Rights Organisation, 'Religious Persecution: A Campaign of Ethnocide Against Chin Christians in Burma', 9

43 Assist News, 'Exiled Chin Protest in Front of Burmese Embassy in India', 26 January 2005

44 Christian Solidarity Worldwide, 'CSW Condemns Crackdown on Churches in Rangoon', 15 January 2009

45 Martin Smith, *Burma: Insurgency and the Politics of Ethnicity*, 2ed Books, 1999, 45

46 Benedict Rogers, 'Carrying the Cross: the military regime's campaign of restriction, discrimination and persecution against Christians in Burma', Christian Solidarity Worldwide, 2007, 17

47 Christian Solidarity Worldwide, 'Burma: CSW UK/Australia Visit to the Chin and Kachin Refugees in India', 2–9 March 2004

48 Daniella Nayu, 'An enduring byproduct of war', Democratic Voice of Burma, 20 July 2009

49 Human Rights Watch, 'Burma: "We Are Like Forgotten People" – The Chin People of Burma: Unsafe in Burma, Unprotected in India', 2009, 33

50 Daniella Nayu, 'An enduring byproduct of war', Democratic Voice of Burma, 20 July 2009

51 Christian Solidarity Worldwide, 'Burma: Visit to the India–Burma Border', 10–25 November 2009

52 Chin Human Rights Organisation, 'On the Edge of Survival: The Continuing Rat Infestation and Food Crisis in Chin State, Burma', 2009, 1

53 Ibid., 2

54 Benny Manser, 'Lessons not learnt from Cyclone Nargis and Karen State', *Burma*, 29 October 2008

55 Christian Solidarity Worldwide, 'Burma: Visit to the India–Burma Border', 10–15 November 2009

56 Chin Human Rights Organisation, 'On the Edge of Survival: The Continuing Rat Infestation and Food Crisis in Chin State, Burma', 2009, 2

57 Christian Solidarity Worldwide, 'Burma: Visit to the India–Burma Border', 15–30 November 2010

58 Chin Human Rights Organisation, 'On the Edge of Survival', 12

59 Christian Solidarity Worldwide: 'Burma: CSW, HART and Norwegian Mission to the East Visit to the India–Burma Border', 3–9 March 2006

60 Christian Solidarity Worldwide, 'Burma: Visit to the India–Burma Border', 15–30 November 2010

61 Ibid.

62 Christian Solidarity Worldwide, 'Burma: Visit to the Thailand–Burma Border and Malaysia', February 2008

63 Christian Solidarity Worldwide, 'Burma: Visit to the India–Burma Border', 10–25 November 2009

Chapter 6: A Stateless People

1 Christian Solidarity Worldwide, 'Burma: Visit to the Bangladesh–Burma Border', 26–31 August 2008

2 Ibid.

3 Refugees International, 'Rohingya: Burma's Forgotten Minority', 18 December 2008

4 Chris Lewa, 'Testimony to the US Commission on International Religious Freedom', 3 December 2007

5 Christian Solidarity Worldwide, 'Burma: Visit to the Bangladesh–Burma Border', 26–31 August 2008

6 Ibid.

7 Ibid.

8 Ibid.

9 National Coalition Government of the Union of Burma, Office of the Prime Minister, Position Paper on Persecution of Muslims in Arakan State, 24 September 1992

10 Ibid.

11 Euro-Burma Office, 'The Rohingyas: Bengali Muslims or Arakan Rohingyas?', EBO Briefing Paper No.2, 2009

12 Ibid.

13 Dr Abdul Karim, 'The Rohingyas: A Short Account of their History and Culture', Arakan Historical Society, Chittagong, 2000, 7

14 Ibid., 14

15 Arakan Rohingya National Organisation, 'NCGUB pushing the Rohingya from the frying-pan into the fire', 13 February 2009 – http://www.rohingya.org/index.php?option=com_content&task=view&id=229&Itemid=39

16 Martin Smith, 'The Muslim Rohingya of Burma', paper delivered at a conference organised by Burma Centrum Netherlands, 11 December 1995 – http://www.rohingya.org/index.php?option=com_content&task=view&id=75&Itemid=33

17 San Oo Aung – http://sanooaung.wordpress.com/2008/01/22/burmas-first-president-sao-shwe-thaikes-support-of-burmese-muslims/, 22 January 2008

18 Euro-Burma Office, 'The Rohingyas: Bengali Muslims or Arakan Rohingyas?', EBO Briefing Paper No.2, 2009

19 Martin Smith, 'The Muslim Rohingya of Burma', paper delivered at a conference organised by Burma Centrum Netherlands, 11 December, 1995

20 Errol da Silva, 'Why the Muslims are fleeing Burma', *Bangkok Post*, 31 May 1981

21 Christian Solidarity Worldwide, 'Burma: Visit to the Bangladesh–Burma Border', 26–31 August 2008

22 *Nation*, 'Thailand says 126 Rohingya boat people "escorted" to sea already', 23 January 2009

23 CNN, 'Probe questions fate of refugees in Thailand', 26 January 2009 – http://

edition.cnn.com/2009/WORLD/asiapcf/01/25/thailand.refugees/index.
html#cnnSTCVideo

24 Ibid. – http://edition.cnn.com/2009/WORLD/asiapcf/01/25/thailand.refugees/
index.html#cnnSTCText

25 John Carlin, 'The terrifying voyage of Burma's boat people', *Independent*, 24
November 2009

26 ALTSEAN Burma, 'Rohingya, Asylum Seekers & Migrants from Burma: A
Human Security Priority for ASEAN', 30 January 2009

27 *Mizzima News*, 'Burmese consular says Rohingya do not belong to Burma',
13 February 2009 – http://www.mizzima.com/news/breaking-and-news-
brief/1708-burmese-consular-says-rohingya-do-not-belong-to-burma.html
and http://democracyforburma.wordpress.com/2009/02/14/burmese-consular-
says-rohingya-do-not-belong-to-burma/

28 Bertil Lintner, 'Religious Extremism and Nationalism in Bangladesh', a paper
presented at an international workshop on Religion and Security in South
Asia at the Asia Pacific Center for Security Studies in Honolulu, Hawaii, 19–22
August 2002 –http://www.asiapacificms.com/papers/pdf/religious_extremism_
bangladesh.pdf

29 Bertil Lintner, 'Bangladesh: breeding ground for Muslim terror', *Asia Times*, 21
September 2002 – http://www.atimes.com/atimes/South_Asia/DI21Df06.html

30 Euro-Burma Office, 'The Rohingyas: Bengali Muslims or Arakan Rohingyas?',
EBO Briefing Paper No.2, 2009

31 Christian Solidarity Worldwide, 'Burma: Visit to the Bangladesh–Burma
Border', 26–31 August 2008

32 Ibid.

Chapter 7: Defectors, Deserters and Child Soldiers

1 Samuel Blythe, 'Myanmar's army document spotlights low morale', *Jane's
Defence Weekly*, 4 April 2007

2 Min Lwin, 'Burmese Armed Forces Day Celebrated in Naypyidaw', *Irrawaddy*,
27 March 2009

3 Kachin News Group, 'Ethnic soldiers in Burma Army discriminated against', 29
September 2009

4 Kachin News Group, 'Twenty fresh desertions from Burmese Army in Kachin
State', 24 September 2009

5 Narinjara News, 'Burma army faces increasing desertion', 15 September 2007

6 Christian Solidarity Worldwide, 'Visit to the Thai-Burma Border', November
2002

7 Benedict Rogers, *A Land Without Evil: Stopping the Genocide of Burma's Karen
People*, 238

8 Ibid., 239

9 Christian Solidarity Worldwide, 'Visit to the Thai–Burma Border', November 2002

10 Christian Solidarity Worldwide, 'Visit to Kachin State, Burma', 25 August–1 September 2006

11 Christian Solidarity Worldwide, 'Visit to the Thai-Burmese Border', 19 October–4 November 2005

12 Ibid.

13 Christian Solidarity Worldwide, 'Visit to the Thailand–Burma Border', 16–28 November 2007

14 *Mizzima News*, 'Ailing Prime Minister to go back to Burma, Rangoon commander ousted', 1 October 2007

15 Associated Press, 'Generals, soldiers detained for refusing to shoot monks in Myanmar', 10 October 2007

16 Matthew Weaver, 'Burmese army major defects to Thailand', *Guardian*, 3 October 2007

17 BBC, 'Diplomat resigns over Burmese monks', 9 October 2007

18 Christian Solidarity Worldwide, 'Visit to the Thailand-Burma Border', 16–28 November 2007

19 Christian Solidarity Worldwide, 'Visit to the Chin and Kachin Refugees in India', 2–9 March 2004 – Appendix: Testimony of a Defector

20 Christian Solidarity Worldwide, 'Visit to the Thailand-Burma Border', 20 January–10 February 2009

21 Radio Free Asia, 'We All Want Democracy', 30 July 2009 –http://www.rfa.org/english/news/burma/democracy-07302009190128.html?textonly=1

22 Richard Lloyd Parry, 'Burma: Than Shwe "ordered troops to execute villagers"', *The Times*, 7 June 2008

23 Aung Lynn Htut, 'Than Shwe Maneuvers to Retain Power', *Irrawaddy*, 24 June 2009

24 Democratic Voice of Burma, 'Engaging with the military regime', 23 September 2008 –http://english.dvb.no/news.php?id=1781

Chapter 8: The Torture Chambers

1 BBC Burmese.com, 'Student activists claim they have half a million signatures', 24 October 2006

2 Democratic Voice of Burma, ''88 Generation to step up peaceful protests', 21 May 2007

3 Richard Lloyd Parry, 'Burma activists sentenced to 65 years each in draconian crackdown', *The Times*, 12 November 2008

4 Assistance Association for Political Prisoners (Burma), 'ABFSU member sentenced to 104 years in jail', 14 January 2009 – http://www.aappb.org/ABFSU_member_sentenced_to_104_years.PDF

5 Assistance Association for Political Prisoners (Burma), 'Political Prisoner Profile: U Khun Tun Oo', 11 July 2009 – http://www.aappb.org/bio_pdf/Khun_Tun_Oo_bio_11_July_2009.pdf

6 BBC, 'Burmese comic jailed for 45 years', 21 November 2008 – http://news.bbc.co.uk/1/hi/7741653.stm

7 Ibid., 9

8 Andrew Harding, 'On the run in Burma', 22 September 2007 –http://news.bbc.co.uk/1/hi/programmes/from_our_own_correspondent/7006506.stm

9 Human Rights Watch, 'Burma's Forgotten Prisoners', 26

10 Than Htike Oo, '88 generation activist Nilar Thein arrested', *Mizzima News*, 11 September 2008

11 Human Rights Watch, 'Burma's Forgotten Prisoners', 27

12 Andrew Buncombe, 'Burmese democracy activist: "I don't know how I kept my sanity"', *Independent*, 25 September 2008

13 Richard Lloyd Parry, 'Burma activists sentenced to 65 years each in draconian crackdown', *The Times*, 12 November 2008

14 Peter Popham, 'Burmese cameraman jailed for defying regime', *Independent*, 18 November 2009

15 Awzar Thi, 'Breaking Burma's Official Secrets', United Press International, 5 February 2009

16 *Mizzima*, 'Another 20-year prison term for undercover reporter Hla Hla Win', 5 January 2010

17 Assistance Association for Political Prisoners (Burma), 'Burma's Prisons and Labor Camps: Silent Killing Fields', May 2009, 2

18 Assistance Association for Political Prisoners (Burma), 'Eight Seconds of Silence: The Death of Democracy Activists Behind Bars', 29

19 Christian Solidarity Worldwide, 'Burma: Visit to the Thai-Burmese Border', November 2006

20 Assistance Association for Political Prisoners (Burma), 'Female political prisoner Tin Tin Htwe Mae Pae died in prison', 24 December 2009

21 Amnesty International, 'Urgent Action: Medical Treatment Needed Immediately', 3 December 2009

22 Human Rights Watch, 'Burma's Forgotten Prisoners', September 2009

23 Radio Free Asia, 'Burmese prisoners killed after cyclone', 30 January 2009

24 Radio Free Asia, '"Burma dissidents" visits restricted', 17 March 2009

25 Phil Thornton, 'The forgotten political prisoners', *Bangkok Post*, 30 August 2009

26 Ko Bo Kyi, 'Lifting Burma sanctions will not silence the screams', *Nation*, 31 October 2009

27 email correspondence with the author, 3 November 2009

28 Assistance Association for Political Prisoners (Burma), 'The Darkness We See: Torture in Burma's Interrogation Centers and Prisons', 2005

29 Ibid., 15

30 Ibid., 15

31 Ibid., 15

32 Democratic Voice of Burma, 'They forced me to kneel like a dog', 2 November 2009

33 Human Rights Watch, 'Burma's Forgotten Prisoners', 10

34 Christian Solidarity Worldwide, 'Burma: Visit to the Chin Peoples on the India-Burma Border', 3–9 March 2006

35 Christian Solidarity Worldwide, 'Burma: Visit to the India-Burma Border', 14–21 September 2007

36 Christian Solidarity Worldwide, 'Burma: Visit to the Chin Peoples on the India-Burma Border', 3–9 March 2006

37 Christian Solidarity Worldwide, 'Burma: Visit to the India-Burma Border', 14–21 September 2007

38 Christian Solidarity Worldwide, 'Burma: Visit to the Chin Peoples on the India-Burma Border', 3–9 March 2006

39 Christian Solidarity Worldwide, 'Burma: Visit to the India-Burma Border', 14–21 September 2007

40 Christian Solidarity Worldwide, 'Burma: Visit to the Chin Peoples on the India-Burma Border', 3–9 March 2006

41 Christian Solidarity Worldwide, 'Burma: Visit to the India-Burma Border', 14–21 September 2007

42 Assistance Association for Political Prisoners (Burma), 'The Darkness We See: Torture in Burma's Interrogation Centers and Prisons', 16

43 Christian Solidarity Worldwide, 'Burma: Visit to the Thai-Burmese Border', November 2006

44 Ibid.

45 Phil Thornton, 'The forgotten political prisoners', *Bangkok Post*, 30 August 2009

46 Assistance Association for Political Prisoners (Burma), 'The Future in the Dark: The Massive Increase in Burma's Political Prisoners', September 2008

47 Assistance Association for Political Prisoners (Burma), 'Chronology of Political Prisoners in Burma', February 2009

48 ALTSEAN, 'New US Policy: An Alibi for Regional Complacency', 5 November 2009

49 ALTSEAN, 'Burma Bulletin', Issue 33, September 2009

50 Christian Solidarity Worldwide, 'Burma: Visit to the Thai-Burmese Border', November 2006

51 James Mawdsley, *The Heart Must Break: The Fight for Democracy and Truth in Burma*, 147

52 Ibid., 159

53 Ibid., 308

54 Ibid., 369

55 Ibid., 372–3

56 Wa Wa Kyaw, 'Junta Exacts Revenge on American Citizen', *Nation*, 10 December 2009

57 Ibid.

58 Glenn Kessler, 'Little focus put on U.S. man jailed in Myanmar', *Washington Post*, 24 December 2009

59 Ko Bo Kyi, 'Lifting Burma sanctions will not silence the screams', *Nation*, 31 October 2009

60 Tom Parry, 'Suu Kyi's Right Hand Man', *Irrawaddy*, 19 September 2009

Chapter 9: Bloody Spots and Discarded Flip-Flops: The Saffron Revolution

1 Christian Solidarity Worldwide, 'Burma: Visit to the Thailand-Burma Border and Malaysia', February 2008

2 Christian Solidarity Worldwide, 'Burma: Visit to the Bangladesh-Burma Border', 26–31 August 2008

3 Human Rights Watch, 'Crackdown: Repression of the 2007 Popular Protests in Burma', 34

4 National Coalition Government of the Union of Burma (NCGUB), Human Rights Documentation Unit, 'Bullets in the Alms Bowl: An Analysis of the Brutal SPDC Suppression of the September 2007 Saffron Revolution', 27

5 Human Rights Watch, 'Crackdown: Repression of the 2007 Popular Protests in Burma', 35

6 Ibid., 37

7 Christian Solidarity Worldwide, 'Burma: Visit to the Bangladesh-Burma Border', 26–31 August 2008

8 Human Rights Watch, 'Crackdown: Repression of the 2007 Popular Protests in Burma', 38

9 Ibid., 40

10 Christian Solidarity Worldwide, 'Burma: Visit to the Thailand-Burma Border and Malaysia', February 2008

11 Human Rights Watch, 'Crackdown: Repression of the 2007 Popular Protests in Burma', 40

12 Ibid., 41

13 Ibid., 42–3

14 Ibid., 44

15 All Burma Monks Alliance, 'Statement of People's Alliance Formation Committee to the Entire Clergy and the People of the Whole Country', 21 September 2007

16 Human Rights Watch, 'Crackdown: Repression of the 2007 Popular Protests in Burma', 53

17 National Coalition Government of the Union of Burma (NCGUB), Human Rights Documentation Unit, 'Bullets in the Alms Bowl: An Analysis of the Brutal SPDC Suppression of the September 2007 Saffron Revolution', 47

18 Ibid., 48

19 Christian Solidarity Worldwide, 'Burma: Visit to the Bangladesh-Burma Border', 26–31 August 2008

20 Ibid.

21 Ibid.

22 Christian Solidarity Worldwide, 'Burma: Visit to the Thailand-Burma Border and Malaysia', February 2008

23 Christian Solidarity Worldwide, 'Burma: Visit to the Thailand-Burma Border', 16–28 November 2007

24 Christian Solidarity Worldwide, 'Burma: Visit to the Thailand-Burma Border and Malaysia', February 2008

25 Christian Solidarity Worldwide, 'Burma: Visit to the Bangladesh-Burma Border', 26–31 August 2008

26 Ibid.

27 Christian Solidarity Worldwide, 'Burma: Visit to the Thailand-Burma Border and Malaysia', February 2008

28 Ibid.

29 Ibid.

30 Christian Solidarity Worldwide, 'Burma: Visit to the Thailand-Burma Border', 16–28 November 2007

31 Christian Solidarity Worldwide, 'Burma: Visit to the Bangladesh-Burma Border', 26–31 August 2008

32 Christian Solidarity Worldwide, 'Burma: Visit to the Thailand-Burma Border', 16–28 November 2007

33 Christian Solidarity Worldwide, 'Burma: Visit to the Thailand-Burma Border and Malaysia', February 2008

34 Ibid.

35 Ibid.

36 Christian Solidarity Worldwide, 'Burma: Visit to the Bangladesh-Burma Border', 26–31 August 2008

37 Ibid.

38 Christian Solidarity Worldwide, 'Burma: Visit to the Thailand-Burma Border', 16–28 November 2007

39 Ibid.

40 BBC, 'Burma censor chief calls for more media freedom', 8 October 2011 – http://www.bbc.co.uk/news/world-asia-pacific-15227175

41 Christian Solidarity Worldwide, 'Burma: Visit to the Thailand-Burma Border and Malaysia', February 2008

Chapter 10: Cyclone Nargis

1 Steve Jackson, 'Was Burma's cyclone predicted?', BBC News, 6 May 2008 – http://news.bbc.co.uk/1/hi/world/asia-pacific/7386695.stm

2 Cardinal Keith Patrick O'Brien, Cardinal Archbishop of the Archdiocese of St Andrews and Edinburgh, Report on Pastoral Visit to Myanmar/Burma, 19–31 January 2009

3 Ibid.

4 Christian Solidarity Worldwide, 'Burma: Visit to the Thailand-Burma Border',

20 January–10 February 2009

5 Emergency Assistance Team (EAT) and Johns Hopkins Bloomberg School of Public Health, 'After the Storm: Voices from the Delta', March 2009, 8

6 Ibid., 33

7 Christian Solidarity Worldwide, 'Burma: Visit to the Thailand-Burma Border', 20 January–10 February 2009

8 Free Burma Rangers, 'As thousands suffer the effects of Cyclone Nargis, villagers suffer continued brutality by the Burma Army in Karen State', 9 May 2009 – http://www.freeburmarangers.org/Reports/2008/20080509b.html

9 ABC News, 'Burma aid curbs driving up death toll: Opposition', 10 May 2008 – http://www.abc.net.au/news/stories/2008/05/10/2241057.htm

10 Benedict Rogers, 'Ignore the junta', *Guardian*, 13 May 2008 – http://www.guardian.co.uk/commentisfree/2008/may/13/ignorethejunta

11 Benedict Rogers, 'Tea with a dictator', *Guardian*, 31 May 2008 – http://www.guardian.co.uk/commentisfree/2008/may/31/teawithadictator

12 Matthew Weaver, 'Cyclone Nargis: one month on, US accuses Burma of criminal neglect', *Guardian*, 2 June 2008 – http://www.guardian.co.uk/world/2008/jun/02/burma.cyclonenargis

13 Alan Brown, 'Myanmar cyclone: Burma junta is killing its own people, says West', *Daily Telegraph*, 17 May 2008 – http://www.telegraph.co.uk/news/worldnews/asia/burmamyanmar/1976611/Myanmar-cyclone-Burma-junta-is-killing-its-own-people-says-West.html

14 David Cameron, 'If the generals will not let in the aid, they must face trial', *Independent*, 1 June 2008 – http://www.independent.co.uk/opinion/commentators/david-cameron-if-the-generals-will-not-let-in-the-aid-they-must-face-trial-837683.html

15 Elana Schor, 'Laura Bush urges Burma to accept US aid', *Guardian*, 5 May 2008 – http://www.guardian.co.uk/world/2008/may/05/burma.usa

16 UN News Center, 'Myanmar's leader agrees to open access to foreign aid workers – Ban Ki-moon', 23 May 2008 – http://www.un.org/apps/news/story.asp?NewsID=26773&Cr=Myanmar&Cr1

17 The Center for Peace and Conflict Studies, 'Listening to Voices from Inside: Myanmar Civil Society's Response to Cyclone Nargis', 152

18 Ibid., 175

19 Al-Jazeera, 'Myanmar hosts cyclone aid meeting', 25 May 2008 – http://english.aljazeera.net/news/asia-pacific/2008/05/200861503218669523.html

20 'Co-operation with United Nations Cornerstone of Myanmar's Foreign Policy', *New Light of Myanmar*, 24 October 2008

21 'The enemy who is more destructive than Nargis', *New Light of Myanmar*, 8 June 2008

22 The Center for Peace and Conflict Studies, 'Listening to Voices from Inside: Myanmar Civil Society's Response to Cyclone Nargis', 150

23 Emergency Assistance Team (EAT) and Johns Hopkins Bloomberg School of Public Health, 'After the Storm: Voices from the Delta', March 2009, 9

24 Ajesh Patalay, 'Children of the Cyclone', *Telegraph Magazine*, 21 May 2009

25 Christian Solidarity Worldwide, 'Burma: Visit to the Thailand-Burma Border', 20 January–10 February 2009

26 Myanmar/Burma Emergency Aid Network, 'Cyclone Nargis relief and early recovery work – report from the field', 10 May–31 July 2008 – www. BurmaRelief.org

27 The Centre for Peace and Conflict Studies, 'Listening to Voices from Inside: Myanmar Civil Society's Response to Cyclone Nargis', 188

28 Human Rights Watch, 'Burma's Forgotten Prisoners', September 2009, 19

29 Ibid., 21

30 Matt Prodger, 'Storm victims' misery turns to fury', BBC, 2 June 2008 –http:// news.bbc.co.uk/1/hi/7430867.stm

31 Human Rights Watch, 'Burma's Forgotten Prisoners', September 2009, 10

32 Human Rights Watch, ' "I Want To Help My Own People": State Control and Civil Society in Burma after Cyclone Nargis', April 2010, 30

33 Andrew Marshall, 'Burma's Woes: A Threat to the Junta', *Time*, 20 May 2008

34 The Centre for Peace and Conflict Studies, 'Listening to Voices from Inside: Myanmar Civil Society's Response to Cyclone Nargis', viii

35 Ibid., 188

36 The famous story of a man who is on a beach covered with hundreds of stranded starfish. He starts picking up starfish and throwing them back into the sea, and someone asks him how he can possibly expect to make a difference when there are so many starfish on the beach. He picks up another starfish and as he does so he replies: 'It makes a difference to this one.'

Chapter 11: Out of Uniform but Still in Power

1 VOA News, 'Thailand Suggests Road Map for Burma', by Ron Corben, 20 July 2003

2 *Asiaweek*, 'Myanmar: No Talking Here', 8 December 1995

3 Fink, 74

4 Ibid., 75

5 Christian Solidarity Worldwide, 'Burma: Visit to Kachin State', May 2009

6 Human Rights Watch, 'Vote to Nowhere: The May 2008 Constitutional Referendum in Burma', 21

7 Institute for Political Analysis and Documentation (IPAD), 'No Real Choice: An Assessment of Burma's 2008 Referendum', 26

8 Human Rights Watch, 'Vote to Nowhere: The May 2008 Constitutional Referendum in Burma', 23–4

9 The Public International Law & Policy Group, 'Burmese Constitutional Referendum: Neither Free Nor Fair', May 2008, 10–11

10 Ibid., 35

11 Ibid., 37

12 *Irrawaddy*, 'Massive cheating reported from referendum polling stations', 10 May 2008 – http://www.irrawaddy.org/article.php?art_id=11923

13 Institute for Political Analysis and Documentation (IPAD), 'No Real Choice: An Assessment of Burma's 2008 Referendum', 34

14 Ibid., 23

15 Ibid., 36

16 Ibid., 37

17 Christian Solidarity Worldwide, 'Burma: Visit to the Bangladesh-Burma Border', 26–31 August 2008

18 Zipporah Sein, 'Burma's New Constitution: A Death Sentence for Ethnic Diversity', *Irrawaddy*, 13 October 2009

19 Human Rights Watch, 'Vote to Nowhere: The May 2008 Constitutional Referendum in Burma', 44–5

20 Ibid., 46

21 International Center for Transitional Justice, 'Impunity Prolonged: Burma and its 2008 Constitution', 3

22 Ibid., 4

23 Saw Yan Naing, 'Constitutional crisis over the Border Guard Force?', *Irrawaddy*, 16 July 2009

24 U Win Tin, 'An "Election" Burma's People Don't Need', *Washington Post*, 9 September 2009

25 National Coalition Government of the Union of Burma (NCGUB), 'Proposal for National Reconciliation: Towards Democracy and Development', 2009, 1 - http://www.ncgub.net/NCGUB/mediagallery/download85d1.pdf?mid=20091023154306771

26 Christian Solidarity Worldwide, *Burma:* 'Visit to Kachin State', May 2009

27 Richard Lloyd Parry, 'Spy novels, an out-of-tune piano and meditation: Suu Kyi faces another 18 months of solitude', *The Times*, 12 August 2009

28 Andrew Heyn, 'Burma's USDP is heading for election victory, by hook or by crook', *Guardian*, 3 November 2010 – http://www.guardian.co.uk/world/blog/2010/nov/03/burma-usdp-election

29 Christian Solidarity Worldwide, 'Burma: Visit to the India-Burma Border', 15–30 November 2010

30 ALTSEAN-Burma, Election Watch 2010 – Political Parties Statements – http://www.altsean.org/Research/2010/Resources/Statements/Parties.php?pageNum_rs_statements=5

31 U Win Tin, 'An "Election" Burma's People Don't Need', *Washington Post*, 9 September 2009

32 'Myanmar's First Budget in Decades', AFP, 12 February 2012

33 Phoebe Kennedy, 'Supporters receive a message of hope from their heroine', *Independent*, 15 November 2010

34 Kenneth Denby, 'Suu Kyi challenges generals: politics belongs to everyone', *The Times*, 15 November 2010

35 BBC, 'Suu Kyi: Burma democracy in my lifetime', 5 January 2012

36 AFP, 'Myanmar's Suu Kyi "could get government role"', 8 January 2012

37 BBC, 'Suu Kyi: Burma democracy in my lifetime', 5 January 2012

38 Quoted in *Irrawaddy*, 'Is Than Shwe Still Pulling the Strings?', 9 December 2011 – http://www.irrawaddy.org/article.php?art_id=22629

39 As quoted in Shway Yoe, *The Burman: His Life and Notions*, Macmillan, 1910, 383

Chapter 12: The Future?

1 Associated Press, 'Suu Kyi says Myanmar's powerful military could still halt progress to democracy', 5 January 2012

2 Kenneth Denby, 'Democracy reforms are a ploy by generals to scupper Suu Kyi's power, activist warns', *The Times*, 5 January 2012

3 Andrew Drummond, 'Glenys Kinnock smuggles Suu Kyi video from Burma', *The Times*, 11 November 1996

4 'The Protest Network: social networking is an awesome tool for democracy. In their support for Egyptian protestors, Google and Twitter have emerged as powerful political actors', *The Times*, 2 February 2011

5 Aung San Suu Kyi, *Freedom from Fear*, 212

6 Quoted in Malavika Karlekar, 'Imagining the Lady: the media have made Suu Kyi's struggle visible', *Telegraph*, 8 January 2012

Epilogue

1 Archbishop Charles Bo, 'Burma needs tolerance to reach its potential', *Washington Post*, 13 June 2014 – http://www.washingtonpost.com/opinions/burma-needs-tolerance-to-reach-its-potential/2014/06/13/6e5d3c92-ea90-11e3-93d2-edd4be1f5d9e_story.html

2 Human Rights Watch, 'All You Can Do is Pray: Crimes Against Humanity and Ethnic Cleansing of Rohingya Muslims in Burma's Arakan State', 22 April 2013 – https://www.hrw.org/report/2013/04/22/all-you-can-do-pray/crimes-against-humanity-and-ethnic-cleansing-rohingya-muslims

3 Ibid.

4 Saw Yan Naing, 'UNHCR Rejects Rohingya Resettlement Suggestion', *Irrawaddy*, 13 July 2012 – http://www.irrawaddy.org/burma/unhcr-rejects-rohingya-resettlement-suggestion.html

5 Fortify Rights, 'Policies of Persecution', February 2014 – http://www.fortifyrights.org/downloads/Policies_of_Persecution_Feb_25_Fortify_Rights.pdf

6 Fortify Rights, 'Myanmar: Abolish Abusive Restrictions and Practices Against Rohingya Muslims', 25 February 2014 – http://www.fortifyrights.org/publication-20140225.html

7 Michelle Nicholls, 'Rohingya camp conditions in Myanmar "appalling" – UN official', Reuters, 18 June 2014 – http://in.reuters.com/article/2014/06/17/myanmar-un-aid-idINKBN0ES2NW20140617

8 BBC, 'Burma camp for Rohingyas "dire" – Valerie Amos', 5 December 2012 – http://www.bbc.co.uk/news/world-asia-20615778

9 UN, 'UN rights expert urges Myanmar authorities to address signs of backtracking', 18 March 2015 – http://www.un.org/apps/news/story.asp?NewsID=50364#.VdIP3vlViko

10 Burmese Rohingya Organisation UK, 'Briefing on The Humanitarian Crisis in Rakhine State', December 2014 – http://burmacampaign.org.uk/media/The-Humanitarian-Crisis-Of-Rohingya-In-Rakhine-State.pdf

11 BBC, 'Buddhist mobs "target aid workers" in Myanmar's Rakhine', 27 March 2014 – http://www.bbc.co.uk/news/world-asia-26763083

12 Physicians for Human Rights, 'Massacre in Central Burma: Muslim Students Terrorised and Killed in Meiktila', May 2013 – https://s3.amazonaws.com/PHR_Reports/Burma-Meiktila-Massacre-Report-May-2013.pdf

13 BBC, 'One killed in Burma Oakkan town religious violence', 1 May 2013 – http://www.bbc.co.uk/news/world-asia-22362992

14 Mizzima, 'Hidden hands stoked Mandalay communal violence: NGO', 23 March 2015 – http://www.mizzima.com/news-domestic/%E2%80%98hidden-hands%E2%80%99-stoked-mandalay-communal-violence-ngo

15 Christian Solidarity Worldwide, 'Burma: Visit Report, April 2013', – file:///C:/Users/Ben%20Rogers/Downloads/csw-briefing-burma-april-2013.pdf

16 BBC, 'Ashin Wirathu: Myanmar and its vitriolic monk', 23 January 2015 – http://www.bbc.co.uk/news/world-asia-30930997

17 CNN, 'Top UN official slams Myanmar monk over "whore" comments', 22 January 2015 – http://edition.cnn.com/2015/01/22/world/myanmar-united-nations-wirathu/

18 Lawi Weng, 'The Rise and Rise of the Ma Ba Tha Lobby', *Irrawaddy*, 10 July 2015 – http://www.irrawaddy.org/commentary/the-rise-and-rise-of-the-ma-ba-tha-lobby.html

19 Feliz Solomon, 'Burma Parliament Approves Contentious Race and Religion Bills', *Irrawaddy*, 20 August 2015 – http://www.irrawaddy.org/burma/burma-parliament-approves-contentious-race-and-religion-bills.html

20 BBC, 'Myanmar court finds trio guilty of insulting religion', 17 March 2015 – https://www.youtube.com/watch?v=c3DcChXNyYQ

21 CSW, 'Democracy activist given prison sentence', 5 June 2015 – http://www.csw.org.uk/2015/06/05/news/2612/article.htm

22 Statement of the Special Rapporteur on the Situation of Human Rights in Myanmar, 26 July 2014 - http://www.ohchr.org/EN/NewsEvents/Pages/DisplayNews.aspx?NewsID=14909&

23 BBC, 'Burmese leader defends "anti-Muslim" monk Ashin Wirathu', 24 June 2013 – http://www.bbc.co.uk/news/world-asia-23027492

24 Benedict Rogers, 'Indonesia and Myanmar: Tackling Religious Violence', Tony

Blair Faith Foundation, 1 April 2015 – http://tonyblairfaithfoundation.org/religion-geopolitics/commentaries/opinion/indonesia-and-myanmar-tackling-religious-intolerance

25 Christian Solidarity Worldwide, 'Burma: Visit Report, April 2013', – file:///C:/Users/Ben%20Rogers/Downloads/csw-briefing-burma-april-2013.pdf

26 BBC, 'Burma's President Thein Sein warns "extremists"', 28 March 2013 – http://www.bbc.co.uk/news/world-asia-21968040

27 *Wall Street Journal*, 'Myanmar Cardinal Charles Maung Bo To Work Toward Religious Tolerance', 7 January 2014 – http://www.wsj.com/articles/myanmar-cardinal-charles-maung-bo-to-amplify-plea-for-religious-tolerance-1420611495

28 BBC, 'Myanmar's strongman gives rare BBC interview', 20 July 2015 – http://www.bbc.co.uk/news/world-asia-33587800

Bibliography

Ad hoc Commission on Depayin Massacre. 'Preliminary Report of the Ad hoc Commission on Depayin Massacre (Burma), July 4, 2003'. Bangkok. 2004.

ALTSEAN Burma. 'Rohingya, Asylum Seekers & Migrants from Burma: A Human Security Priority for ASEAN'. Bangkok. 30 January 2009.

Amnesty International. 'Crimes against humanity in eastern Myanmar'. London. 5 June 2008.

Assistance Association for Political Prisoners (Burma). 'Burma's Prisons and Labour Camps: Silent Killing Fields'. Thailand. May 2009.

———.'The Future in The Dark: The Massive Increase in Burma's Political Prisoners'. Thailand. September 2008.

———. 'Eight Seconds of Silence: The Death of Democracy Activists Behind Bars'. Thailand. May 2006.

———. 'The Darkness We See: Torture in Burma's Interrogation Centers and Prisons'. Thailand. December, 2005.

Aung Moe Htet, ed. *To Stand and Be Counted: The Suppression of Burma's Members of Parliament*. Bangkok: All Burma Students' Democratic Front (ABSDF) Documentation and Research Centre, 1998.

Aung San Suu Kyi. *Freedom from Fear and Other Writings*. London: Penguin Books, 1991.

———. *The Voice of Hope: Conversations with Alan Clements*. London: Rider, 2008.

Aung Shwe, *et al.*, trans. and eds. *Letters to a Dictator, Correspondence from NLD Chairman Aung Shwe to the SLORC's Senior General Than*

Shwe. Bangkok: All Burma Students' Democratic Front (ABSDF) Documentation and Research Centre, 1997.

Back Pack Health Worker Team. 'Chronic Emergency: Health and Human Rights in Eastern Burma'. Mae Sot, Thailand. 2008.

Callahan, Mary. *Making Enemies, War and State Building in Burma*. Ithaca and London: Cornell University Press, 2003.

Centre for Peace and Conflict Studies. 'Listening to Voices from Inside: Myanmar Civil Society's Response to Cyclone Nargis'. 2009.

Charney, Michael. *A History of Modern Burma*. Cambridge: Cambridge University Press, 2009.

Chin Human Rights Organisation. 'Religious Persecution: A Campaign of Ethnocide Against Chin Christians in Burma', by Salai Za Uk Ling and Salai Bawi Lian Mang. 2004. www.chro.ca.

———. 'Critical Point: Food Scarcity and Hunger in Burma's Chin State'. 2008. www.chro.ca.

———. 'On the Edge of Survival: The Continuing Rat Infestation and Food Crisis in Chin State, Burma'. 2009. www.chro.ca.

Christian Solidarity Worldwide fact-finding reports – see www.csw.org.uk.

EarthRights International. 'Total Impact: The Human Rights, Environmental and Financial Impacts of Total and Chevron's Yadana Gas Project in Military-Ruled Burma (Myanmar)'. September 2009. www.earthrights.org.

Egreteau, Renaud and Jagan, Larry. 'Back to the Old Habits: isolationism or the self-preservation of Burma's military regime'. Institute of Research on Contemporary South East Asia (IRASEC), Occasional Paper No. 7, 2008.

Emergency Assistance Team (EAT) and Johns Hopkins Bloomberg School of Public Health. 'After the Storm: Voices from the Delta'. March 2009.

Euro-Burma Office. 'The Rohingyas: Bengali Muslims or Arakan Rohingyas?' EBO Briefing Paper, No. 2, 2009.

Fink, Christina. *Militarisation in Burma's Ethnic States: Causes and Consequences*. London: Routledge, 2008.

———. *Living Silence in Burma: Surviving Under Military Rule*, Second Edition. London: Zed Books, 2009.

Gore-Booth, Paul. *With Great Truth and Respect: The Memoirs of Paul*

Gore-Booth, London: Constable, 1974.

Houtman, Gustaaf. *Mental Culture in Burmese Crisis Politics: Aung San Suu Kyi and the National League for Democracy*. ILCAA Study of Languages and Cultures of Asia and Africa Monograph Series No. 33. Tokyo: Institute for the Study of Languages and Cultures of Asia and Africa, Tokyo University of Foreign Studies, 1999.

Human Rights Foundation of Monland. Women and Child Rights Project (WCRP). 'Nowhere Else To Go: An Examination of Sexual Trafficking and Related Human Rights Abuses in Southern Burma'. Thailand, August 2009.

———. 'Catwalk to the Barracks: conscription of women for sexual slavery and other practices of sexual violence by troops of the Burmese military regime in Mon areas'. Thailand, July 2005.

Human Rights Watch. 'Sold to be Soldiers: The Recruitment and Use of Child Soldiers in Burma'. New York, Washington, London and Brussels, 2007.

———. 'Crackdown: Repression of the 2007 Popular Protests in Burma'. New York, Washington, London and Brussels, 2007.

———. 'Vote to Nowhere: The May 2008 Constitutional Referendum in Burma'. New York, Washington, London and Brussels, 2008.

———. 'Burma: "We Are Like Forgotten People" – The Chin People of Burma: Unsafe in Burma, Unprotected in India'. New York, Washington, London and Brussels, 2009.

———. 'Burma's Forgotten Prisoners.' New York, Washington, London and Brussels, 2009.

———. ' "I Want To Help My Own People": State Control and Civil Society in Burma after Cyclone Nargis'. New York, Washington, London and Brussels, 2010.

Institute for Political Analysis and Documentation. 'No Real Choice: An Assessment of Burma's 2008 Referendum'. 2008.

International Human Rights Clinic, Harvard Law School. 'Crimes in Burma'. Cambridge, MA, May 2009.

Kachin Environmental Organisation. 'Damming the Irrawaddy'. Chiang Mai, Thailand, 2008.

Kin Oung. *Who Killed Aung San?* Bangkok: White Lotus, 1996.

Kivimaki, Timo and Morten Pedersen. 'Burma: Mapping the Challenges and Opportunities for Dialogue and Reconciliation'. A report by Crisis Management Initiative and Martti Ahtsaari Rapid Reaction Facility, 2008.

Koehler Johnson, Bernice. *The Shans: Refugees Without a Camp*. New Jersey: Trinity Matrix, 2009.

Lintner, Bertil. *Aung San Suu Kyi and Burma's Unfinished Resistance*. London: Peacock Press, 1990.

———. *The Rise and Fall of the Communist Party of Burma (CPB)*. Ithaca, NY: Southeast Asia Program, Cornell University, 1990.

———. *Burma in Revolt: Opium and Insurgency since 1948*. 2nd ed. Chiang Mai: Silkworm Books, 1999.

———. 'The Staying Power of the Burmese Military Regime'. Paper presented at a public forum on Burma, Aichi Gakuin University, Nagoya, Japan, 11–17 March 2009.

Lintner, Bertil and Black, Michael. *Merchants of Madness: The Methamphetamine Explosion in the Golden Triangle*. Chiang Mai: Silkworm Books, 2009.

Maung, Aung Myoe. 'A Historical Overview of Political Transition in Myanmar since 1988'. Asia Research Institute Working Paper Series No.95. Singapore: Asia Research Institute, National University of Singapore, August 2007.

Mawdsley, James. *The Heart Must Break: The Fight for Democracy and Truth in Burma*. London: Random House, 2001.

National Coalition Government, Union of Burma. Human Rights Documentation Unit. 'Bullets in the Alms Bowl: An Analysis of the Brutal SPDC Suppression of the September 2007 Saffron Revolution', March 2008.

Phan, Zoya. *Little Daughter: A Memoir of Survival in Burma and the West*. London: Simon and Schuster, 2009 (published in the United States under the title *Undaunted*).

Public International Law and Policy Group. 'Burmese Constitutional Referendum: Neither Free Nor Fair'. May 2008.

Rogers, Benedict. *A Land Without Evil: Stopping the Genocide of Burma's Karen People*. Oxford: Monarch Books, 2004.

———. 'Carrying the Cross: The military regime's campaign of restrictions, discrimination and persecution against Christians in Burma'. A report by Christian Solidarity Worldwide, 2007.

——. *Than Shwe: Unmasking Burma's Tyrant*. Chiang Mai: Silkworm Books, 2010.

Sakhong, Lian H. *In Search of Chin Identity: A Study in Religion, Politics and Ethnic Identity in Burma*. Denmark: Nordic Institute of Asian Studies, 2003.

Sargent, Inge. *Twilight Over Burma: My Life as a Shan Princess*. Honolulu: University of Hawaii Press, 1994.

Selth, Andrew. *Burma's Armed Forces, Power Without Glory*. Norwalk, CT: East Bridge, 2002.

Shan Herald Agency for News (SHAN). 'Dispossessed: a report on forced relocation and extrajudicial killings in Shan State'. Chiang Mai, Thailand, April 1998.

Shan Women's Action Network (SWAN). 'Licence to Rape'. Chiang Mai, Thailand, 2001.

——. 'Forbidden Glimpses of Shan State'. Chiang Mai, Thailand, 2009.

Shwe Yoe. *The Burman: His Life and Notions*. New York: W.W. Norton & Company, 1963.

Silverstein, Josef. *Burma, Military Rule and the Politics of Stagnation*. Ithaca, NY: Cornell University Press, 1977.

——. *Burmese Politics, the Dilemma of National Unity*. New Brunswick, NJ: Rutgers University Press, 1980.

Slim, William. *Defeat Into Victory: Battling Japan in Burma and India 1942–1945*. New York: Cooper Square Press, 2000.

Smith, Martin. *Burma: Insurgency and the Politics of Ethnicity*. London: Zed Books, 1999.

——. *The Muslim Rohingya of Burma*, paper delivered at a conference organised by Burma Centrum Netherlands, 11 December, 1995

South, Ashley. *Ethnic Politics in Burma: States of Conflict*. Routledge, 2008.

——. *Mon Nationalism and Civil War in Burma: The Golden Sheldrake*. London: Routledge, 2003.

Steinberg, David. *Burma: The State of Myanmar*. Washington, DC: Georgetown University Press, 2001.

Thailand Burma Border Consortium. 'Protracted Displacement and Chronic Poverty in Eastern Burma'. 2010. www.tbbc.org.

Thant, Myint-U. *The River of Lost Footsteps: A Personal History of Burma*. London: Faber and Faber, 2008.

Tinker, Hugh. *The Union of Burma: A Study of the First Years of Independence.* Oxford: Oxford University Press, 1967.

Turnell, Sean. *Fiery Dragons; Banks, Moneylenders, and Microfinance in Burma.* Hawaii: University of Hawaii Press, 2009.

Win Min. 'Looking Inside the Burmese Military'. *Asian Survey* 48, no. 6 (2008): 1018–37.

Women's League of Chinland. 'Unsafe State: state-sanctioned sexual violence against Chin women in Burma'. India, March 2007.

Yawnghwe, Chao-Tzang. 'Ne Win's Tatmadaw Dictatorship'. Master's thesis, University of British Columbia, April 1990.

News Sources

ABC News
Asian Wall Street Journal
Asiaweek
Assist
Associated Press
Australian, The
Bangkok Post
BBC News
Burma Debate
Chin Human Rights Organisation
Christian Science Monitor
Daily Telegraph
Democratic Voice of Burma
Deutsche Press Agentur
Economist, The
Free Burma Rangers
Guardian
Independent
International Herald Tribune
Irrawaddy
Jane's Defence Weekly
Kachin News Group
Mizzima
Narinjara

Nation, The
New Light of Myanmar, The
New York Times, The
Outlook (India)
Radio Free Asia
Reuters
Shan Herald Agency for News (S.H.A.N)
The Times
Time
Times of India, The
United Press International
Voice of America
Washington Post
Working People's Daily

Further Information

Advocacy Organisations

The Alternative ASEAN Network for Burma (ALTSEAN)

ALTSEAN-Burma (Alternative ASEAN Network on Burma) is a network of organisations and individuals based in ASEAN member states working to support the movement for human rights and democracy in Burma. The network comprises human rights & social justice NGOs, political parties, think tanks, academics, journalists and student activists. The organisation was formed at the conclusion of the Alternative ASEAN Meeting on Burma held at Chulalongkorn University, Bangkok, in October 1996.
PO BOX 296
Lardprao Post Office
10310 Bangkok
Thailand
Tel : +66 81 850 9008
www.altsean.org

Burma Campaign Australia

Burma Campaign Australia is a network of groups and individuals located around Australia campaigning for peace, democracy, good governance and human rights in Burma. Burma Campaign Australia includes human rights advocates, academics, aid agencies and a broad range of Australia-based ethnic and pro-democracy groups from Burma.

c/o Burma Office
Trades Hall
Suite 110
4 Goulburn St
Sydney
NSW 2000
Australia
Tel & Fax: 0061 9264 7694
www.aucampaignforburma.org

Burma Campaign UK

Burma Campaign UK works for the promotion of human rights, democracy and development in Burma.

28 Charles Square
London, N1 6HT
United Kingdom
Tel: (+44) (0)207 324 4710
www.burmacampaign.org.uk

Christian Solidarity Worldwide

CSW is a Christian organisation working for religious freedom through advocacy and human rights, in the pursuit of justice. An international human rights organisation, CSW has offices in London, Brussels and Washington, DC and affiliates and partners in Hong Kong, Nigeria, Norway, Denmark and India.

PO Box 99
New Malden
Surrey KT3 3YF
United Kingdom
Tel: (+44) (0)845 456 5464
www.csw.org.uk

The U.S. Campaign for Burma

The United States Campaign for Burma (USCB) is a US-based organisation dedicated to empowering grassroots activists around the world to rally for human rights and to bring an end to the military dictatorship in Burma.

1444 N Street NW, Suite A2
Washington, DC 20005
United States
Tel: (+1) (202) 234-8022
www.uscampaignforburma.org

AID ORGANISATIONS

The Free Burma Rangers

The Free Burma Rangers (FBR) is a multi-ethnic humanitarian service movement. They bring help, hope and love to people in the war zones of Burma. Ethnic pro-democracy groups send teams to be trained, supplied and sent into the areas under attack to provide emergency assistance and human rights documentation. Together with other groups, the teams work to serve people in need.

P.O. Box 14, Mae Jo
Chiang Mai 50290
Thailand
www.freeburmarangers.org

Humanitarian Aid Relief Trust

HART works to provides targeted aid-work and international advocacy for those who are, or who have been, suffering oppression and persecution. The focus is on those who are trapped behind closed borders, not served by other major aid organisations, and largely neglected by the international media.

3 Arnellan House
144–146 Slough Lane
Kingsbury
London NW9 8XJ
United Kingdom
Tel: +44 (0) 208 204 7336
www.hart-uk.org

Partners Relief and Development
Partners Relief and Development is a registered charity in Australia, Canada, New Zealand, Norway, the United Kingdom and the United States, working with communities impacted by war in Burma.
www.partnersworld.org

The Phan Foundation
The Phan Foundation was founded by the four children of Padoh Mahn Sha, the General Secretary of the Karen National Union, and Nant Kyin Shwe, in memory of their parents. The Foundation has four main objectives: to alleviate poverty; provide education; promote human rights; protect Karen culture.
Phan Foundation
28 Charles Sq
London N1 6HT
United Kingdom
www.phanfoundation.org

Prospect Burma
Prospect Burma is a non-political education charity dedicated to supporting the education of Burmese students.
Prospect Burma
Porters' Lodge
Rivermead Court
Ranelagh Gardens
London SW6 3SF
United Kingdom
Telephone: +44 (0) 20 7371 0887
www.prospectburma.org

Index